# Sociological Snapshots 5

# Sociological Snapshots 5

*Seeing Social Structure and Change in Everyday Life*

 **Jack Levin**

*Northeastern University*

 PINE FORGE PRESS
An Imprint of Sage Publications, Inc.
Los Angeles • London • New Delhi • Singapore

*For information:*

Pine Forge Press
A SAGE Publications Company
2455 Teller Road
Thousand Oaks,
   California 91320
E-mail: order@sagepub.com

SAGE Publications Ltd.
1 Oliver's Yard
55 City Road
London EC1Y 1SP
United Kingdom

SAGE Publications India Pvt. Ltd.
B 1/I 1 Mohan Cooperative
   Industrial Area
Mathura Road, New Delhi 110 044
India

SAGE Publications Asia-Pacific Pte. Ltd.
33 Pekin Street #02-01
Far East Square
Singapore 048763

Printed in the United States of America.

*Library of Congress Cataloging-in-Publication Data*

Levin, Jack, 1941-
Sociological snapshots 5 : seeing social structure and change in everyday life/Jack Levin.
     p. cm.
Includes bibliographical references and index.
ISBN-13: 978-1-4129-5649-9 (pbk.)
   1. Sociology. 2. Social change. 3. Social structure—United States.
4. United States—Social conditions—1980- I. Title.

HM585.L48 2008
301—dc22                                    2008008556

This book is printed on acid-free paper.

08   09   10   11   12   10   9   8   7   6   5   4   3   2   1

| | |
|---|---|
| *Acquisitions Editor:* | Benjamin Penner |
| *Editorial Assistant:* | Nancy Scrofano |
| *Production Editor:* | Karen Wiley |
| *Copy Editor:* | Melinda Orman |
| *Proofreader:* | Caryne Brown |
| *Typesetter:* | C&M Digitals (P) Ltd. |
| *Indexer:* | Gloria Tierney |
| *Cover Designer:* | Gail Buschman |
| *Marketing Manager:* | Jennifer Reed Banando |

# Contents

# Preface

Sociology is a vitally exciting field. You may know that, and I may know that. The trick is getting our students to realize it. Usually, instructors who teach introductory sociology hope that they will develop in their students some enthusiasm for the contributions of the field, but the question is always *how*.

I wrote this book with at least two specific outcomes in mind, both of which relate to the general goal of getting the students to understand and appreciate the sociological perspective: to serve as a springboard to more abstract thinking about society and to encourage student interest in learning more about the field of sociology.

It is an important function of sociology to help broaden the educational experience of all college students, but especially those in fields of study that may be narrow in scope and purpose. One measure of the effectiveness of an introductory sociology course is the extent to which students come to view their world with a sociological eye.

When students truly see the sociology in things, they are also being helped to develop their abstract thinking skills—the very skills of vital importance in any job or career. Unfortunately, students too often get little help from their introductory courses in enhancing their ability to think at an abstract level. Instead, they are asked to read and memorize long lists of terms that seem more to obfuscate and complicate than to clarify reality.

The snapshots in this book are casual and informal, but they are designed to ease students into the formal world of sociological analysis. Each essay relates some abstract sociological concepts to the concrete problems confronting ordinary people. Social structure and social change are introduced as major variables but almost always in the context of everyday life.

At the same time, the snapshots are grounded in sociological data and theorizing. The introductory essays that begin each section are intended to emphasize the importance of the formal sociological literature. Indeed, the entire book serves as a springboard from the informal, concrete world of the student to the more formal, abstract world of sociological theory and method.

Students also need active ways of developing their ability to see and articulate abstractions and for analyzing data about social reality. The physical and biological sciences usually include a lab component in their courses in which students are given an opportunity for hands-on experience. Sociologists should attempt, wherever possible, to do the same.

For this reason, each section of the book contains ideas for student writing and research assignments. There is nothing fancy or complicated about the proposed tasks. They are designed to get introductory students to begin to write from a sociological perspective or to collect data about their everyday lives. We can only hope that they will decide to go on to bigger and better sociological things.

To the extent that the first outcome is realized, students will, I hope, also achieve the second: They will be eager to learn more about the sociological perspective. Some will take more sociology courses or even major in the discipline.

Unlike the situation in many other fields, sociology simply cannot depend on students' prior familiarity with the study of behavior to provide a background of information or enhance their interest. In high school, very few had the opportunity to select a sociology course. Some may have a vague idea that sociologists study human behavior or that sociology is somehow related to social work, but that's about it.

Partly as a result of their lack of familiarity, only a small number of students declare a sociology major when entering college. More typically, students who enroll in introductory sociology courses represent a range of disciplines and interests. It is therefore a major function of the introductory sociology course—for many undergraduates, perhaps their only point of formal contact—to persuade students to take upper-level courses in the field. This places a special burden on instructors to provide a positive learning climate—one in which student interest is encouraged.

Writing the fifth edition of *Sociological Snapshots* has given me another chance to make some important changes. Most of the snapshots found in the fourth edition have been retained, though almost all have been modified or updated. Moreover, there are five new snapshots in this edition—about bullying in the schools, the immigration debate, celebratory rioting among college students, pathological bigotry, and the community responses to sexual predators. Most of the new essays have a comparative perspective, emphasizing differences and similarities in societies around the world.

A number of people were important in making *Sociological Snapshots 5* a reality. At *Bostonia,* I am grateful to Laura Fried, who gave me the opportunity to write a regular column on behavior for a first-rate magazine; to Keith Botsford, who permitted me to carry on the tradition; and to Lori Calabro and Janice Friedman, under whose skillful editorship the quality of my writing always improved. I also thank David Gibson at *Northeastern University Magazine* for helping me to write the essay concerning the sociology of soap operas. Rachelle Cohen encouraged me to do "Americans Are Moving to the Margins of Society" for the *Boston Herald,* and Marjorie Pritchard encouraged me to write "Who's Minding the Kids" for the *Boston Globe.*

In previous editions, I depended a great deal on the insightful comments and suggestions of the following reviewers: Paul Baker, Illinois State University; Agnes Riedmann, Creighton University; Anne Hastings, University of North Carolina at Chapel Hill; Robert Emerick, San Diego State University; Judith Richlin-Klonsky, University of California at Los Angeles; William R. Aho, Rhode Island College; Russ Crescimanno, Piedmont Community College; Diane Carmody, Western Washington University; Judith Lawler Caron, Albertus Magnus College; Mary Rogers, University of West Florida; Michael L. Sanow, Towson State University; Rich Eckstein, Villanova University; and Shirley Varmette, Southern Connecticut State. In this revision, I was guided a great deal by the insightful suggestions of the following reviewers: Steve Beach, Kentucky Wesleyan University; Brenda Chaney, Ohio State University; Bob Carothers, Kent State University; Joel See, University of New England; Cheryl Albers, Buffalo State College; Bill Nye, Hollins University; Marsha Rose, Florida Atlantic University; and Larry Leavitt, Holyoke Community College.

I am grateful to Betty and the late Irving Brudnick for encouraging me to search for solutions to the troublesome problems—hate, bigotry, and prejudice—that divide human beings from one another. Having chosen to lead their lives with selflessness and respect for differences, Betty and Irv are my role models and my heroes.

My colleague Arnie Arluke deserves a special note of praise for suggesting the title of this book. Gordana Rabrenovic, Jamie Fox, and Bill Levin were generous with both their encouragement and their ideas.

I take this opportunity to express my gratitude to Steve Rutter, who skillfully served as the editor in the first edition of *Snapshots,* and to Jerry Westby and Ben Penner, who, with considerable expertise, inspired and monitored all of the important changes in the present incarnation of the work. I feel fortunate to have worked with such talented and dedicated editors.

I wish to thank the thousands of students I have had the pleasure of teaching. They have taught me a great deal about sociology and about life, and they have certainly given my career all of the excitement and energy that I ever hoped to find in my work.

And last but far from least, my wonderful wife, Flea, and my terrific children, Andrea and Mike (and now, Jaden), Bonnie and Brian (and now, Benjamin), and Michael have been more than patient, tolerating all of my many idiosyncrasies. I am grateful for their love, understanding, and support during times both troubling and trouble-free.

# The Sociological Eye

Among my several hobbies, photography is my favorite. I've never tried to take formal or posed pictures. Instead, the heart of my interest—what I have always found most satisfying—is the art of taking snapshots: informal, often candid photos of everyday life. I particularly enjoy capturing on film the problems experienced by ordinary people and the spontaneous, unguarded moments in the lives of loved ones.

The essays in this book are snapshots too, but they are sociological snapshots. Each one is a 3 × 5 glossy of a social situation encountered by the people we meet every day—the circumstances of ordinary people caught up in ordinary (and, occasionally, not so ordinary) social events. You will find essays about family and class reunions, television soap operas, behavior in elevators, children who have unpopular names, the people who do dirty work in occupations, spectators at football games, bystander apathy, people who act in deviant ways while driving in automobiles, heartburn, fads through the generations, popular rumors about shopping malls, contemporary images of fat people, and so on. At the extreme end, you will also discover a few essays concerning such topics as the death penalty, mass killers, and hate crimes (sadly, in today's society, even ordinary people have to be aware of such extraordinary topics).

The essays in this book are snapshots in another sense as well; most take a casual, informal approach with respect to the presentation of statistical evidence. Many appeared originally in *Bostonia* (a magazine of culture and ideas). Others were opinion pieces that I earlier published in newspapers. Some were written specifically for this book. All were designed to bridge the existing gap between the two cultures of academic sociology and everyday life. As a result, in every snapshot you will find a mix of both social science and journalism. There are very few references, quantitative data, and formal evidence, the kind that you typically expect to find in an introductory sociology textbook. Sometimes the essays in the book present only anecdotal confirmation—illustrations and examples rather than hard, statistical facts.

Some are speculative pieces about changes in society or about the future. Others seek to illustrate a new perspective on aspects of society that may have seemed obvious to you before. None are meant to replace the technical journal articles written for professional sociologists. All are meant to motivate students, to help them see the contribution of the sociological approach, and to ease them as gently as possible into the more formal world of sociological analysis.

After teaching classes in sociology for a number of years, I have noticed that many students are troubled by what they regard as the abstractness of sociological insight. They often complain about not being able to see how social structure touches their everyday lives or how culture contributes to ordinary events. No longer are they asked to examine the structure of individuals but of entire groups, organizations, institutions, communities, or societies.

What I believe is missing, from a pedagogical viewpoint, are the snapshots of culture and social structure that bridge the gap existing in many students' minds between what may appear to be vast sociological abstractions on the one hand and everyday experiences on the other. Hence, the central purpose of this book is to relate abstract sociological concepts to the concrete problems confronting ordinary individuals in our society.

Please don't be fooled into believing that these snapshots represent the personal opinions of the author alone. On the contrary, all of them are based on sociological thinking, sociological data, or both. The essays that introduce each section of the book and the annotated suggested readings at the end (Focus: Suggestions for Further Reading) are meant to emphasize the importance of the sociological literature. Indeed, they direct the student to it. You will find that the suggested readings include not only the more formal sources on which the snapshots were based but also important general works from the sociological literature. I have tried to describe them in enough detail so that interested students will understand why they are worth reading. Once again, no snapshot is meant to replace the technical journal articles—the formal portraits—written for professional sociologists, but all are grounded in them.

This book was not written to replace the standard introductory text. Instead, *Sociological Snapshots* was intended to serve as a springboard into the formal course material, whether presented in a single text or as a series of monographs. To move back and forth between levels of abstraction, each section of the book has been organized in a consistent format. First, there is an introductory essay in which the basic sociological concepts are defined, discussed, illustrated, and then linked with the snapshots for that particular section. Second, there are the snapshots themselves.

Next, there are suggestions for further reading, extensively annotated (see the References for publication information for each reading). Finally, there are ideas for student writing and research assignments in Developing Ideas. By the way, most of these assignments require the students to apply a sociological eye to their everyday lives or to begin, in a preliminary way, to collect data using a sociological method.

There is one final sense in which the essays in this book are snapshots. They often reflect, frequently in an explicit way, the ideas that the "photographer" considers valuable or problematic. In taking pictures of the world around me, I often take photos of my family and friends, and occasionally of the unusual circumstances of daily life, but always with a point of view implicit in my choice of subject. In other words, my snapshots are, in part, a reflection of my values—the things that I appreciate or cherish. They are often addressed to preserving and understanding the images of the people I love, the problems in everyday life that bother me, or the things I believe need changing.

Like all scientists, sociologists have values. They are human beings too, having grown up in a particular social setting and been exposed selectively to certain kinds of ideas. Max Weber, a turn-of-the-century German sociologist who contributed a great deal to our understanding of religion, inequality, and social change, strongly believed that sociology could be value free. He fully recognized that the subjects sociologists chose to study were frequently influenced by their personal values. For example, it would not be surprising that a sociologist who grew up in extreme poverty might decide to study inequality; a rape victim might conduct research into the causes of sexual violence; an African-American sociologist might specialize in race relations; and so on.

But when Weber talked about value-free sociology, he really wasn't talking about the selection of a subject about which to conduct research. Instead, he meant that sociologists must not permit their values, biases, or personal opinions to interfere with their analysis of that subject. They must, instead, attempt to be objective in collecting and analyzing information; they must seek out and consider all of the evidence, even evidence that might contradict their personal opinions. Weber would have advised that we must let the chips fall where they may. I hope "The Sociological Eye" personal biases have determined only the subjects of my snapshots, not the conclusions that I reach about them.

Now that you understand the snapshot part of the title of this book, *Sociological Snapshots 5*, I ask that you stop a moment longer and consider the sociological part as well. As you probably already surmise—even if you have never taken a course in it—psychology deals with the behavior and personality of individual human beings. Psychologists might study a person's attitudes, hostility, attractiveness, moods, helpfulness, learning styles, prejudices, and so on. In contrast, sociologists focus not on any one individual but on what happens between two or more individuals when they interact.

Sociologists might study the relationship between husband and wife, interaction in a small task group at work, the peer groups in a high school, family relations, prison culture, relations between managers and workers, and so on.

To explain the unique and important contribution of sociology, allow me to reveal a little bit about my everyday routine. Every time I drive from my suburban home to my office in the city, I think about how painfully predictable and orderly my daily commuting routine has become. I live some 25 miles from downtown, so I have plenty of time, while sitting in bumper-to-bumper traffic, to think. In my darker, more impatient moments, I play "what if" games: What if I had sold my house and moved into the city? What if I were teaching in a college located in a remote, rural area? What if I had taken the train into work? What if I could change my schedule to avoid the rush-hour commute? Would I still be stuck in traffic? Probably not.

As a sociologist, I recognize that the interesting thing about my predicament is the fact that it is shared by so many other people. This, of course, explains why traffic jams happen on a daily basis. Tens of thousands of residents have similar work schedules, live in the suburbs, and drive their cars to work in the city. They get up at about the same time every morning, take a shower, brush their teeth, and have a cup of coffee. Then they take to the roads—most of them at the same time that I do! Sociologists seek to understand the predictable and patterned aspects of what happens between people when they get together; sociologists even have a term for it: *social structure.* And in the case of sitting in maddening bumper-to-bumper traffic every day, social structure has become my biggest headache.

The smallest unit of social structure informs us that every member of society is expected to behave in a certain way, depending on the social position he or she occupies at any given time. Known as a *role,* this bundle of expected behaviors varies, from stopping at red lights and yielding the right-of-way at intersections, if you are a driver, or giving lectures and grading exams, if you are a teacher, to conversing informally and being supportive, if you are a friend. In the role of physician, an individual is expected to give physical exams and treat illnesses, whereas in the role of homemaker, an individual is expected to feed children and provide shelter. Dentists can stick their fingers in your mouth, but only during working hours. Shoe salesmen can measure your foot size, unless they happen to be in church. And judges can order you in contempt of court, except when they are eating in a restaurant or mowing the lawn at home. In truth, everybody plays a number of different roles every day.

The same person who is a dentist may also be a parent, someone's child, a member of the PTA at school, a part-time student at night, a member of a religious congregation, a vice president of a professional organization, a patient, a customer in stores and restaurants, a good friend, a brother or sister, a spouse, and so on. Each and every role played has its own set of expected behaviors, and, typically, we play large numbers of roles every day.

In "Just How Powerful Is a Role?" we learn that many people will go to great lengths, acting in uncharacteristic and bizarre ways, simply to behave in the socially expected manner. The experiment described in this essay suggests that roles can be very powerful in terms of determining how we behave and may also help us understand how the most hideous atrocities are sometimes committed by normal, even healthy and stable, individuals.

The negative consequences of social structure can be seen in other ways as well. In "Better Late Than Never," we see that college students are usually expected to bloom on time. That is, they are supposed to excel academically from an early age and to enter college by the age of 18 or 19. Indeed, if they vary from the expected pattern, students are given a name. They are called late bloomers.

Of course, whether or not a student is ultimately successful in the classroom (and in a career) is partially a matter of individual effort, talent, and luck. But there is definitely an important sociological side to being successful as well. You probably won't excel academically if you are denied the opportunity to do so.

Traditionally, men were much more likely than women, no matter how qualified in terms of grades and test scores, to be given any opportunity for higher education. Similarly, it was far more probable for individuals born into wealthy circumstances to attend college than for their economically less fortunate counterparts.

Opportunity also varies by society. In most societies, blooming on time is strictly enforced, no matter how much potential an individual might have. You either go to college at the age of 18 or not at all; you either get As and Bs by the time you're 12 years old or receive a trade school education, at best. In American society, we still prefer blooming on schedule—the majority of college students fit the mold, but we also allow some flexibility as to timing. In fact, 25% of all college students are now over 30, and close to 20% of college freshmen had Cs and Ds in high school.

Of course, social structure also has its desirable aspects. Because social life is somewhat predictable, we are able to count on instructors meeting their classes, doctors making their appointments, final exams beginning and ending pretty much on time, and so on. Because of the strict scheduling of time in an educational context, school administrators definitely benefit, because they can predict with some degree of certainty precisely how many textbooks, classrooms, and teachers they will need for an upcoming academic year. In fact, it would not be too much of an exaggeration to suggest that life without some degree of social order—social structure—would be utterly chaotic and therefore impossible over the long run. Perhaps the rush-hour commute is unpleasant, but at least we can be fairly sure that classes will be held when scheduled and that shops, stores, and restaurants will be open when they are expected to be.

In "Heartburn and Modern Times," I suggest that even basic biological processes (the regurgitation of stomach acid into the esophagus causing the burning sensation we call heartburn) may be influenced by a weakening of social structure. French sociologist Émile Durkheim, who lived at the turn of the 20th century, used the term *anomie* to describe a social situation in which the traditional rules of everyday life have broken down and individuals have become confused as to how to behave. Because of a sudden and dramatic change in lifestyle, their old patterns of social interaction are disturbed, and new patterns have not yet been established.

Individuals caught in an anomic condition are therefore at a loss to know how they are expected to behave. Social life is, for them, no longer patterned, shared, or predictable. A state of anomie can be brought on by any of several different circumstances—for example, a war, a physical disaster, a dramatic drop in income, or the loss of family and friends. Communities that attract large numbers of transients, drifters, and migrants often experience anomic conditions. For example, many who move great distances from home for the sake of a job have left behind all sources of guidance and support—their friends, extended kin, church, and fraternal organizations. After arriving in Los Angeles or Miami or Houston, they may have no place to turn for counsel or advice.

In his classic work, Durkheim discovered that anomie actually provoked some individuals to commit suicide. More precisely, he found that the rate of suicide in an area increases during periods of rapid social or economic change and also among those who are recently divorced or widowed.

If anomie affects the rate of suicide, it should be less than shocking to discover that anomie produces high rates of antacid use as well. Indeed, anomic circumstances seem to be associated with all forms of pathology, including crime, suicide, and even heartburn. Notice, by the way, that I address the rate of pathology, including antacid use, rather than any individual who experiences heartburn. I am not suggesting that the newcomers in any metropolitan area necessarily suffer from heartburn (though this is possible), only that their presence in large numbers will increase the likelihood that the heartburn rate is generally high. Maybe it's the transients and drifters who have heartburn, or perhaps they give it to more stable members of the population. As a sociologist, I am characterizing the metropolitan area as a whole, even if I never look at an individual case. In sum, the state of some characteristic of the area (its degree of migration) may have some influence on its rate of acid indigestion, not to mention its rate of suicide, homicide, and divorce.

# Just How Powerful Is a Role?

## Ask the Prisoners and Guards on Campus

Is it possible for people who are ordinarily decent, caring, and kind to behave as though they are sadistic and cruel, just because we expect them to be? Can the structure of social situations make normal people do crazy, sickening, immoral things? At the Nuremberg trials for crimes against humanity perpetrated in the concentration camps during World War II, Nazi leaders typically looked normal, ordinary, so much like the rest of us. Yet they were eventually found guilty of organizing and carrying out mass executions. In addition, thousands of German citizens went along and obeyed orders, even if it meant committing atrocities.

An important study by Philip Zimbardo and his associates at Stanford University may help shed light on the phenomenon of normal people doing abnormal, even horrific, things to others. Zimbardo and his colleagues turned the basement of a building on campus into a mock prison. They created a number of cells by installing bars and locks on each room and then placing a cot in each one.

Twenty student volunteers—all chosen for their mature and stable personalities—were selected to participate in the study. On a purely random basis (i.e., the flip of a coin), half of the students were assigned to play the role of guards, and the other half were assigned to play the role of prisoners. The experiment actually started at the homes of the 10 student prisoners.

To increase the realism of the study, all of them were arrested, put in handcuffs, read their rights, and then driven to jail in police cars. They were then completely stripped, sprayed with disinfectants, issued prison uniforms, and placed into locked cells.

Everyone knew that the experiment was artificial and that it was supposed to end in 2 weeks. Nobody was really a prisoner; nobody was really a guard. It was pure make-believe, having been decided by the flip of a coin. Yet after only a few days, both the prisoners and the guards were playing their roles with frightening determination.

Guards were told only to keep order. Instead, they began to humiliate and embarrass the prisoners, coercing them to remain silent on command, to sing or laugh in front of the other inmates, and to clean up messes made by the guards. In some cases, the guards would verbally and physically threaten and intimidate the prisoners, apparently for the purpose of asserting their authority.

For their part, the prisoners became more and more passive and compliant. In accord with the roles to which they had been assigned, the prisoners obeyed orders and accepted commands, no matter how unreasonable. They began to feel totally powerless to fight back. After only 6 days, four of the prisoners had to be excused from the study, having suffered serious episodes of anxiety, anger, or depression. In fact, the entire experiment was ended in less than 1 week when it became clear that the guards had become abusive and the prisoners were emotionally at risk.

Interviews conducted after the experiment ended were revealing. Both the prisoners and the guards told Zimbardo and his associates that they were both shocked and ashamed at how they had behaved. None of them would have predicted that they were capable of such cruelty, in the case of the guards, or obedience to authority, in the case of the prisoners. Remember that all of the student volunteers had been selected for their mature and stable personalities. Yet they all acted according to the roles created by the structure of prison life.

How powerful is a role? Just ask the students who volunteered to participate in Zimbardo's study. Then think of the atrocities committed in Nazi Germany, Rwanda, or the former Yugoslavia.

# Better Late Than Never

## Misery Can Be a Turning Point for Academic Success

It was a Thursday afternoon in March when Jennifer came to my office. The young woman's parents had urged her to see me for some advice about improving her dismal academic record. She had approached the end of her freshman year and was on the verge of flunking out. After speaking with her and reviewing her transcript, I was convinced that Jennifer was intelligent enough to succeed but was totally uninvolved with campus life. I thought that she might benefit from changing to a major she genuinely enjoyed and from participating more in campus activities. Within a week of our meeting, Jennifer had taken my advice: She changed her major from English to speech communication and joined the campus chorus. By the end of the term, she had dropped out of school.

What Jennifer failed to tell me (and I failed to ask) was that she was having an awesome time and didn't feel any particular need to remain in college. While enrolled in a full-time program (and attending classes only when she "felt like it"), she also held a part-time job that gave her plenty of spending money, was dating her supervisor at work, and was otherwise preoccupied with partying. Her parents paid most of her bills, and she hadn't really considered what she wanted to do as a career. From her point of view, there simply was no incentive to give up all the good times in favor of spending many hours in the library.

I have long wondered how we might get the Jennifers of the world to become committed students. To this end, Professor Bill Levin at Bridgewater State College and I interviewed a sample of honor college students who represent a particular variety of *educational late bloomers*—serious-minded, dedicated college students who had compiled only mediocre academic records while in high school. As late bloomers, many of these honor students had earlier "gone through the motions" of pursuing a college education. Borrowing from sociologist Robert Merton's typology of modes of adaptation, they had rejected the goal of academic success while continuing to attend college in a merely perfunctory or formalistic manner. Such a person remains in school because that is what middle-class Americans are expected to do.

Clearly, many young people with potential never bloom because they lack the economic resources to do so. Their parents simply cannot pay the cost of a college education. Thus, educational ritualism is largely a middle-class phenomenon. Yet opportunity varies not only from individual to individual but also from society to society. Almost everywhere outside the United States, the timing of academic success is inflexible. Students must achieve high grades and achievement test scores early in their academic careers; they must also enter college by a specified age.

Thus, in England, India, and Japan, students who have not excelled by the time they reach high school have traditionally been effectively disqualified as college material. What is more, students in such countries have been expected to enroll in college by their late teens and have not been given opportunities to do so later in life, regardless of their academic potential.

In American society, we at least tolerate some degree of late blooming. Since 1970, the number of college students over 25 years of age has increased from 28% to 44% (Owen, 2003). Almost 20% of all American college students were C and D students in high school. When they get to college, many of them—some 28%—take remedial courses in reading, writing, or mathematics. Moreover, hundreds of thousands of students who begin at community and junior colleges later transfer to four-year institutions. The number of such students is disproportionately represented among African-Americans, Hispanics, and Asian-Americans.

Based on our interviews with late-blooming honor students at Northeastern University, Bill Levin and I have identified a number of precipitants—situations or events that served as turning points for late academic success. A few of these precipitants were positive. In one case, for example, a young woman bloomed after developing a close relationship with a boyfriend who expected her to be a serious student. In another case, a late bloomer gave credit to a new and exciting course that inspired him to study hard and to change his major.

Even when positive turning points could be located, however, they were almost always accompanied by negative precipitants as well. Indeed, many of our late bloomers were, at least on a temporary basis, intensely frustrated, upset, and disappointed before they succeeded. In a word, they were first *miserable,* and then they bloomed.

Many of the honor students we interviewed were a few years older than their schoolmates, having dropped out of college for a year or two, transferred from another college, or spent a few years in the military. At some point prior to matriculating (or rematriculating), they began to acknowledge the importance of their educational deficiency, viewing it as an obstacle, a failing, a major shortcoming to overcome. While out of school, some had been forced by circumstances to take jobs that were low paying, boring, or unpleasant. They then realized that their career opportunities would be greatly enhanced by returning to school and studying toward a college degree.

Because Northeastern University is an institution that stresses cooperative education, most of the late bloomers in our sample had taken a job for a 6-month period while undergraduates. Many suggested to us that their work experience "on co-op" had showed them, perhaps for the first time, the strong connection between grades and the work they were likely to be doing after they graduated. A large number of co-op experiences were positive. But an unpleasant co-op was particularly motivating; it forced the student to deal with the likelihood that, unless things changed drastically, this was the kind of monotonous job he or she might be forced to fill for the rest of his or her life.

There are probably numerous college students who are miserable enough to want to succeed in school. Relatively few will do so. Instead, they lower their level of aspiration, change their goals to those that do not require a college degree, or find some source of satisfaction outside of their jobs. Those who cannot adjust and remain miserable, in their quest for acceptance and success, may become deviants.

Many potential late bloomers simply do not know how to succeed. They may not know how to study, they may not know how to take good notes, they may not have friends who support and encourage their success, they may not know what to read, or they may be timid about changing their major in line with their personal interests and goals. Those who have dropped out of school may not easily be able to find sources of encouragement and support. Even those still in school may continue to act from the negative self-concept they held in the past.

Once a student is ready to accept the importance of educational success, therefore, instructors, advisors, counselors, and close friends have a special opportunity to become agents of change. This is when they ought to intervene to provide structure and support. Timing is crucial. Some will look for tutoring and advice. Others will want support and encouragement. If they find what they need, they may succeed. If not, they may remain miserable.

In closing, allow me to return to the case of Jennifer, a student who came to me for advice and then dropped out of school. After leaving college, Jennifer got a full-time job as a waitress in a pizza restaurant. Her parents stopped sending money, and her boyfriend left. She was suddenly less than happy with her life. She began to ask, "Is this the kind of boring, tedious, underpaid job that I might have to take the rest of my life?" Ten months later, Jennifer went back to Northeastern University. She changed her major, changed her friends, changed her thinking about school, and became a straight-A student. She is now a practicing attorney in a large law firm in Philadelphia.

# Heartburn and Modern Times

## Don't Blame the Tex-Mex

According to a Gallup survey, the ailment known as heartburn is a chronic source of pain and suffering for almost 62 million American adults. Fifty-four percent of them pin the blame on spicy foods; others single out overeating, indigestion, gas, or poor diet. Many regularly take an antacid in pill or liquid form.

For the sufferer, heartburn clearly has a biological basis. It frequently occurs after a meal when acid backs up from the stomach into the esophagus, causing a burning sensation in the chest or throat. From a sociological point of view, however, there may be a good deal more to heartburn than just the discomfort of spicy foods and excessive acidity. Like many other physical ailments, the symptoms of heartburn may be influenced by the stresses and strains frequently associated with residential mobility undertaken to enhance a career or supposedly to improve the quality of life.

I ranked 197 metropolitan areas of the United States on the National Rolaids Heartburn Index, a measure based on an area's per-capita sales of all brands of over-the-counter antacids, and then compared these metropolitan areas on a grid of important social, economic, and demographic characteristics. Most striking, I found important regional differences in heartburn rates. For example, despite their reputation for having a laid-back pace of life, most major cities located in the far West—San Francisco, Sacramento, Fresno, Seattle, Los Angeles, and Phoenix—had particularly high rates of antacid use. Indeed, 40% of all high-heartburn metropolitan areas were located in western states. Also having particularly high rates were southern cities such as Charlotte, North Carolina; Richmond, Virginia; and New Orleans, Louisiana.

By contrast, midwestern cities had extremely low rates of heartburn. Green Bay, Wisconsin; Sioux City, Iowa; Columbia, Missouri; and Fort

Smith, Arkansas, placed close to the bottom. In fact, almost half of the metropolitan areas with the lowest rates of heartburn were located in Midwestern states. El Paso, Texas, however, even with its penchant for spicy Tex-Mex cuisine, turned out to have the lowest level of heartburn of any city in the United States.

Data on northeastern cities were also surprising. Overall, those cities seldom exhibited either high or low heartburn levels. Only 11% of both the highest heartburn metropolitan areas and the lowest heartburn areas were located in the Northeast. New York City, for example, registered only a moderate rate of heartburn, though it is well known for its fast-paced, hectic way of life.

How can these variations in rates of antacid use by metropolitan areas be explained? Differences in diet and physical environment might contribute to the overall level of heartburn. Over-the-counter antacid use may not be an accurate measure of heartburn (a few people without heartburn take these antacids, and many with heartburn do not).

Despite such methodological problems, a major contributing factor to the rate of heartburn in an area can be found in what might be called gold-rush fever. All of the cities with a high incidence of heartburn have recently experienced tremendous population growth as a result of migration from other cities and regions of the country. For the sake of a job or a better way of life, former Midwesterners and Easterners have gone West.

They have packed their bags, left behind family and friends, and traveled thousands of miles to cities on the West Coast. This may explain why most of the most attractive and appealing metropolitan areas also have the highest rates of heartburn. They attract individuals who are dissatisfied with their present lives and are willing to move to enhance them.

Cities with stable populations are more likely to have a low incidence of heartburn. These cities appeal less to individuals who want to increase their economic opportunities. In such cities, construction comes to a standstill as the demand for real estate remains constant. Of the top 15 housing markets, not one is located in a low-heartburn metropolitan area, but 5 are in the high-heartburn group. The city of El Paso never experienced the oil-based, boom-and-bust cycle of heartburn-plagued Texas cities such as Dallas or Houston.

Wherever there are large numbers of transient, rootless people, there is also likely to be anxiety, stress, and frustration—and high levels of heartburn. Sociologists call this state of affairs *anomie,* a social condition that prevails where newcomers to an area are confused as to the rules of living. When things are anomic, there is widespread disorganization and isolation, a breakdown in order.

One indicator of anomie is the presence of social pathology. Thus, high-heartburn areas were more likely than their low-heartburn counterparts to also have high rates of violent crime, divorce, and alcohol consumption. Heartburn may be another, albeit more subtle, indicator that something is wrong.

Other researchers have noticed that the pathology varies by specific metropolitan areas. Social psychologist Robert Levine of California State University compared cities in terms of their level of psychological stress. He found that 6 of his 10 cities with the highest stress were located in the far West. He determined that stress was especially high in those metropolitan areas that contained large numbers of migrants, residents who were born out of state. Not coincidentally, the Western states had the greatest percentage of migrants—gold-rush fever strikes again! Whenever the population flow to the far West begins to reverse itself, Easterners and Midwesterners will cease exporting their heartburn to other areas of the country. Who knows? In the future, New York, Philadelphia, or Boston might even become the next heartburn capital of the United States.

# FOCUS

## ✧ Suggestions for Further Reading ✧

The classic prison role experiment conducted by Philip Zimbardo and his colleagues Craig Haney and William Banks is described in detail in "A Pirandellian Prison" in the *New York Times Magazine* (1973). For a recent update, read Zimbardo's (2007) *The Lucifer Effect: Understanding How Good People Turn Evil*. For a famous study of obedient role-playing, also read Stanley Milgram's *Obedience to Authority: An Experimental View* (1974) and *Obedience to Authority: Current Perspectives on the Milgram Paradigm* edited by Thomas Blass (2000). In Milgram's study, 60% of a sample of normal Americans were willing to administer a severe electrical shock to a stranger, simply because they were told to do so by an authority figure in a lab coat.

Concerning "Better Late Than Never," Bill Levin and I published our ideas about late blooming in an article titled "Sociology of Educational Late-Blooming," in *Sociological Forum* (1991). Then, I wrote more about the triggering incidents for late blooming in "Misery as a Turning Point for Academic Success," in *Journal of Research in Education* (1993).

Eviatar Zerubavel's book *Hidden Rhythms: Schedules and Calendars in Social Life* (1981) offers insights into a much-neglected topic, the sociology of time. For a social-historical analysis of the rise of age consciousness in American society, read Howard Chudacoff's *How Old Are You?* (1989). In this fascinating work, Chudacoff reminds us that there was a time when people didn't know their precise ages and when birthdays were left uncelebrated. Prior to the 20th century, people rarely sent birthday cards to one another or had birthday parties.

The data reported in "Heartburn and Modern Times" concerning rates of antacid use by metropolitan area were originally collected by pollster ACNielsen. I was hired by Warner-Lambert to analyze these data and then report my results. In 2004, I consulted for Novartis Consumer Health in a similar capacity. This time, however, I examined the sale of cough and cold medicines in metropolitan areas across the country. Once again, I discovered that many balmy California cities led the field. Bakersfield, Monterey, and San Diego were all cough and cold capitals, whereas the residents of much frostier cities like Minneapolis, Buffalo, and Lincoln, Nebraska, were substantially less likely to come down with a cold (*Nursing Home & Elder Business Week*, 2004).

The link between illness and anomie is a new variation on an old theme. Anomic circumstances have long been associated with high rates of pathology.

In his classic study *Suicide: A Study in Sociology* (1951), Émile Durkheim introduces a sociological theory to explain differences in the rate of suicide by time and place. One of his major types is called anomic suicide because it results from a sharp break, a profound disruption in the social bond.

The powerful attraction of social structure is poignantly illustrated in Debra Renee Kaufman's excellent *Rachel's Daughters* (1991). Her subjects were women who returned to religious orthodoxy out of a sense that structure was missing from their lives. By contrast, the extraordinary women in Mary Catherine Bateson's *Composing a Life* (1990) chose a different course in response to ambiguities in the female role. Making the best of the severe discontinuities in their lives, they improvised opportunities for creativity and innovation but not without experiencing pain.

# DEVELOPING IDEAS

## ✦ About Social Structure ✦

1. Research topic: One of the most fundamental forms of social order is contained in the concept of role, the set of expected behaviors associated with a particular social position, such as teacher, doctor, son, mother, student, and so on. What is OK in one role may be totally inappropriate in another. For example, we expect students to take exams, write papers, and attend class. We do not expect them to stick their fingers in someone's mouth. But dentists do it every day (we actually pay dentists to stick their fingers in our mouths), and we don't expect dentists to write papers.

   What is proper or improper depends on the role. As you know, there is even a role of elevator rider. Similarly, there is a role of passenger, whether on a bus, a train, or an airplane. While riding with strangers on public transportation, we are expected to behave in a certain way. To examine the requirements of this role, take a ride on a bus or another form of public transportation (if this is too difficult, try riding in an elevator). While acting as a passenger, notice how other riders are sitting or standing, whether there is any conversation (if so, about what and under what circumstances?), and how you feel when the vehicle is crowded and why you feel that way. If you are not too embarrassed to do so, you might try starting a conversation with another passenger. What is the reaction?

2. Writing topic: In the essay about educational late bloomers, I presented several factors that seem to contribute to succeeding behind schedule, including intellectual capacity, opportunity, a precipitating incident, and social support. Think of someone you know (perhaps a friend or a relative) who

possessed the intelligence to bloom educationally but never did. In a short essay, explain how his or her position in the social structure (gender identity, age, socioeconomic status, societal membership) may have helped prevent his or her educational success.

3. Writing topic: In the essay about heartburn, I focused on per-capita antacid use by metropolitan area. How do you think a psychologist who was interested in the causes of heartburn would have conducted this study? Would he or she have examined a number of metropolitan areas? What do you think he or she would have looked for in those individuals who suffered from heartburn? What conclusions might a psychologist have drawn, and how might they have differed from those derived by a sociologist?

4. Research topic: One measure of the importance of being on time is just how precisely individuals keep their clocks and watches running. Because the importance of precise time varies from society to society, it is possible that the precision of watches and clocks also varies from place to place. Because it is unreasonable to ask you to travel to another society, instead, compare the clocks and watches in your own home, apartment, or dormitory floor with those in someone else's home, apartment, or dormitory floor. (You might, for example, compare men's and women's floors to determine the influence of gender on the importance of time, or you might compare different kinds of office buildings.) In writing, record the error (from actual time) on each clock or watch, and then take an average for each place. Also include the number of watches and clocks in a state of disrepair. Now, identify the winner!

5. Writing topic: Instant millionaires—those who win the Megabucks lottery— aren't always as happy as you might believe. Many of them experience tremendous anomie. In a short essay, speculate as to exactly how the lives of instant millionaires might abruptly change for the worse. Also indicate what you think they might do to diminish the pain of suddenly being wealthy.

6. Research topic: Interview someone who has recently experienced a dramatic change in lifestyle—an individual who has moved thousands of miles, has been recently widowed or divorced, or has even been married. (It would be great, but very difficult, to interview an instant millionaire!) Try to determine whether the abrupt change in that person's way of life has had any negative effects of which he or she is aware. Where does he or she go for help and guidance? Is he or she more anxious about the future? How does that person fill the hours of the day with meaningful activities? If he or she has had little or no trouble adjusting, you might want to determine why. Through friendships, religion, fraternal organizations, or a commitment to work, has that person found a new source of structure in his or her life?

# PART I

## Culture

S everal of the students in the course I teach on the sociology of violence came from other countries to attend school in Boston. Two were from Asia, one was from Europe, one was from South America, and another was from an island in the Caribbean. About 15 minutes into our first meeting, I realized that their presence in the classroom would make a difference in the way I approached the course. It really didn't take a psychic to figure out that communication would be more difficult. From the first day, there were lots of bewildered looks and blank stares to remind me. Then there were questions.

At first, I considered the problem to be only one of language. In plain English, I believed that my plain English was, to them, not so plain. By the end of our first session together, however, I recognized that the problem was more profound than just misunderstood words and phrases. Indeed, from the types of questions they were asking, I concluded that some of the international students in my class also lacked familiarity with those practices, objects, and ideas that most Americans share on an everyday basis and therefore take for granted as the American way of life. My foreign students were, in a word, *unfamiliar* with American culture.

Consider a concrete example. In our discussion of the manner in which mass killings are reported by the mass media, I introduced James Huberty's rampage through a McDonald's fast-food restaurant located in a suburb of San Diego. I noted that several newspapers around the country had referred to Huberty's killing spree (he killed 21, mostly Hispanic children) as Mass McMurder and The Big Mac Attack. The American students immediately understood the glib, possibly offensive aspects of these newspaper headlines, but three of the international students had only questions: What is a Big Mac? one asked. Not knowing the logo of this famous hamburger chain, another wanted to know why the paper called Huberty's attack McMurder. Before continuing our discussion of mass killings, therefore, we spent several minutes talking about fast-food hamburgers.

Now, it is true that degree of familiarity with American culture varies quite a bit among the peoples of the world. And among my international students, I noticed immense variation in this respect. In fact, the young woman from Western Europe was quite familiar with American values and customs, at least much more so than her counterparts from Asia or South America. Though she had been in the United States only a few days before the course began, she had eaten many times in American fast-food restaurants (McDonald's restaurants are located throughout Europe and increasingly in other areas of the world), had watched American television, and was also acquainted more with the American brand of humor. That's because the values and customs in her country were so similar to ours. They are likely to be, of course, because we Americans have had enormous contact with

Europe and have derived much of our culture from it. The process whereby cultural traits spread from one society to another (e.g., from the mother country England to the United States) is known as *cultural diffusion.*

Clearly, we can thank (or blame) cultural diffusion for giving us many important ideas and objects that originated in, or at least passed first through, Europe. In "The Immaculate Americans," we discover that it was the British who, during the Industrial Revolution, were plumbing pioneers. By the early part of the 20th century, however, the idea of plumbing for the masses had traversed the Atlantic Ocean, and American society had taken the lead in developing private bathrooms for the majority of its citizens. For the first time in history, the home bathroom was regarded as a middle-class necessity. Also in "The Immaculate Americans," we learn that collective tolerance for odor varies from place to place, from one society to another. In some other parts of the world, Americans are viewed as neurotically concerned with their personal cleanliness. We certainly do use tremendous amounts of deodorant and mouthwash; such products have become part of our culture.

The ideas that we often take for granted or believe to be constants in nature—for example, our ideas about cleanliness—may actually originate in the culture that we learn. But what is the origin of culture? We know that people aren't born with it—although they are born with the capacity for culture. Only humans seem to have the full-blown capability; other animals often share a way of life but not one that is learned and passed along to the next generation. For the most part, animals are programmed from birth to act and react in social situations. (For example, birds don't learn to fly by watching other birds do it first; nor do mother birds teach them. They develop the ability for flight by instinct alone.) The origin of a particular type of cultural content—whether one or another thing is regarded as proper and right—is also a fascinating topic.

Some sociologists and anthropologists believe that economics may play a major role in determining the particular character of a culture. The important 19th-century theorist Karl Marx argued, in writing about the rise of communism, that the economic system of a society determines almost everything about other social institutions. He believed that religion, family life, and the press were all handmaidens to the prevailing economic system; that is, they existed essentially to support and maintain the economic status quo, to make sure that it survived. From a Marxian point of view, therefore, the Protestant belief about work—the religious conviction that hard work is a sign of personal salvation—exists only because capitalism needs a way to dupe or mislead workers (that is, a way of motivating workers to tolerate their terrible working conditions, accept their exploitation by the owners of production, and be achievement oriented in the interest of maximizing corporate profit). You don't have to accept Marxism to agree that he was right to emphasize the role of the economy in determining the complexion of mass culture—popular art and music—in a capitalistic society like ours.

Middle-aged and senior citizen rock musicians such as Van Morrison, Paul Simon, Mick Jagger, and Billy Joel may not help to preserve capitalism, but their continuing popularity is probably a result of the appeal they have to huge numbers of people who grew up in the 1960s and 1970s and who are willing to spend their hard-earned money in the interest of nostalgia.

In "Baby Boomers" we are introduced to a possibly important source of cultural expression. The baby boomers—that generation of people born between 1946 and 1964—continue to have a certain amount of cultural clout but only so long as they spend their money. How will they be treated if they give up their credit cards? Only time will tell.

Culture often takes on human form and substance. The cultural values cherished by Americans are embodied in the heroes we choose to revere on a collective level. During the opening decades of the 20th century, our cultural heroes were what sociologist Leo Löwenthal in 1961 called idols of production—industrial tycoons who served as role models for citizens who accepted some version of the American Dream and aspired to be successful and wealthy just like their heroes. By mid-century, however, Americans had instead shifted from idols of production to idols of consumption—the entertainers and sports figures who filled our leisure hours with their music, drama, and athletic prowess.

In "The Demise of Bystander Apathy," I speculate that we have recently undergone yet another major shift in our selection of cultural heroes. Coming out of an era of spectatorship and passivity, we now seem to admire idols of activism, those men and women who are seen as having taken control of their destiny, who aren't afraid to step forward and stand apart from the crowd to take a firm position. In the face of big business, big government, and the threat of terrorism, we respect individuals who take charge of their everyday lives because we hope to be able to do the same. In "Making Monsters Into Celebrities," however, I argue that our cynicism is showing when we place the worst sorts of murderers in places where we formerly put our most virtuous heroes.

Culture has thus far been associated with an entire society. Yet even the smallest social settings can develop a shared set of rules for behavior—that is, a culture. In "Elevator Culture," I discuss the proper way to behave in an elevator when riding with other passengers. Surprisingly, perhaps, it turns out that elevator culture permits very little positive guidance for behavior; in fact, there may be only one socially correct way to stand in an elevator. No wonder some people prefer to take the stairs! Before turning to the snapshots of culture in this first section of the book, let's return for a moment to the situation of having a number of international students in the small seminar that I teach. In introducing this section of the book, I emphasized the communication problems posed by my students' lack of familiarity with American culture. What I failed to stress, however, was that their presence in my seminar also had an important positive impact by bringing to bear on our classroom discussions the experiences of the diverse cultures they represented. In some cases, students from other countries added to our discussions by reinforcing the universal validity of our sociological generalizations. Their own experiences suggested that what was true about American society might also apply to their homelands. In other cases, however, my students added a cautionary input. Based on their experiences, certain relationships discussed in our class could probably not be generalized beyond American, or perhaps Western, culture. As a sociologist, I can safely say that I learned a great deal from being immersed, even if only on a secondhand basis, in cultures from around the world.

# The Immaculate Americans

## Being Cleaner Doesn't
## Mean We're Better

B ody odor is big business. Every year, we immaculate Americans spend
more money on deodorants and mouthwashes than we contribute to
the United Way. In addition, we probably pass more time scrubbing, wash-
ing, spraying, bathing, squirting, and gargling than any other people in the
history of the world. Every American, in fact, learns from an early age that
cleanliness is considered next to godliness—a sign that an individual is
morally pure and sinless. No wonder Americans spend more than $1 billion
annually on soap—it's part of our culture.

In other parts of the world, however, we are regarded as neurotically concerned with our personal cleanliness. In some European countries, for example, American tourists are easily identified by their demands for a room with
a private bath. Meanwhile, their European counterparts more often stay in
rooms where they wash up daily in a small sink and take their baths down
the hall. In their own countries, anyone caught showering twice a day would
probably be regarded as either eccentric or ill.

Notwithstanding our present-day preoccupation, Americans can hardly
take credit (or blame) for inventing a concern for cleanliness. Arab interme-
diaries, in arranging a marriage, sometimes rejected a prospective bride who
didn't smell nice. Sniffing and nose kissing have long been practiced by the
Inuit of Canada, Philippine Islanders, and Samoans who recognized the
desire for a pleasant odor. And bathing for purification is an ancient custom
practiced by the early Hebrews, Muslims, and Hindus.

Medieval royalty even took baths but only on occasion. In England, for
example, King John bathed three times a year, always before a major religious festival. But church authorities and medical practitioners in the Middle

Ages generally frowned on bathing, denying the general population access to the few existing baths. Instead, medieval people stuffed their nostrils with strong perfumes to disinfect the air and reduce the onslaught of black plague. Even after the Middle Ages, Queen Elizabeth I of England bathed only monthly (whether she needed it or not).

Major efforts to overcome the problem of personal cleanliness for the masses really weren't made until the mid–19th century. During the Industrial Revolution, the British were the plumbing pioneers. For those who lacked private facilities, the state built public bathhouses consisting of individual bathrooms with centrally controlled plumbing. By the early part of the 20th century, however, cultural diffusion had taken effect, and America had taken the lead in developing private bathrooms for the majority of citizens. For the first time in history, the home bathroom was no longer viewed as a status symbol but was regarded as a middle-class necessity.

Of course, everything is relative when it comes to culture, and some Americans have acquired such lofty cultural standards today that they think foreigners smell. Perhaps they are right, at least when judged by a national norm that refuses to tolerate any body odor at all. The odorous outsiders (who, by the way, probably smell pretty much like human beings are intended to) are then regarded by some Americans as dirty, slovenly, or perhaps even morally impure.

The bias is not new. Odor has often been used to discredit entire groups of people. During the Middle Ages, for example, European Jews were widely believed to have drunk the blood of Christian children as part of the Passover ritual to rid themselves of an odor of evil. It was also rumored that after their conversion to Christianity, the Jewish malodor miraculously disappeared.

Closer to home, American blacks, Latinos, Hawaiians, and Native Americans have all been stereotyped in cultural images at one time or another as smelling different. And one of the most offensive olfactory images is that of elderly citizens—especially nursing home residents—who are too often stereotyped as reeking from incontinence, indifference, and the ravages of age.

Just how accurate are such cultural images of group differences in odor? Is it possible that the members of different ethnic and racial groups really do have distinctive smells? Consider, for example, the possible effect on the quality and quantity of perspiration of dietary differences or of jobs requiring strenuous physical activity. Such differences do vary by group; they might even differ by ethnicity or social class. Yet the perception of such group differences in odor seems entirely out of proportion to their actual occurrence, if they happen at all.

More likely, the charge of minority malodor is needed by bigots who are eager to justify discriminatory treatment against a group of people by dehumanizing them. The reasoning is simple enough: Animals, not human beings, give off a stench. Human beings must be treated according to the rules of civilized society, but animals can be mistreated, even slaughtered, at will. The members of group X give off a stench (they don't bathe and live like pigs); therefore, they can be mistreated.

The sociological question is answered best by recognizing that perception of odor is only one component in the much larger repertoire of cultural racism. Our beliefs about various groups are often supported by deeply rooted emotions acquired early that can linger throughout life. In the Jim Crow South, white Southerners had an intense emotional reaction to the possibility of desegregating their public facilities. Black skin was regarded almost as a contagious physical condition, something dirty that might rub off and contaminate those individuals who were fortunate enough to be white—hence the need for norms requiring separate public conveniences that imply close contact, such as restaurants, theaters, buses, water fountains, and restrooms.

In his analysis of race relations in the United States, James Comer, himself a black American who overcame poverty and discrimination to become a well-known psychiatrist and author, recounts the story of a white teenage girl who was scolded by her father for having put a coin in her mouth. He yelled, "Get that money out of your mouth—it might have been in a nigger's hand!" His reaction reminds us of an important principle of human behavior: You really don't have to smell like a skunk to be treated like one.

# Baby Boomers

## A Generation Without a Gap

Rock music has long been a symbol of adolescent rebellion. The greasers of the 1950s wouldn't have been caught dead listening to recordings of Glenn Miller, Woody Herman, or any other musician reminiscent of their parents' day. Similarly, members of the 1960s hip generation were too intent on distancing themselves from what they saw as oppressive traditional authority to regard tunes by Fats Domino and Chuck Berry with more than historical curiosity.

That's why it is so intriguing that for the last couple of decades, high school and college students didn't reject—and, in fact, embraced—the popular music of yesteryear. Of course, they still identified with the superstar songsters of their own age—Backstreet Boys, Hanson, Spice Girls, Fiona Apple, Oasis, and the like. But amazingly, they also admired longtime rock idols of the 1960s and early 1970s who were well into what we euphemistically call the prime of life, otherwise known as middle age. During the 1990s, oldsters such as Pink Floyd, Fleetwood Mac, Aerosmith, Carly Simon, the Grateful Dead, Mick Jagger, Van Morrison, Bonnie Raitt, George Harrison, and Paul Simon all had top-selling CDs or videos. Paul Simon's Grammy-winning album *Graceland* was a top-ranked CD. And according to *Billboard* magazine, among the top concert moneymakers of the 1990s were middle-agers Billy Joel, Bob Seger, the Eagles, and David Bowie. During the same period, concerts by such 1960s oldies legends as 51-year-old Gene Pitney and Shirley Alston Reeves, former lead singer of the Shirelles, drew sellout crowds. In the late 1990s, the top concert draws continued to include an overrepresentation of such late middle-agers as the Rolling Stones, Paul McCartney, Barbra Streisand, and Fleetwood Mac. Even more recently, Bruce Springsteen, Elton John, and Billy Joel have held sold-out concerts around the country.

Part of the continuing popularity of the 1960s rock stars was their nostalgic appeal to the moving human population explosion we now call the baby boomers, 76 million American men and women born between 1946 and 1964. Many of them were just coming of age during the 1960s as the Beatles, the Rolling Stones, and Bob Dylan entered the music scene or later as Woodstock launched their generation into the 1970s.

Even as their oldest members now approach their early 60s, the baby boomers wax nostalgic. They have glowing memories of the formative period in their lives and the music that it spawned. The passage of decades has not changed their appetite for the rock 'n' roll songs on which they were raised.

But it isn't only nostalgic baby boomers who have craved the sounds of the 1960s and 1970s; their younger brothers and sisters and in some cases their children also did—and in a big way. Only a few years ago, for example, the weather vane of adolescent opinion, *Teen* magazine, reported the results of a survey of its readers' favorite entertainers. Among the names of idols in the entertainment world were names associated with a previous generation, many of whom were 30 years older than their teenybopper fans— Kenny Rogers, Alabama, Bill Cosby, the Judds, and Cybill Shepherd. Similarly, a poll of the youthful audience for a popular MTV all-request music program named "Heart and Soul" by the Monkees as its top video of the year and 42-year-old Davy Jones as its choice for cutest guy. As recently as 1998, *Seventeen* magazine raved about concerts by oldsters from Janet Jackson to Tina Turner and focused on the future of youthful Deadheads in the aftermath of Jerry Garcia's death. Even more shocking, senior citizen singer Tony Bennett has during recent years made a spectacular comeback, enjoying popularity even in the teenage music market.

Baby boomer nostalgia has also inspired many of the top advertising agencies to include pop oldies in their commercials. The fast-food company Burger King has used the Everly Brothers' "Wake Up Little Susie," the laxative Senokot made use of a rendition of James Brown's "I Got You (I Feel Good)," Toyota featured a version of Sly and the Family Stone's "Everyday People," Applebee's played an adaptation of Creedence Clearwater Revival's "Suzie Q," and Sears employed the lyrics of Roy Orbison's "You Got It." In 2007 alone, TV commercials featured the music of the Everly Brothers, Buddy Holly, Elvis, the Lovin' Spoonful, and Van Morrison.

During the 1960s, long before they were given a label, today's baby boomers had not only large numbers (half the population of the United States was under 25) but also plenty of disposable income. And they often disposed of it on 35-mm single-lens reflex cameras, stereo components, bell-bottom jeans, miniskirts, Hula Hoops, and so on. Business interests were, of course, thoroughly pleased with such free-spending habits—so pleased, in fact, that such commercials as the Oil of Olay ads promised that you would not look over 25! And in his best-selling work *The Greening of America*, law professor Charles Reich raised the possibility that our entire society would soon be transformed in the image of youthful hippies of the day.

During the closing years of the 1960s, there was reason to make such a prediction. The baby boomers were role models for everyone who emulated their teenage children's appearance. Middle-aged women donned bell-bottom jeans, tie-dyed shirts, sandals, and love beads while their husbands wore their hair shoulder length, their ties psychedelic, and their sideburns to the end of their earlobes. Many also grew beards and mustaches to lengths that today would be regarded as thoroughly outrageous. Indeed, the style of the day was the style of the baby boomer generation: It seemed as if everybody was either young or wanted to be.

Into the new millennium, however, the baby boomers have finally lost at least some of their cultural clout. They still boast large numbers and spend lots of money on microwave ovens, compact disc players, home theaters, and personal computers. But the most important factor influencing the recent decline in their cultural clout is the competition they have gotten from their own offspring who are now in their teenaged years or older.

The children of the baby boomers (sometimes referred to as the baby boomerang generation) hardly match the huge numbers associated with their parents but are nevertheless a mini–baby boom of their own, representing more than 17 million of the nation's high school students and almost 20 million college students. And as with their mothers and fathers, the fact that the baby boomers' teenagers have plenty of disposable income has attracted the attention of commercial interests around the country who are eager to sell them cars, cosmetics, and fast food.

As a result, the popular music industry has undergone a dramatic change, no longer depending almost exclusively on baby boomers for inspiration or consumption. The oldies format has all but vanished from radio and with it the sounds of Elvis, Motown, and the Beach Boys (Fisher, 2007). Middle-aged rock artists continue to appeal, but they share the spotlight with a whole new group of youthful rappers—Ludacris, Joe Budden, 50 Cent, Obie Trice, The White Stripes, The Streets, Nelly, and Lil' Kim—whose names are as foreign to baby boomers as are the musicians of Asia or the Middle East. Moreover, the characters on primetime television and the models in commercials are once again as likely to be young as they are middle-aged. The likes of Katie Couric, Andie MacDowell, and Adam Sandler continue to enjoy popularity, but so do younger entertainers like Kelly Clarkson, Christina Aguilera, Lindsay Lohan, and Miley Cyrus.

Recognizing the possibly diminishing influence of the boomers, the American Association of Retired Persons—whose membership consists of Americans 50 and older—has begun to promote concerts and radio formats for elders. In 2007, the organization sponsored a Tony Bennett national concert tour and stage shows featuring Earth, Wind & Fire and Rod Stewart. Moreover, boomers continue to buy lots of CDs, while their youthful counterparts are instead increasingly downloading music from the Internet. There are also signs that certain rock stations in major cities may return to an oldies format, simply because teenagers have reduced their interest in listening to music on broadcast radio. Among the top recording artists in July 2007 were boomer favorites Pink Floyd, The Rolling Stones, and Bob Marley. Since the year 2000, a number of seasoned songsters have attracted large audiences. Boomers continue to flock to live concerts given by Jimmy Buffett, ZZ Top, Ozzy Osbourne, the Village People, Tina Turner, U2, Paul McCartney, Prince, and Bruce Springsteen. The continuing popularity of boomer artists may be helped along by a fundamental shift in the thinking of youngsters. Until recently, teenagers and their parents hardly crossed the lines that separated their musical tastes. For example, most boomers of the 1960s wouldn't have been caught dead admitting they listened to Eddie Cantor or Al Jolson, popular singers from their parents' generation. By contrast, today's young people are less inclined to conceive of music in chronological terms. All of the musical trends of the last five decades seem to coexist.

What is the future course of events likely to be for aging baby boomers? Though now forced to share the cultural spotlight with their own teenaged children, the baby boomers still have large numbers on their side. By the year 2025, when they achieve senior citizenship, more than 20% of the population will be over 65.

Yet it is a sad truth that numbers alone are as likely to ensure poverty as power. In fact, elder Americans living 200 years ago commanded much greater respect and privilege than they do today, despite (or perhaps because of) the fact that only 10% of the population lived to celebrate their 60th birthday. Granted, this figure is skewed somewhat by high rates of infant mortality. Nonetheless, under Puritanism, old age was regarded as a sign of election and a special gift from God. But when longevity increased and more sizable numbers of people survived to old age, the cultural clout of elders declined. Specifically, preferential seating arrangements in public vehicles for older people were abolished, mandatory retirement laws appeared, youthful fashions were preferred, and eldest sons lost their inheritance advantages.

More than sheer numbers, then, graying baby boomers of the future will need to maintain the free-spending habits that endeared them to commercial interests if they are to maintain any of their cultural clout. Not only will they need plenty of money, but they must be willing to spend it as they did in the past. If they are anything like previous generations of older Americans, however, this may not be realistic. Senior citizens tend to become economy conscious by reducing their use of credit and by shopping for price. Even if many baby boomers refuse to retire at 65 or 70, they will likely decide to temper their consumerism in favor of preparing for an uncertain future in terms of health care, economic depression, inflation, and the like. Depending on the course of public policy over the next few decades, even financially secure individuals may become quite conservative in their spending habits. This does not mean that aging baby boomers will be asked to live in poverty, only that they may be forced to give up their place as the cultural kingpins of American society.

# The Demise of Bystander Apathy

## We Admire Idols of Activism

In 1964, in a now classic case, Kitty Genovese was stabbed to death in the middle of the night while 38 of her neighbors listened from the safety of their apartments. Although the victim screamed for help and her assailant took almost 30 minutes to kill her, no one even reported the incident to the police, never mind fought off Genovese's killer.

Social scientists of the day argued that this apparent indifference was a result of what they called diffusion of responsibility. That is, although they may have been concerned for the victim, Genovese's neighbors also felt a lack of personal responsibility to intervene. They reasoned, Why should I risk my neck when there are other witnesses who will surely come to the rescue? However it was explained at the time, the Genovese case was the first nationally recognized episode of bystander apathy—one of the most distasteful by-products of the American preoccupation with spectatorship.

Although it was first acknowledged then, bystander apathy is a phenomenon not peculiar to the 1960s, nor is it exclusive to any one generation of people. Just by going through recent newspaper stories, it would not be difficult to argue that people still do not help one another.

Take the Manchester, New Hampshire, woman who was brutally raped in a yard just steps away from her apartment. Apparently, she was in full view of several of her neighbors, but they ignored her pleas for help.

In Raleigh, North Carolina, a motorcyclist injured in an accident lay on a crowded highway and counted 900 cars over a 3-hour period before anyone stopped to assist him. In Boston, a third-year medical student was jumped by four teenagers while riding his bicycle home from the hospital. Many people watched, but none of them intervened. In New York City, a group of jeering and joking youths watched while a 30-year-old man was electrocuted on the third rail of the subway station at Times Square. And on and on.

Observers of the social scene have used such cases in arguing for the existence of a destructive and callous side of human nature. Based in part on the writings of Freud and, more recently, of such ethnologists as Konrad Lorenz, who emphasize the evolutionary basis for aggressive behavior, they have focused on bystander apathy to illustrate how people are moving away from one another. This point of view is sometimes so thoroughly one-sided, however, that it ignores the fact that altruism is a value in virtually all human societies and forms the basis for most of the world's great religions. Americans have long institutionalized altruism by awarding medals for outstanding acts of selfless heroism as, for example, in the medals awarded by the Carnegie Hero Fund Commission or, during wartime, in the U.S. Armed Forces' awarding of the Congressional Medal of Honor.

While some observers dwell on the seedier side of human nature, hundreds of others donate one of their kidneys for transplantation into another human being. Thousands more have donated their blood at some personal expense and inconvenience. And millions regularly donate money to their favorite charities.

Following September 11, 2001, the nation's charities were swamped with checks, cash, clothes, and even frequent-flier miles. During the first two weeks alone, donations hit $500 million. By August 2002, the 10 largest charities claimed they had collected $2.3 billion.

And the sources were so diverse: race drivers donating helmets, an all-star rock concert at Madison Square Garden, school bake sales in Wyoming, and, in Massachusetts, Congressman Marty Meehan's Education Fund to help the victims' families.

The response to Hurricane Katrina in August 2005 was no less substantial. Hundreds of thousands of evacuees were welcomed by the residents of communities around the country. Americans donated money, medical supplies, blood, and clothing.

Today, some 40 years after the Genovese case, these acts of generosity and selflessness seem more abundant than ever. In addition, there seems to be less tolerance for those individuals who respond to others with indifference or selfishness. In fact, bystander apathy seems fast becoming the exception to what may be a new norm of social life: being willing to risk inconvenience, embarrassment, and even personal safety to come to the rescue of the victims of crimes and accidents. The evidence is, at this point, admittedly anecdotal and informal, but it is nonetheless highly suggestive. There have been numerous reports recently of acts of great heroism and courage performed by average citizens who haven't otherwise stood apart as paragons of virtue. The members of this breed of Good Samaritans are very serious about taking personal responsibility for the plight of others, refusing to take refuge in the anonymity of the crowd or the masses.

We used to see purse snatchers and muggers; now we also see bystanders who chase and catch the mugger. We used to read about physicians who drive past automobile accidents because of the fear of a lawsuit; now we also read about doctors who come to the rescue of accident victims and, in the process, may suffer injuries of their own. We used to see corruption in government and industry; now we also see whistle-blowers who risk being fired to expose practices that they believe to be dangerous to the public.

An example of personal altruism is the behavior of Richard Young, a New York City fireman, who risked serious injury to rescue a total stranger—a truck driver who hung by his arms from the steering wheel of the cab of his truck as it dangled over the edge of a bridge. Arriving on the scene, Young threw himself under the truck driver's body to break his fall. In saving the man's life, Young received a broken leg, a broken ankle, and severe back injuries.

In 1997, 53-year-old Harvey Randolph saw his neighbor Jill Fitzgerald being viciously attacked and bitten by four pit bulls. The 155-pound plumbing contractor rushed to Jill's side, where he was finally able to drag her to safety. The brutal attack left Jill with 113 wounds to her head, neck, back, arm, and legs, requiring 188 stitches. Harvey suffered an injury to his elbow, requiring surgery, and wounds to his hands and right leg.

In 1998, Bruce Fitzell was fishing down river from Healdsburg Veterans Memorial Beach in Sonoma County, California, when he spotted a swimmer helplessly slip below the surface. Bruce immediately swam to the spot where the swimmer had gone under and found him lying on the bottom of the river. He then pulled the drowning man to the surface and got him to shore, where a bystander administered cardiopulmonary resuscitation (CPR) until the swimmer had regained consciousness and was breathing on his own.

In 2003, Daniel Creange, an off-duty Bogota, New Jersey, patrolman, observed a car swerve across lanes and strike two curbs and several traffic signs before coming to rest on the grass median of an off-ramp. The driver, 37-year-old Jimmy Mak, had suffered a seizure and lost control of his vehicle. Creange and another passersby pulled the unconscious man from his car and, seeing that he was not breathing, began CPR. Minutes later, paramedics stabilized Mak and drove him to Hackensack University Medical Center.

In 2007, an anonymous bystander in Arlington Heights, Virginia, saw a 7-year-old girl floating face down in an apartment swimming pool. He brought the unconscious girl to the side of the pool, where he performed CPR until she awoke. By the time she was transported to a nearby hospital, the youngster was in good condition. The anonymous spectator had saved her life.

Also in 2007, 50-year-old Wesley Autrey witnessed a teenager suffer a seizure and collapse onto subway tracks at Broadway's 137th Street Station in New York City. Autrey immediately jumped down onto the tracks and attempted to pull the teenager, still in the throes of a seizure, to safety. Recognizing there was not enough time to avoid an approaching train, Autrey pulled the teenager into the center of the tracks and lay on top of him. Two cars passed over the men before it stopped, leaving only about 2 inches to spare. Quick thinking on Autrey's part saved him and his fellow commuter from certain death.

What characteristics distinguish these Good Samaritans from the rest of humanity? Social scientists have discovered that individuals who intervene in a dangerous situation are likely to have had training in first aid, lifesaving, or police work. In addition, they tend to be exceptionally tall and heavy. These attributes give them the sense of competence or efficiency—through training and strength—necessary to be injected into potentially hazardous situations. Good Samaritans also tend to be adventurous types who have taken other risks with their personal safety. The most important conditions accounting for the rise of the Good Samaritan may be found in the types of heroes they choose to emulate.

Researchers have discovered a common factor among German Christians, who, during World War II, helped rescue the victims of their Nazi persecutors; civil rights activists of the 1950s and 1960s (called Freedom Riders); and altruistic children: the presence of someone to serve as a model of altruism. In the case of a child, that model is likely to be an intensely moralistic parent with whom the Good Samaritan can closely identify. In adults, models for appropriate behavior are also found in the national heroes they choose to emulate.

On the national level, we continue to have our *idols of consumption*—those bigger-than-life images on the screen, tube, or field of play whose accomplishments fill our leisure hours with music, comedy, and drama.

But there is now a new breed of national hero as well. Today, we have *idols of activism*—individuals who are admired and revered not for their ability to keep us entertained but for their courage to take active charge of their own lives and the lives of others. In the face of overwhelming and impersonal social, political, and economic forces, such as the threat of terrorism, big government, and corporate malfeasance, we feel increasing admiration for those who come forward from their place among the spectators.

The September 11 attack on the United States has given us new idols of activism—firefighters, police officers, the volunteers at ground zero, the family members of victims, and our military in Afghanistan and Iraq. The 40 doomed passengers and crew on Flight 93 have been honored for their heroic efforts in refusing to allow terrorists to fly into the White House or the Capitol. The final words of passenger Todd Beamer on an onboard phone call to the FBI became legendary when an operator overheard him say, "Let's roll." Shortly afterwards, Flight 93 crashed into a field in a rural area near Pittsburgh, killing everyone on board. The passengers had apparently wrested control of the plane from the terrorists.

This change in our culture may have made heroes out of the cinematic images of Kate Winslet in *Titanic*, Jeff Bridges in *Fearless*, Denzel Washington in *John Q*, Ben Affleck in *Daredevil*, Tobey Maguire in *Spider-Man*, Brandon Routh in *Superman Returns*, and Tom Cruise in *Mission: Impossible III*, but it has still made us admire the very real courage of the passengers on Flight 93.

# Elevator Culture

## You Really Can't Do Anything Else But Stare at the Door

Social psychologists conducted an experiment in which they gave elevator riders at Ohio State University an opportunity to help themselves to a coupon good for a complimentary Quarter Pounder with cheese. After entering the elevator, riders saw a poster reading "Free McDonald's Burger" and a pocket underneath it in which coupons for one Quarter Pounder were located. All they had to do was take one.

Fifty-six people entered the elevator alone. Of this number, 26 were randomly permitted to ride without other passengers, 16 rode with one other passenger, and 14 rode with two other passengers (all of the other passengers were really confederates of the experimenters who decided on a random basis whether subjects rode with 2, 1, or no other riders).

Results obtained in this experiment showed that individuals riding alone were much more likely to help themselves to a coupon for a cheeseburger than were riders in the presence of other passengers. In fact, of those individuals riding by themselves, 81% took a free coupon. With one other passenger present, however, only 38% took a coupon, and with two other passengers present, only 14% helped themselves to a coupon.

Why would elevator passengers avoid doing something to their advantage— taking a coupon for a free cheeseburger—just because other riders were present? The answer seems to involve the influence of elevator culture—a set of unspoken, unwritten rules of behavior that are widely shared and generally observed by people in elevators who ride with other passengers. The riders in this experiment were eager to avoid doing something that might call attention to themselves in the public setting of the elevator, even if it meant sacrificing a free fast-food lunch. They didn't want to be deviant; they desired to avoid being embarrassed; they didn't want to look different.

Actually, there isn't very much you can do that is right in an elevator, especially if you are among strangers. Almost all of the rules of elevator riding seem to be proscriptive—things you are definitely not supposed to do. The only prescriptive—positive—rule involves standing quietly while facing the elevator door, and that is precisely what most passengers will do. Unless they want to be regarded as weirdos, most riders avoid talking to anyone they don't know, staring at anyone, touching anyone, and even breathing on anyone (they wouldn't want to violate the personal space of other riders, even in a crowded elevator).

One interesting thing about elevator culture is that it extends far beyond the elevator walls. Actually, almost any public setting—whether walking on the streets of a city, eating in a restaurant, or sitting in the park—carries a set of rules that severely limit the quality and quantity of social interaction: In all of these places, there is little, if any, talking to, touching, or even looking at strangers. As a result, strangers in a big city who are physically close might as well be miles apart as far as interaction is concerned.

Of course, individuals also have some control over their culture; they don't passively have to conform to it. In an early study of conformity, Solomon Asch (1952) studied a group of eight people, in a classroom situation, who were asked to match the length of a line drawn on the blackboard with one of three comparison lines drawn on an index card. All judgments were made out loud and in order of seating in the room.

Actually, only one participant in the Asch study was a naive subject, and he voiced his judgment after hearing several other students state theirs first. (These others were confederates of Asch who had been instructed to respond incorrectly when asked to match the length of the lines.) Over a number of trials with different groups, approximately one third of the naive subjects made incorrect estimates in the direction of the inaccurate majority—in other words, about one in three conformed. But when a lone dissenter gave support to the naive subject by going against the majority judgment, the rate of conformity dropped dramatically to less than 6%.

Thus, if even one person waiting in line for a table in a restaurant starts talking to other customers, he or she might serve as a role model for other customers to imitate. Who knows? Maybe lots of people will take a chance and get involved in the conversation. And if one rider in a crowded elevator has the courage to take a coupon for a free cheeseburger, everybody might conceivably end up having lunch on McDonald's.

# Making Monsters Into Celebrities

## Popular Culture Is Saturated With Images of Infamy

### Jack Levin and James Alan Fox

More than 30 years ago, when he predicted that everyone would some-day be world famous for 15 minutes, even Andy Warhol could not have foreseen the astounding rise of celebrity as it would come to pervade turn-of-the-century mass culture. In response to the growing influence of the entertainment industry, a new genre of "star" biographies, gossip columns, magazines, television programs, and souvenirs—saturated with images of "mega-fame" and "mega-stardom"—has established itself in America's popular arts.

At the same time, it is nothing new for Americans to single out certain of its most virtuous members for special attention. Not unlike the residents of other Western nations, Americans have lavished celebrity status on a range of human beings considered exemplary or extraordinary, including military leaders, politicians, business leaders, scientists, entertainers, and leading sports figures.

In America's recent preoccupation with celebrity, however, the most villainous figures—those who have committed particularly repulsive and despicable crimes—are being granted the same sort of celebrity status traditionally accorded to heroes. A recent example occurred in October 2002 when, over a period of three weeks, two snipers shot to death 10 innocent people in the Washington, DC, area. Even before 42-year-old John Muhammad and his 17-year-old partner John Lee Malvo had been identified and apprehended, they were already dubbed "the Tarot card killer" on the cover of *Newsweek* magazine. Moreover, not to be "scooped" by its competition, *U.S. News & World Report* similarly reserved its cover story for the "I am God" message found scrawled on a Tarot card at one of the snipers' crime scenes. Leading newspapers further deified the DC snipers by using their arrogant statement as their "quote of the week." Given such a memorable and glamorized depiction, the DC snipers Muhammad and Malvo are sure now to take their place among the many other serial killers who have become household names—the Son of Sam, the Green River Killer, the Hillside Strangler, and the Unabomber, to name only a few.

The around-the-clock media saturation surrounding the DC sniper case was not without justification, of course. Even though the print and electronic media may have been criticized for their excessive coverage, news journalists still performed a vital function, at least for those who lived in the area that for weeks was enveloped by fear.

While a killer is on the loose, poised to strike at any moment, it is not only the right but also the responsibility of the mass media to inform a terrified public about a clear and present danger in their midst—about the latest details concerning the killer's movement and the progress of the investigation. But transforming a serial killer into a national celebrity is surely another matter entirely. It may even inspire him to take more lives, to enlarge his body count, so that he can maintain and enhance his stature as a national superstar.

Serial killers appear quite aware of their media impact as well as their celebrity. Lawrence Bittaker and accomplice Roy Norris tortured and murdered a string of teenage girls in 1979 in Southern California, dumping one mutilated body on a suburban lawn to encourage media coverage.

After Bittaker was caught, he signed autographs from his prison cell, "Pliers Bittaker." Clifford Olson, who raped and murdered 11 children in British Columbia in the early 1980s, begged to be referred to as "Hannibal Lecter." In order to justify his desired position as the "grand champion" of serial murder, Olson actually confessed to slayings he could not possibly have committed.

Becoming a popular-culture celebrity is an important part of the motivation that inspires serial killers to continue committing murder. Once they are identified with a superstar moniker, their frequency of murder increases. No longer satisfied with obscurity, they seek to prove that they deserve the superstar status to which they have been assigned. Los Angeles's 1984–85 Night Stalker, Richard Ramirez, reportedly said to one of his victims as he assaulted her, "You know who I am, don't you? I'm the one they're writing about in the newspapers and on TV."

The damage done by granting celebrity status to serial killers goes beyond motivating their evil deeds. In addition, it helps inspire other ignored and alienated Americans to become copycat killers in order to achieve their own degree of infamy. Making monsters into celebrities teaches our youngsters—especially alienated and marginalized teenagers—a lesson about how to get attention. "Want to be noticed? Want to feel important? Simple. Shoot lots of your classmates. Then, you'll be on the cover of *People* magazine, you'll be interviewed by CNN, and you'll make headlines all over the nation, if not the world!"

On February 2, 1996, for example, in the obscure town of Moses Lake, Washington, Barry Loukaitis, a 14-year-old student at Frontier Junior High who had long been teased, shot to death two classmates and his math teacher. The fact that a 14-year-old boy could commit multiple homicide at school was so abhorrent that it sparked a national orgy of media coverage, inspiring a string of copycat multiple murders, which included tragic episodes in such unlikely places as West Paducah, Kentucky, Pearl, Mississippi, Jonesboro, Arkansas, Springfield, Oregon, Littleton, Colorado, and Santee, California.

The copycat effect may be particularly strong for those teenagers around America who have suffered humiliation, if not physical abuse, at the hands of their insensitive classmates. Some alienated youngsters come to view school snipers—like Dylan Klebold and Eric Harris, who shot and killed more than a dozen classmates at Columbine High in Littleton, Colorado—as their heroes. After all, they had the guts to take matters and guns into their own hands and strike back against the nasty bullies and mean-spirited teachers. Even more, they're famous for it. Like other schoolyard killers, Klebold and Harris received a massive amount of media attention, albeit posthumously. Their images now appear on "trenchcoat Mafia" T-shirts, referring to the name they had given their small group of misfits, nerds, and outsiders at Columbine High. Although adults may look at the image of a school sniper plastered on a magazine cover and consider it the ultimate humiliation for the youngster and his family, many children, in their immature view of the world, may instead consider the youthful assailant as a big shot. Those high school students in small-town America who had been teased and bullied were inspired by the shootings they watched on the network newscasts and in the headlines.

The Virginia Tech massacre of 32 students and faculty in 2007 seems to have received much inspiration from the early rampage of Klebold and Harris through Columbine High. Seung-Hui Cho was given a model for achieving a sense of power and importance through the barrel of a semiautomatic. In order to secure his place in infamy, the Virginia Tech killer sent to NBC News a set of photos he had taken of himself, portraying him as a powerful and dangerous person, certainly not someone to be ignored.

It is no coincidence that so many of the tragic school shootings were committed by teenagers residing in obscure areas around the United States. These were areas of the country that had felt immune to what they regarded as big-city crime. Unlike large cities, where residents had taken measures to reduce juvenile violence, small towns and suburbs had not prepared for the onslaught and were caught totally off guard.

Along with sociologist Jason Mazaik, we recently studied the 1,300 covers of *People* magazine published over its first 25 years. During the 1970s, only one killer was featured on its cover. In the 1990s, by contrast, *People* printed more than two dozen different cover stories about vicious killers.

Its readership of 36 million weekly makes *People* magazine an especially influential form of American popular culture. Yet to single out this magazine for criticism would be unfair and inaccurate. To an increasing extent, violent criminals are gratuitously being featured in places where we used to place our heroes. Through the Internet, it is now possible to buy action figures, calendars, trading cards, and T-shirts bearing the likenesses of such despicable killers as Ted Bundy, the law student who killed dozens of women in several states; Jeffrey Dahmer, the cannibal who strangled to death and consumed 17 men in his Milwaukee apartment; and Andrei Chikatilo, the Russian serial killer who took the lives of 53 people. Dahmer has also been featured in a comic book depicting him engaged in sexual acts with his victims (who are in fact identified by name).

Moreover, there are individuals who are so fascinated with serial murderers that they will purchase any item associated even remotely with a killer's hideous crimes. Bricks taken from Jeffrey Dahmer's apartment building were considered by some as prized souvenirs. Even before his execution by the state of Illinois, the self-portraits painted by John Wayne Gacy, who killed 33 men and boys, were sold for as much as $2,000 each.

And Richard Speck's oil paintings went for $3,000—only because he had murdered eight nurses in Chicago. Danny Rolling, a serial killer who murdered and mutilated five college students in Gainesville, Florida, coauthored (with his adoring girlfriend) a book of sketches and poetry: Like many other murderers, Rolling even has his own Web site.

Unfortunately, Americans seem to have become infatuated with infamy. Some have suggested that scandalous celebrities serve a social comparison function for audience members who work out their own moral issues by speculating about the personal lives of the "stars." This is, however, not the whole story. By granting celebrity status to villains, not only do we add insult to injury by further denigrating the memory of the victims, but we may be inadvertently providing our young people with a dangerous model for gaining national prominence and fame. We may also be giving to the worst among us exactly what they hope to achieve—celebrity status. One serial killer made this intention and his frustration known when he asked in a letter to the local police, "How many times do I have to kill before I get a name in the paper or some national attention?"

# FOCUS

## ✧ Suggestions for Further Reading ✧

Many of the ideas and evidence found in "The Immaculate Americans" were based on Gale Largey and David Watson's excellent 1972 article "The Sociology of Odors" in *American Journal of Sociology*. In this article, Largey and Watson make a very strong case that olfactory sensitivities vary from culture to culture. The use of images of odor to discredit a group of people is only one form of dehumanization. For a visual version of this phenomenon, see Sam Keen's *Faces of the Enemy: Reflections of the Hostile Imagination* (1986).

Evidence for the tremendous influence of baby boomers can be found in *Great Expectations: America and the Baby Boom Generation* (1980) by Landon Y. Jones. To focus specifically on women at the leading edge of the baby boom generation, I recommend Winifred Breines's excellent book *Young, White, and Miserable: Growing Up Female in the Fifties* (1994). For a cultural-materialist view of social customs more generally, read Marvin Harris's fascinating work *Cultural Materialism* (1979). Harris suggests that the variety of cultural behavior around the world is a result of the adaptations that societies make to their particular environments. For example, in 1487, the Aztecs suffered from a profound shortage of animal protein in their diet; they were not able to raise cattle, sheep, goats, horses, pigs, or llamas. In response, they continued to incorporate cannibalism into their warfare. After a battle, they would eat their enemies—thousands of them—as an alternative source of animal protein.

The trend toward activist cultural heroes as introduced in "The Demise of Bystander Apathy" is beginning to show up in the sociological literature. For example, Myron Peretz Glazer and Penina Migdal Glazer, in their important book *The Whistleblowers: Exposing Corruption in Government and Industry* (1989), have studied the growing phenomenon of ethical resisters—those courageous workers who expose corruption in high places. Despite harassment and a strong possibility of defeat, these whistle-blowers operate out of a sense of moral responsibility to challenge the status quo. If you are interested in learning more about altruism and empathy in everyday life, read Alfie Kohn's book *The Brighter Side of Human Nature* (1990). He convincingly presents evidence from sociology, psychology, and biology to suggest that human beings are more caring and generous than we give ourselves credit for. According to Kohn, helping others occurs as often as hurting others. Samuel Oliner's penetrating work *Do Unto Others: How Altruism Inspires True Acts of Courage* (2003) examines hundreds of individuals who helped rescue victims of the Nazis during Hitler's reign of power. Oliner emphasizes that the rescuers had a deep-rooted empathy for other people's problems that they had developed in their childhood homes. Their parents were profoundly moral individuals who often acted on their beliefs; in our terms, they were everyday versions of idols of activism.

A work by Robert Bellah, Richard Madsen, William Sullivan, Ann Swidler, and Steven Tipton, *Habits of the Heart: Individualism and Commitment in American Life* (1985), analyzes both the tradition and the direction of our cultural values. According to Bellah et al., we have lost touch with our cultural commitment to community in favor of a preoccupation with rugged individualism. In the process, we have ignored the very traditions that might help us today. A related argument has been put forward by Robert D. Putnam (2000) in his excellent analysis *Bowling Alone: The Collapse and Revival of American Community*.

Our cultural recognition of rugged individualism (and perhaps cynicism) can be seen historically in images of criminals who have received inordinate public attention. In many cases, they were regarded as "Robin Hood" types, whose victims—banks and large corporations—were widely viewed as exploitative and unethical (Kooistra, 1989). In some cases, of course, very influential villains also received attention but only so long as they were newsworthy and only in media specializing in news of a political, an economic, or a legal character. For example, Adolf Hitler made 7 covers of *Time;* Joseph Stalin was on 12.

In "Making Monsters Into Celebrities," we examined a more recent phenomenon—that of heaping attention on the "accomplishments" of brutal and sociopathic murderers. Such villains are not noteworthy for their pervasive political or economic influence, nor are they admired because they attack victims who are themselves widely regarded as exploitative or evil. Instead, these celebrity criminals—not unlike their counterparts who sing, dance, or perform in major motion pictures—simply entertain the masses with their spectacular and bizarre criminal behavior.

Yet featuring villainous celebrities may represent only part of a larger trend in American popular culture, in which nastiness has more generally come to assume a prominent position. In the face of intense competition for sales and ratings, the producers of the popular arts, eager to capture the largest possible share of the media market, have introduced more and more horrific depictions. The old-fashioned "good against evil" morality plays are harder to locate, having been replaced by one despicable professional wrestler brutalizing another despicable professional wrestler or one miserable talk-show guest berating (if not fist-fighting) another miserable talk-show guest. Moreover, TV reality shows like *Fear Factor* play on the sadistic impulses of audience members who delight in the suffering of contestants.

# DEVELOPING IDEAS

## ✧ About Culture ✧

1. Writing topic: Name five of your heroes from such fields as business, sports, entertainment, religion, and politics or from everyday life. Then write an essay in which you identify the particular cultural values reflected in their heroic accomplishments. To start, consider whether they are idols of production, consumption, or activism.

2. Writing topic: We have seen how much cultural clout the baby boomers have had in American society. Thinking about music, art, comedy, and television, identify some of the contributions that your generation has made to American popular culture.

3. Research topic: Let's say you are a sociologist studying the culture of your campus. Construct a one-page questionnaire to identify some of the values and practices that are widely shared among the students at your college. Then give the questionnaire to a sample of students. (To get at how values operate in everyday life, you might want to ask such questions as how many hours a week your respondents spend doing things like studying, partying, watching TV, and so on. You might also ask them to rank order certain activities—getting good grades, having a date, being well liked, or making lots of money—in terms of how important they are.)

4. Research topic: Pick up a recent issue of a supermarket tabloid—preferably the *National Enquirer* or the *Star*. Analyze all of the profiles in that issue with respect to the human qualities and problems that they emphasize. First, determine how many profiles feature celebrities.

   How many of these are entertainers, business leaders, or politicians? How many would you regard as idols of consumption? Next, find out how many profiles feature ordinary people who do extraordinary things. How many were Good Samaritans? How many performed miracles or great acts of courage? How many would you regard as idols of activism?

5. Research topic: Taking September 11, 2001, as a dividing point, compare the celebrities on the covers of *People* for the 12-month period before versus after the attack on the United States. This will probably require going to the library and photocopying more than 100 *People* covers. Be sure to discard any cover that does not feature a particular individual—that is, a cover that contains several celebrities all given equal emphasis or a cover that does not feature human beings. You might hypothesize that the September 11 terrorist attack caused Americans to focus more on our traditional heroes rather

than criminals. If so, then, in comparison to the 12-month period prior to September 11, you would expect to find fewer murderers, rapists, and other criminals on the cover of *People* in the year following the attack on America.

# PART II

## Socialization

I t was a disquieting scene: Three African-Americans waiting for a bus and, across the road, a young white child—he couldn't have been more than 2 or 3 years old—shouting racial slurs at the top of his lungs as he took bites from a 3 Musketeers bar. Just as the trio got aboard the bus, the boy's mother rushed over, picked him up, and carried him away. At first, she was furious that he had left her side without asking permission. But then she smiled as he continued to yell racial slurs and point in the direction of the bus as it sped away.

Just like the child at the bus stop, we aren't born knowing the content of our culture; we learn it. We absorb our culture—we learn love of country, motherhood, apple pie, and racism through a process of interacting with others—parents, teachers, friends, and television characters—that we call socialization.

In "Can Hate Be Healed?" we see that children can be socialized to hate. From an early age, they overhear jokes and epithets that belittle and degrade the members of other groups; they are told that people who are different in terms of race, religion, sexual orientation, or disability status are inferior; they come to restrict their informal relations to individuals within their own groups and to distance themselves from people who are different. At the extreme, hate can become pathological, reflecting not only the cultural standards of a society but also the psychological abnormalities of the hatemonger.

Much socialization is by necessity somewhat parochial. Few of us grow up with a representative sample of life experiences. So, many Americans don't realize, for example, that Caucasians are a minority among the world's racial groupings or that Christianity is a minority religion worldwide. They believe incorrectly that most of the world looks the way they and their family and friends look.

In "Teaching Students They Are Not at the Center of the Universe," my colleague Will Holton and I discuss a course that we developed to help change our students' views of people who are different with respect to race, religion, and ethnic background. The effect of any distortions in our perception may be profound: Many of the decisions we make in everyday life are in part a result of what we believe the world to be like. If, for example, we exaggerate the likelihood of being a victim of violence, we might decide to carry a handgun. If we overestimate the wealth of our nation, we may oppose programs that aid the homeless. And if we incorrectly believe that most of the members of another race or ethnic group are rapists and murderers, we might avoid them like the plague.

Socialization is absolutely essential for individuals to become humanized members of their society. Without internalizing culture, we would all be sociopaths, essentially unsocialized individuals who lack conscience, human warmth, and empathy for the problems of other people. Yet just because individuals accept the values and norms of their group doesn't necessarily mean that they will automatically reject violence. Indeed, even the most brutal, most repulsive behaviors have been taught during the normal course of socialization. A good deal of socialization occurs at school, where a child typically spends much of the day with teachers, classmates, friends, and counselors.

Sadly, there is also far too much violence in the school environment, even at the elementary level. In response, principals have instituted programs and policies that aim at resolving dangerous conflicts and teaching students techniques for preventing any future acts of violence. But administrators don't always recognize the need for after-school activities—sports, music, drama, student government, and so on—to provide alienated and unsupervised youngsters with a safe alternative to violence.

Especially in the elementary years—kindergarten through 5th grade—such programs are usually missing. And even where after-school activities exist at the middle and high school levels, they are generally treated as a privilege for the "good" students rather than as a cost-effective violence prevention program in which all students learn values and establish models for healthy relationships.

Any discussion of the way in which values are transmitted to the members of American society would be incomplete if it failed to include a discussion of the mass media. In particular, television has an immense influence as an agent of socialization, if for no other reason than that the average child spends 4 to 5 hours daily in front of the tube. I often hear concerned Americans voice their criticism of television for what it supposedly does to children. And much of this criticism is well deserved. But let's put the effect of television in perspective: There is far less street crime in Japan, yet Japanese television is even more violent than ours. Why? Perhaps because fewer Japanese parents use television as a baby-sitter.

Instead, they sit with their children while they watch the tube, ready to monitor, interpret, and discuss. It isn't so much that American television is so strong but that our other institutions—family, business, religion, and schools—aren't doing their part, which may be at the heart of the problems we now face. Socialization does not come to an abrupt end just because someone grows up.

To some degree, adults continue to change throughout life, and they too are very much influenced by what they watch on the tube. "Confessions of a Soap Opera Addict" suggests that the fantasy on TV is often seen as the reality. In the extreme case, soap opera characters become our good friends. We may even send them gifts.

In "Adult Socialization Can Be Murder," I examine an extreme example of development into adulthood gone awry—the case of murderers who don't start killing until they reach their 30s, 40s, or even 50s. I ask, If early child-hood is really the critical factor, why didn't these killers begin their murder sprees when they were 12 or 18 or even 24? Why did they wait until they were middle-aged adults? To some extent, most Americans share an overall way of life. They accept at least some values and practices from the dominant culture as their own. At the same time, Americans are not rubber stamps of one another. Just as they share in the dominant culture, their worldviews are also colored by their belonging to a subculture—a group whose members have their own particular set of values, objects, and practices.

In "Sticks and Stones May Break . . ." we see the importance of member-ship in subcultures for establishing an individual's personal identity. The question, Who am I? is often answered in subcultural terms: I am Irish-American, I am Latin-American, and so forth. These subcultural names are important in symbolic terms for their ability to express the shared conscious-ness and pride of a group in society whose members may struggle with their subcultural identity.

Charles Horton Cooley, writing at the turn of the last century, suggested that our self-image is developed through the looking-glass process. That is, we form a sense of self by interacting with others. In this process, we come to make a judgment of ourselves—that we are smart, attractive, moral, and so forth—based on the judgments that others make of us. Thus, the other people in our lives are, in a sense, a mirror in which we see our own reflec-tion. Cooley called the result of this process the looking-glass self.

If self-esteem develops in social interaction, names can hurt you as much as sticks and stones. In "Sticks and Stones May Break . . ." we see that children who are given unpopular or unusual names may be treated in a neg-ative way. In response, they develop poor self-esteem and actually act as pre-dicted: badly. The entire process becomes a self-fulfilling prophecy.

When applied to a group of people, names often contain a cultural stereo-type—an unflattering image that the members of a society learn from their parents, their teachers, their friends, and the mass media. The racial slur shouted by the toddler in the bus-stop scene that opened this section is only a name. But it contains one of the nastiest cultural stereotypes ever taught to our children.

# Can Hate Be Healed?

## The Difference Between Cultural and Pathological Prejudice

*Jack Levin and Arnold Arluke*

L ast week, a 30-year-old Pakistani-American, Naveed Haq, went on a shooting rampage at a Jewish Federation office in Seattle. After a forced entry, he shouted, "I am a Muslim-American, angry at Israel" and opened fire, killing one woman and wounding five. Haq had frequently told colleagues that he despised Jews. His parents told reporters that their son had long suffered from bipolar disorder. Cases like this happen close to home, too. In February, an 18-year-old man went on a crime spree, assaulting patrons inside a gay bar in New Bedford, Massachusetts, and killing two people in a gun battle with Arkansas police before killing himself. Jacob Robida, the killer, hated gays, blacks, and Jews. He collected Nazi memorabilia and filled the walls of his bedroom with swastikas. Robida had also been severely depressed.

We deplore such acts of hate as perpetrated by Robida and Haq in part because they are considered purposeful. According to some psychiatrists and psychologists, hate is also a mental illness causing bigots to become totally irrational and destructive.

Most hate is cultural. Normal people learn to hate from an early age from parents, teachers, friends, coworkers, and the media. They might never translate their bigotry into behavior beyond using stereotypic epithets and telling bigoted jokes.

But some hate is pathological. It becomes so severe that it takes control of a person's life, causing him to become isolated, fearful, self-destructive, and dangerous to others. Haq and Robida seem to have suffered from pathological hate.

Mental health researchers now propose medicalizing the most extreme and dysfunctional forms of prejudice by treating pathological hate as an official psychiatric diagnosis. Edward Dunbar, a psychologist at the University of California, Los Angeles who has treated dozens of patients for "racial paranoia," suggests that dangerous forms of hate can be reduced by administering an appropriate form of psychotherapy. Alvin Poussaint, a psychiatrist at Harvard Medical School, argues that patients who suffer from pathological hate might benefit from antipsychotic medications and other forms of therapy.

Opponents assert that this diagnosis would only allow bigots to evade responsibility for their nasty and illegal behavior. They express a concern that the hatemongers would be treated as victims rather than perpetrators, even when they are tried for assaulting members of the groups they despise.

But it is already the case that a defendant's mental illness can be a mitigating factor in a judge's sentencing decisions. For example, killers may get a lighter sentence, even when not diagnosed as hatemongers, if they can show they were abused as children. It is the plea of "not guilty by reason of insanity"—not a diagnosis of mental illness—that allows defendants to avert criminal responsibility. And only 1% of all felony defendants attempt the insanity defense.

More important, the threat from individuals like Haq and Robida would be reduced by treating pathological hate as a mental disorder. First, it would help to discredit and stigmatize the prejudices of individuals whose persistent fears of other groups are regarded as a product of disease rather than rational thought. Their stereotyped views of blacks, Muslims, Jews, or gays would be viewed as delusional, entirely lacking in any reality, rather than as a normal case of prejudiced thinking. Also, extremely hateful individuals would no longer be ignored by the mental health profession or treated only for depression but would be more likely to receive the attention that they so sorely need to combat their delusional beliefs.

Even if Haq and Robida had received effective treatment in the form of psychotherapy or antipsychotic medication, they would probably still have held bigoted views. But they might not have gone on a rampage.

# Teaching Students They Are Not at the Center of the Universe

## We Construct the World in Our Own Image

*Jack Levin and Wilfred Holton*

Segregation is a fact of life on college campuses around the country. Visit a crowded cafeteria at almost any college or university, even the most diverse, and you will see students "of a feather" sitting and eating together—whites with whites, blacks with blacks, Latinos with Latinos, and Asians with Asians. Even worse, when college students from diverse backgrounds occasionally interact, they often do so under hostile conditions. A survey of 550 colleges conducted by *U.S. News & World Report* found that, over a 1-year period, 71% of the campuses in the United States had at least one hate incident involving a student's race or religion. Of course, it's not just college students who opt for spending quality time with their "own kind." Americans of all ages and backgrounds tend to separate themselves by race and religion in almost every aspect of daily life.

It is not surprising that our beliefs about other human beings are often inaccurate, based more on stereotype than reality. A person who grows up in Boston may come to believe that 60% of all Americans are Catholic because that is what she sees on her street, at her workplace, and in school (the real figure is more like 25% of all Americans). Similarly, someone raised in Washington, DC, may be convinced that 70% of all Americans are black (the real figure is approximately 12%); a New Yorker might swear that half of all Americans are Jewish (the real figure is close to 2%). We tend to apply what we see every day to what we don't see every day.

And television is not very helpful in giving its viewers an accurate portrayal of the entire range of humanity. Communication research conducted for more than a decade indicates that heavy television viewers tend to overestimate the percentage of the world population that is white and male and underestimate the amount of poverty in our country. They are socialized to accept a false view of social reality, because this is precisely what they see on TV every evening beginning at 8 p.m. The world of primetime television is overpopulated by white males who possess more than their share of wealth and power. F. Earle Barcus, in his work *Images of Life on Children's Television: Sex Roles, Minorities, and Families* (1983), discovered that the same could be said of children's television—of the 1,145 characters appearing on 20 children's programs, only 42 were black, and 47 belonged to some other minority group.

Last fall, we teamed up to teach an experimental sociology course that took teams of undergraduate students out of the traditional classroom to provide service to the local community. Yet the emphasis of the course was on changing students, not changing the neighbors. Our objective was to broaden students' perspectives—to give them an opportunity to interact with people of different races, ethnicities, or religions and to do so in a spirit of cooperation, civility, and good will. In short, we hoped to challenge and clarify our students' views of social reality, with the objective of preparing them to live in an increasingly diverse world.

One of the important functions of formal education is to broaden our personal experience, to serve as an agent of socialization with aspects of life that we might otherwise never experience firsthand. And this is precisely why a formal course that combines classroom instruction with firsthand involvement in the life of the community makes so much sense, at least theoretically.

Based on the quality of their personal essays and academic transcripts, 17 undergraduate students were selected to participate in our course. The majority was white, but black, Asian, and Latino students were represented as well. Every week, each student in the course performed five hours of community service and then met together as a class for two hours to discuss issues related to the way that groups interact. Our text was Ruth Sidel's *Battling Bias* (1994), an analysis of diversity on campus. In addition, students wrote logs summarizing their community service experiences for the week and a more inclusive term paper at the end of the quarter. Our final class meeting together consisted of oral team presentations in which students summarized their community experiences and reflected on how those experiences had changed their own feelings and thinking about diversity.

The range of student reactions was as broad and varied as their agency placements. Some reported initially feeling out of place when exposed to an unfamiliar situation in which they were, for the first time ever, the "racial minority." For example, Sally, a white student from a middle-class Boston suburb, helped in peer-mediated conflict resolution with girls at a local high school where most of the young people were either black or Latino. At first, she regarded the students as "nameless girls who frightened me in the hallways." About one girl who had gotten into a fist fight, Sally later remarked, "During our first meeting, I didn't think she wanted me in the room. Now, six weeks later, she calls me her 'big sis' and confides in me." Sally reports that her experience caused her "to look at people in a very different light" and to be "more sensitive to issues of racial, class and social disputes." As a result, she has decided to continue working at the school for the entire year and is applying to graduate school to study juvenile crime.

Other students in our course discovered unexpected civility among the community members they served. Richard, a young man from upstate New York, conducted empathy training as part of a conflict resolution program with racially diverse first graders at an elementary school near Chinatown. Richard's experience changed his perspective. "Perhaps the biggest thing I noticed in working with these kids was just how little race differences matter to them," Richard suggested. "It is not that they don't understand that other people have different skin colors than they do, it's that they don't care. It made it so obvious to me that racial hatred is a learned thing." Some of our students learned a good deal from being part of a project team whose members were diverse. For example, Marjorie, a biracial student who grew up in a part of Maine where there was only a tiny Jewish population, had been exposed to many anti-Jewish stereotypes. But through her partnership in a Cambridge agency with a Jewish woman from New York, she felt comfortable enough to ask her about her religion.

Toward the end of the course, Marjorie remarked, "Now that I possess a better understanding of the Jewish faith and background, I am less likely to believe the stereotypes employed to discredit Jewish individuals." However, not every student left the course with an increased sense of optimism or tolerance. Some were stunned by the depth and pervasiveness of the problems confronting members of the community, especially those who are impoverished. Jamie, a student who worked with battered women at a local hospital emergency room, explained that she was "overwhelmed by the difficulty in ever making wide, far-reaching gains combating this huge problem, yet I am left wanting to help more. It was amazing for me to see how common domestic violence is. . . . I was also struck, however, by the strength some women possessed in surviving tremendous difficulties. It is a shame their strength is wasted on situations they shouldn't have to face." Because they have grown up shielded from those who are different, many young people lack the skills necessary for good citizenship, tolerance, civility, and humanitarianism. They need to be made aware of the existence of poverty and homelessness, flaws in the criminal justice system, prejudice and discrimination, and their own mortality. Most of all, college students need to learn that they are not at the center of the universe. As one of our students concluded after spending 10 weeks working with Boston teenagers, "The greatest content of learning in this course was about myself. I was forced to explore my own prejudices and those of others like me."

# Confessions of a Soap Opera Addict

## The Daytime Serials Are More Than I Bargained For

I've been watching *Days of Our Lives* each day of my life for more than 30 years. It all started when I took a year off to finish my doctoral dissertation. Each afternoon, my wife and I sat together in the living room of our small apartment: She watched soap operas; I wrote my thesis.

Working at home was tough enough, and eavesdropping on midday melodrama didn't help. In fact, it only reinforced my long-held impression that soaps were at about the same intellectual level as Saturday morning cartoons, but these, at least, had action. Did anyone really care whether Julie and David got together again, when Marie would discover that her fiancé was actually her long-lost brother, or whether Missy was pregnant with another man's child? I didn't think so. Soap operas were television's opiate of the masses, I had decided: that medium through which too many Americans vicariously escaped their dreary existences into the make-believe world of the rich and beautiful. While the pressing economic and social problems of our society went ignored, millions of *General Hospital* groupies became Luke and Laura, if only for a few minutes a day. They needed that soap opera fix to make their lives seem exciting and worthwhile. America's daytime serial fanatics were being distracted from improving their own lives by a particularly insidious form of fantasy and escapism.

I was especially annoyed by the depiction of women. They seemed always to be getting pregnant, not for the purpose of having children but to manipulate and control the men in their lives. They used pregnancy to trap boyfriends into unwanted marriages or husbands into maintaining unwanted marriages. In the soaps, single mothers had good jobs and healthy babies. They were neither poorly educated nor poor! In addition, any woman who dared have a career in a field traditionally dominated by men—medicine, law, or business—was either mentally ill or evil. The sex role socialization message was unmistakable: Women were to stay out of the boardrooms and executive offices and stay in the kitchens and bedrooms where they belonged.

It occurred to me that, in some perverse way, soap operas were a mass form of socializing young people to accept the status quo. Even as college students of the 1980s were scheduling or skipping courses to accommodate *General Hospital,* the majority of daytime serial watchers were high school graduates who had never attended college, mostly middle-aged women. Many used the characters on soaps as role models for how to handle their spouses. But what they learned frightened me: first, that infidelity and promiscuity were acceptable, even desirable, modes of sexual behavior; second, that divorce was the answer to any difference, no matter how trivial. If your marriage wasn't smooth as glass, get a divorce. Or a lover. Better yet, get a lover, then a divorce.

By the third or fourth week of watching out of the corner of my eye, I noticed something peculiar was happening to me. If I had to be away during a weekday afternoon, I'd call home for a rundown of that day's episodes. We didn't have a VCR, and TiVos and DVRs hadn't yet been invented. So, I scheduled meetings with colleagues so I wouldn't miss a particular serial. It got to the point where my wife would have to tear me away from my show to take a phone call or answer the door. It was painful to admit, but I was hooked. I was brainwashed. I had become a socialized soapie.

Perhaps as a sort of therapy, I spent a good part of the next few years immersed in the study of soap operas. It was legitimate: I was teaching a course in mass communication, and my students were discussing the impact of television on society. I read what the experts—psychologists, sociologists, and assorted communications specialists—had to say. I even assigned student projects to analyze the characters on daytime serials.

Surprising, to me at least, was their conclusion that soap operas were much better than primetime dramatic series in representing women, minorities, and older people in central roles. While young and middle-aged males were vastly overrepresented on primetime television, in soap operas one half of the characters were women. Even more to their credit, soap operas featured actors and actresses who remained on the show for decades. Many of them aged gracefully and remained thoroughly attractive, while they continued to play roles central to the plot. Indeed, older people were treated much better on soap operas than on most other television fare. And the daytime serials frequently focused on a range of social problems: intergroup conflict, juvenile delinquency, alcoholism, and organized crime—issues that were all but ignored by the soaps' primetime counterparts.

It was soon clear to me why soaps are so appealing to so many. For one, they provide us with the things we find lacking in modern life. Monday through Friday, without fail (barring an occasional murder trial or a presidential news conference), we follow our good friends into their offices, living rooms, and bedrooms. We attend Sammie and Lucas's wedding and visit John in the hospital. We watch Tony argue with Stefano, Rex make love with Mimi, and Nicole plotting to kill Victor. We often get to know more about the personal lives of our favorite soap opera characters than we know about our real neighbors. In an era of anonymity and an eclipse of community, soap operas give us intimacy. Sadly, for those who are socially isolated, this may be the one and only source of intimacy in their lives, but perhaps this is better than nothing.

Soap operas make us feel good about ourselves. Misery loves miserable company, and our own problems are somehow less painful when we're able to compare them with the troubles of those we admire. The world of the daytime serial is the world of the wealthy, beautiful, and powerful—our cultural heroes, the people we aspire to become. Yet these characters have problems with their families and friends, much worse than ours. So we feel better, at their expense, of course.

Soap opera intimacy often takes the form of snooping but only in the most positive sense. By eavesdropping, we're given the opportunity to rehearse our own emotional reactions to problems that may confront us in everyday life. Observing untimely deaths, kidnappings, divorces, and mental illness on television, we learn something about the manner in which we might handle similar problems in our own lives.

At least part of the influence of daytime serials can be attributed to the credibility of television as a form of mass communication. Study after study shows that Americans trust the authenticity of the images they see on the tube. In the process, however, heavy viewers often develop a distorted view of social reality. They tend to exaggerate, for example, the amount of violence they are likely to encounter in everyday life, the proportion of criminal cases that end in a jury trial, and the likelihood that physicians will perform miracle cures. For these viewers, the fantasy world on television becomes the reality. During the 5 years that Robert Young played Dr. Marcus Welby, the actor received more than 250,000 letters asking him for medical advice. Admiring fans were apparently unable to distinguish actor Young from character Welby.

This incredible power of soap operas as an agent of socialization was brought home to me several years ago when I met some of the actors on *Days of Our Lives*. As an interested observer, I couldn't resist asking them the questions that might confirm what I always suspected: Do soap opera addicts confuse the fantasy world of the daytime serials with the real world in which they live? Yes—and often. Whenever a *Days of Our Lives* star either gives birth (it's only a pillow), gets married (a rhinestone wedding ring), or dies (usually a failure to renegotiate the actor's contract), cards and gifts appear at the studio, they said.

For me, soaps have a special appeal. As a sociologist, I investigate problems that have no easy solutions. I spend years studying serial killers, for example, and am troubled that we can't predict from childhood experience who will eventually commit hideous crimes. I research the causes of prejudice and discrimination and still see the number of racist acts of vandalism and desecration increasing. And like others, I see criminals too often get suspended sentences while their victims suffer; the rich get richer as homelessness grows; and the questionable ethics of politicians go unpunished.

And that's how soaps are different. Warm, friendly, predictable, they make sure people get what they deserve.

# Violence in City Schools

## What Principals Are Doing to Stem the Rising Tide

*Jack Levin and Heather Beth Johnson*

L ast year, 64% of elementary school principals in five Massachusetts cities—Boston, Springfield, Worcester, Lowell, and New Bedford—suspended or expelled violent students. At the high school and middle school levels, this figure was close to 96%. In eight public schools, 26 or more students were dismissed for carrying weapons or being violent.

The good news is that these city schools offer a wide array of programs and activities aimed at preventing or resolving violent student behavior. Conflict resolution programs are extremely popular in elementary, middle, and high schools. In addition, especially in the high and middle schools, there are peer-mediation programs, programs to combat hatred and racism, and community volunteers to serve as tutors and mentors.

However, while such after-school programs as intramural athletics, drama, art, music, and student government are offered by 90% of the high schools and 96% of the middle schools, only 14% of the elementary schools sponsor such programs.

The virtual absence of after-school activities in kindergarten through 5th grade leaves many younger children without opportunities for wholesome experiences and activities in the afternoons. Because they generally do not begin until the middle school years, supervised activities after school have not become part of the students' daily routine and therefore may not be seen as "cool" or "hot" by the students who most need them. By the time such programs are available, students have already entered adolescence and may be unwilling to participate in activities supervised by adults, especially by teachers and parents.

Although most urban high schools and middle schools provide at least some after-school activities, such programs are usually restricted to students who are in academic good standing, haven't been troublesome in the classroom, have economic resources, and can find transportation home. In 95% of the schools offering after-school activities, one or more restrictions are placed on the students' eligibility to participate. As a result, students most lacking in healthy alternatives after classes end—those who are impoverished, alienated, and idle—are less likely to participate.

According to school principals, a major reason that so many schools impose eligibility requirements for participating in after-school activities involves a lack of economic resources. Such programs are vastly underfunded.

But another reason has to do with the manner in which such activities are defined by the administrators themselves who fail to recognize after-school programs as violence- or conflict-prevention measures. They are much more likely to view such activities as a *privilege* extended to *deserving* students—those who are achievement oriented, compliant, and well behaved.

More than 40% of all violent crimes committed by teenagers occur between 3 p.m. and 7 p.m. Yet, today, 57% of all juveniles lack full-time parental supervision; they grow up in dual-career families or in single-parent households.

In wealthy communities, many children may be provided with opportunities for healthful after-school alternatives. In areas where economic and human resources are seriously lacking, however, children tend to be on their own until their parents come home from work.

Therefore, expanding the school day to include *all* students in after-school programs would structure our youngsters' days so that their time could be spent on worthwhile activities. What we currently regard as after-school programs should be incorporated into a longer school day during which traditional academics become interspersed among clubs, internships, athletic programs, job apprenticeships, and the arts. By restructuring the school experience so that it is identified with more than academic subjects, the meaning of school would be broadened to include appealing and practical activities from the youngsters' standpoint.

Such an approach requires making a major investment—one that ought to be shared by a wide range of local interests and institutions. The cost would be heavy but not so heavy in human terms as our continuing disinvestment in our children and their future. Some 135,000 U.S. teenagers go to school each day carrying a firearm. It would be a step in the right direction if they traded in their weapons for softball gloves, tennis rackets, and art supplies.

# Sticks and Stones May Break . . .

## In Reality, Names May Indeed Hurt You

What's in a name? Plenty, if you happen to be meteorologist Storm Field, television executive Paul La Camera, psychiatrist Ronald Bliss, or District Court Judge Darrell Outlaw. Whether or not such names inspired career choices, they undoubtedly have provided material for countless after-dinner conversations.

According to psychologist Ron Harré and his associates at State University of New York at Binghamton, and as confirmed in countless other studies, the influence of names begins in childhood. Names that we are familiar with—common names, such as Joseph and Michael—are associated with images of strength and competence, whereas unusual names, such as Ivan and Horace, conjure up weakness and passivity. Consequently, those kids who are unfortunate enough to have been given bizarre or unpopular names are sometimes poorly adjusted and pessimistic about their prospects of being successful in the future; they tend to score lower on achievement tests and get lower grades in school.

This phenomenon extends into adulthood. Men who have strange or unusual names are more likely to suffer from mental illness or to have criminal records. In many cases, a self-fulfilling prophecy may operate during the socialization process. A child is ridiculed because of his name. As a result, he develops a negative attitude toward himself that influences his behavior in the classroom and on the playground. And teachers and peers notice this poor behavior. They assume that kids with unusual names aren't very competent or skillful. So very little is seen, very little is expected, and very little is obtained.

The impact can be very personal. Writing in the December 2007 issue of *Psychological Science,* Leif Nelson and Joseph Simmons demonstrate what they call the "name-letter effect." Their results suggest that people who like their names have an unconscious tendency to prefer words and activities that begin with the same letter. Thus, men named Michael are especially likely to marry someone named Mary, drive a Mustang, and move to Maryland. Students whose names begin with the initials C or D are more likely than those whose names start with A or B to receive a grade of C or D.

The importance of names is nowhere more important than in Hollywood. Consider all the celebrities who weren't born with the right name for the image they want to portray. The former William Bailey is now Axl Rose; Margaret Mary Emily Anne Hyra is Meg Ryan; Marshall Bruce Mathers II calls himself Eminem; Frances Gumm's stage name was Judy Garland; Mark Vincent is better known as actor Vin Diesel; Bob Ritchie became Kid Rock; and Dana Owens was transformed into Queen Latifah.

The flip side of this is that uncommon names sometimes imply uniqueness. One might speculate that Zsa Zsa Gabor, Meatloaf, River Phoenix, Cher, Moon Zappa, Pee-Wee Herman, Jewel, Whoopi Goldberg, Madonna, Eef Barzelay, 50 Cent, and Mr. T owe at least part of their celebrity status to their names.

Names can also convey independence. Fowler and Fuehrer (1997), in interviews with women who decided to keep their last names after marriage, found that name retention was seen as a way to maintain autonomy, assert equality, and resist traditional roles as wives.

Minority groups are also painfully aware of the power of a name to socialize its members to failure and negative self-esteem. People of color prefer to be called black or African-American. They reject labels such as *colored* and *Negro,* contending that they were long ago assigned to them by outsiders. Jesse Jackson recently called for the elimination of the black label in favor of a group identity such as *Afro-American* that would emphasize an African cultural heritage in the same way that white ethnic groups—Irish-Americans, Polish-Americans, and Italian-Americans—choose to stress their European ancestry. Even the term *minority* may be falling out of favor, as more and more people of color refuse to see themselves as playing a minor role in American society. Similarly, many women now resent being labeled *girls, babes,* and *chicks* because of the infantilized image. And older Americans tell survey researchers that they like being called senior citizens rather than *aged* or *elderly,* indicating that old age continues to be a difficult situation for millions.

People who possess a physical disability have often been victimized by harmful and misleading names. Given the negative connotation of the word *cripple,* it is clear why they seek to avoid being referred to in this way. But even the word *handicapped* is not always appropriate, deriving its meaning from an earlier period in which individuals with physical disabilities were forced to the streets, to beg, literally, cap in hand. There are numerous individuals today—blind, deaf, in wheelchairs, and on crutches—who actively seek to maximize their independence and who prefer not being labeled as handicapped.

By characterizing the entire person, the word *disabled* completely ignores the possibility that an individual might possess strengths as well as weaknesses. Yet very few persons are actually disabled in the absolute sense; most possess certain disabilities, some more severe than others, but they also have abilities that can be nurtured and developed if they are not overlooked. A paraplegic may never be able to run in the New York Marathon without the help of a wheelchair, but he or she may still become a brilliant lawyer or physician.

The symbolism in name-calling makes it just as dangerous as sticks and stones. Thousands change the name that appears on their birth certificate; thousands more drop an offensive middle name or use a nickname to avoid the negative attention provided by the formal version of their name. For minority groups, the painful history represented by a label often becomes part and parcel of the consciousness-raising rhetoric of their causes. Socialization counts a great deal: To accept the name is regarded as accepting the stereotyped image that group members have worked so hard to modify or overcome. Under such circumstances, the word may not be the thing, but it certainly has an effect that means the most—an individual's or a group's identity.

Whoever suggested that names will never hurt you must have been named Michael or Emily or maybe even Andrew. It is doubtful that Horace or Hortense would have agreed.

# Adult Socialization
# Can Be Murder

## Development Continues
## Throughout Life

E verything we have learned about the process of socialization suggests that what happens to us while we are very young is extremely important for shaping the rest of our lives. Suffering a horrible experience at the tender age of 2 can leave us with a lifelong phobia. Losing a loved one at 4 or 5 can contribute to making an individual into an emotionally needy adult. Failing the 6th grade can affect our self-image, even many years later.

Yet while early childhood may be critical, we must not forget that development continues throughout life. To focus only on the first few years in the biography of an individual may be to ignore some of the most influential aspects of his or her development.

Erik Erikson, for example, a student of Sigmund Freud and a famous theorist in his own right, proposed that the close personal relationships formed by an individual during young adulthood help determine a sense of intimacy. According to Erikson (1950), if such relationships are not successfully established, the individual will suffer a profound sense of isolation. What is more, in midlife (between the ages of 30 and 50), a failure to master the challenges of work and raising a family can result in an individual's coming to a nonproductive, egocentric sense of self.

To understand what can happen when adult socialization fails, we might examine its most extreme, most deadly consequences. It is interesting to note that most mass murderers—those who massacre large numbers of people—don't kill until they are middle-aged men, in their 30s, 40s, or even 50s. James Huberty, for example, who massacred people, mostly Hispanic children, at a San Ysidro, California, McDonald's, was 41; George Hennard, who opened fire in a Killeen, Texas, cafeteria, killing 23, was 35; and R. Gene Simmons, who exterminated 14 members of his family in Russellville, Arkansas, was 46. If early childhood had been the critical factor, these killers would probably have expressed their murderous impulses much earlier in life—say, by the time they were in their teens or early 20s.

Many mass killers do have profound problems growing up. They may have been abused, neglected, or even abandoned. But so have hundreds of thousands—perhaps even millions—of people who never kill anyone and who never will. The determining factor in the process of creating a mass murderer seems to reside in what happens to a killer when he attempts to make the transition into adulthood or even later. Does he have adequate support systems in place—family, friends, and neighbors—to get him through the tough times, to encourage and support him when he loses a job or an important relationship? Or is he set adrift to fend for himself in an unfamiliar and unfriendly world of anomie? In Erikson's terms, does he suffer a profound sense of isolation at the very time in his life that he needs social support? Also relevant is whether mass killers are successful at home and at work. Actually, most of them have suffered a number of losses in important areas of life—for example, the loss of a close relationship by separation or divorce or a profound financial loss through being fired or terminated. In Erikson's terms, having failed to master the challenges of work and raising a family, they feel a profound sense of stagnation. James Huberty, after losing his job, moved from a small town in Ohio to a suburb of San Diego. After settling in California, he again became unemployed. This time, however, his family and friends were back home in Ohio. He didn't have anyone to give him the psychological boost that he so much needed.

What happens (or fails to happen) in the biography of a mass murderer may give us clues as to what can be done to prevent violence in general, even when committed by otherwise unremarkable members of society. Of course, it would be wonderful if we were able to intervene in the early childhood of every individual in trouble. But we must also not ignore those troubled young people who are already in their teen years and beyond early intervention.

The majority of adult offenders have a juvenile record, but the majority of teenagers with a juvenile record do not later become criminals. Many adolescents who commit deviant acts when they are 14 wouldn't dream of committing the same crimes when they reach 24 or 25. Just because we cannot reach troubled youngsters during the first few years doesn't mean that we should give up on them later. On the contrary, if Erikson is right, we should be doing everything possible to help such teenagers over the obstacles of developing into adults so that they can become productive citizens. In the process, we might even prevent a mass murder.

# FOCUS

## ✧ Suggestions for Further Reading ✧

As suggested in "Sticks and Stones May Break . . . ," labeling children with an unpopular name can sometimes become the basis for a self-fulfilling prophecy. They are expected to perform poorly, are treated accordingly, and eventually come to perform as expected. For a discussion of the looking-glass self, you might read Charles H. Cooley (1902). I would, however, suggest that you first read the work of George Herbert Mead, a University of Chicago social philosopher whose insights into the development of the self continue to provide major direction for sociological research. Particularly germane is his discussion of role taking—the process whereby an individual learns to take another person's point of view. By means of role taking, children come to define themselves in the way that significant others (e.g., mother and father) view them. If Mommy and Daddy see a child as stupid, the child may come to see herself as stupid; if parents see a child as lazy, she is likely to develop a self-image as someone who is lazy. Try *Mind, Self and Society* (1934). It's difficult reading (Mead's students compiled this work from their notes) but completely worthwhile. To see what labeling can do to students' performance, read the modern classic by Robert Rosenthal and Lenore Jacobson, *Pygmalion in the Classroom* (2003). Rosenthal and Jacobson told teachers that certain of their students were bloomers based on their high IQs. Actually, the so-called bloomers had been chosen at random, and their IQs were no higher than those of students not labeled as bloomers at least at the beginning of the study. By the end of the year, however, the IQ scores of bloomers were significantly higher than they had been when they entered the class. Apparently, the expectation given to teachers (that these students are superior) was enough to make the labeled children perform at a higher level.

In "Teaching Students They Are Not at the Center of the Universe," my colleague Will Holton and I discuss a course that we developed to help modify our students' views of people who are different with respect to race, religion, and ethnic background. The course takes as a given that few of us grow up with a representative slice of personal experiences and that each of us is, in a sense, forced to construct our own version of reality.

This, of course, leads to distortion and misunderstanding. In "Can Hate Be Healed?" we see that these distortions are often taught by parents, teachers, friends, neighbors, and the mass media. To see how such factors play out on college campuses around the country, read Ruth Sidel's excellent work *Battling Bias* (1994). To read more about the changing situation of diversity on campus, see Howard J. Ehrlich's *Campus Ethnoviolence and the Policy Options* (1990) and Jack Levin and Jack McDevitt's *Hate Crimes Revisited: America's War on Those Who Are Different* (2002). *Violence on Campus: Defining the Problems, Strategies for Action* (1998), edited by Allan M. Hoffman, John H. Schuh, and Robert H. Fenske, contains a wealth of information about various forms of campus bigotry, including hate speech and hate crimes. For a detailed analysis of violence against lesbians and gays, read the range of articles contained in Gregory Herek and Kevin Berrill's reader, *Hate Crimes: Confronting Violence Against Lesbians and Gay Men* (1992). Gary D. Comstock's *Violence Against Lesbians and Gay Men* (1991) provides research data and many interesting insights. One is worth repeating here: Whereas attacks against the members of different races are usually committed by economically marginal teenagers, violence against gays seems to come from every socioeconomic level. More generally, hate is analyzed by Jack Levin and Gordana Rabrenovic (2004) in *Why We Hate*.

The suggestion to treat extreme forms of hate as a psychiatric illness is part of a larger tendency in our society to medicalize deviant behavior. For example, drug addicts and alcoholics have come to be regarded as sick rather than as criminal. Once a phenomenon is viewed as a medical problem, it is likely to be treated with some kind of medical intervention. Thus, a vulnerable individual—someone who has learning problems, hyperactivity, or extreme hatred—is less likely to be punished and more likely to receive assistance. As a result, more and more social problems have been placed in the hands of medical practitioners—physicians, pharmacists, and the like. Under the medical model, there are both advantages and disadvantages. Drunk drivers may serve their time in a treatment facility rather than in prison. Children with learning disabilities may be seen as dyslexics rather than as stupid. But frail elders may wind up in a nursing home, where they receive inadequate care and poor medical treatment. In addition, many nursing home residents become malnourished. An excellent discussion of this topic can be found in Peter Conrad's *The Medicalization of Society* (2007).

Concerning "Confessions of a Soap Opera Addict," there are plenty of data about the daytime serials in *The Soap Opera* (1983) by Muriel Cantor and Suzanne Pingree and lots of information about *Days* in Maureen Russell's (1995) *Days of Our Lives: A Complete History of the Long-Running Soap Opera*. For a more general treatment of socialization and mass communication, there are many excellent articles in Sandra Ball-Rokeach and Muriel Cantor's *Media, Audience, and Social Structure* (1986). In an article in the *Journal of Popular Culture,* Henriette Riegel (1996) emphasizes the important role of gossip in the appeal of soap operas. Moreover, Mary Strom Larson (1996) examines the disparity between the reality of single mothers' lives, on the one hand, and the perceptions of single motherhood fostered by soap opera characters, on the other hand.

In "Violence in City Schools," Heather Johnson and I present evidence to suggest that after-school programs are missing, especially from elementary schools, and that such activities might have an important impact on the reduction of dangerous conflict and violence. Of course, school violence is often treated with formal social control (law enforcement) responses such as metal detectors and police security. According to P. A. Noguera (2001), however, efforts to socialize youngsters to a less violent alternative can be much more effective than any law enforcement strategy. Rather than send in a police force, it may be more effective to send grandparents as mentors and tutors and role models. For a recent treatment of middle-class delinquency, I recommend Eliott Currie's (2005) *The Road to Whatever.* Many middle-class college students will identify with the teenagers Currie interviews for this volume.

To understand more about the factors in adulthood that contribute to criminality, read Robert Sampson and John Laub's insightful study, *Crime in the Making: Pathways and Turning Points Through Life* (1994). Sociologists interested in how people are influenced during adulthood have paid a good deal of attention to career socialization—how individuals come to adapt the practices and values of their work experiences. In a classic study, Howard Becker and his colleagues attended medical school classes with regular students to observe the lessons that aspiring physicians were being taught as part of their medical training. The researchers determined that the idealistic and humanitarian views of first-year medical students gradually faded and were replaced by a more practical view of medical knowledge and practice. See *Boys in White* (1961), by Howard S. Becker, Blanche Geer, Everett C. Hughes, and Amselm L. Strauss. More recently, Robert Granfield attended classes at a prestigious northeastern law school to determine how law students were being socialized to their careers as attorneys. Not unlike what Becker and his associates had discovered concerning medical students, Granfield found that many law students abandoned their idealism in favor of a more cynical form of thinking. Granfield published his results in "Legal Education as Corporate Ideology" in *Sociological Forum* (1986).

# DEVELOPING IDEAS

## ✧ About Socialization ✧

1. Research topic: Test your knowledge of "social geography." In writing, estimate the percentage of students at your college (or your city)—from 0% to 100%—who are from foreign countries; who are African-American, Asian-American, and Latin-American; and who are women. Now, find a source that can give you an accurate count—the library, the registrar's office, city hall, and so on. How close were your estimates to the actual percentages?

2. Research topic: Communication researchers suggest that television is fixated on appealing to young and wealthy American men, those who buy sponsors' products. As a result, commercial TV does not portray the elderly, minorities, and women as they really are. In fact, many of these groups are virtually absent from the tube. Analyze one episode of any primetime dramatic series. In writing, identify the race, ethnic identity, gender, and approximate age (child, teenager, young adult, middle-aged, or old) of each major character. If possible, also find each major character's occupation and social class (from their job, house, car, and so on). If an alien from Mars knew nothing about American society except what she learned from this one episode, what would she likely conclude about the makeup of the United States?

3. Research topic: Most sociologists believe that the self arises out of social interaction. Cooley's looking-glass self includes this idea. To apply this notion on a personal level, try the following experiment suggested by Manford Kuhn's measure of self-concept, his Twenty-Statements Test. Ask a friend to answer, on paper, the question, Who am I? with 20 different responses. In analyzing your friend's answers, consider how many relate the self to other people: group memberships (fraternity member, sister, son, and so on) or categories (Catholic, Protestant, American, female, and so on). Kuhn says that children tend to define themselves in very specific terms. For example, they might say they are nice to a sister or good at playing cards. Adults tend to define themselves in much more abstract terms—groups or categories of human beings.

4. Writing topic: There is a good deal of evidence that socialization continues throughout life. Robert Granfield and Howard Becker both suggest that students become less idealistic as they are trained formally for a career either in law or in medicine. Thinking about these studies as they might apply to your own behavior and attitudes, write an essay in which you play the role of participant-observer to discuss how your personal values and aspirations might have changed as a result of your classroom experiences. Since you first began taking courses at the college level, have you become more or less idealistic in

terms of your career objectives? If you have changed, exactly what do you believe to be responsible for that change? Does your major have something to do with it? Do you ever feel that your instructors are giving you a subtle, perhaps implicit message about what is important and what is not important in a career, in life? What have you learned from your classmates in this regard?

5. Research topic: Locate a group of several elementary school students— preferably from the same classroom—who are willing to discuss with you any problems involving conflict, violence, and harassment at their school. (Make sure that you have the permission of their parents before you actually begin. In fact, it might be wise to have parents in the room when you talk with their children.) Come to the session prepared with a list of open-ended questions regarding how often they see weapons, what types of weapons they have seen, how teachers and administrators respond to students who carry weapons, how safe they feel at school versus their own neighborhood, what they do after school, whether they are alone—lacking in adult supervision— after school, how often they see violence at school, what types of violence— hair-pulling, punching, stabbing, choking, and so on—they have witnessed, whether they have been involved in a violent confrontation, and so on.

# PART III

## The Group Experience

I've lived in the same house since 1976, and I don't even know my next-door neighbor. It's not that I can't remember his name (though I can't). It's that I don't even know what he looks like. Well, I didn't know, until the other day. I was standing alone in a train station in Boston, when a complete stranger walked up to me and said, "Aren't you Jack Levin?" I, of course, nodded my head and asked him politely how he knew me.

He told me his name and then informed me that he was my next-door neighbor. When I asked him how long he had lived next door, he responded, "For 5 years." Shocked and embarrassed, I welcomed him to the neighborhood. Well, what else was I to do? The amazing thing is that I live in a middle-class suburb—not in a city apartment but in a single-family house on a quiet residential street with other single-family houses. Another amazing thing is that I really like people, including my neighbors. But most of my friends and group memberships are somehow associated either with my job or with my family. There seems to be very little room left over in my everyday interaction for the people on my block.

And, then, there is the assumption—perhaps unwarranted—that most of my neighbors are not any different from me. They have their own lives too—they are away during the day, probably belong to various organizations at work, and probably have a circle of friends and family with whom they share their leisure hours. What kind of an effort have they made to get to know me, I ask? (Boy, am I defensive!)

This section is about the experience of being in groups, ranging from families, roommates, neighbors, and peers, on the informal side of the continuum, to the largest organizations, companies, universities, and government agencies you might possibly envision, on the more formal side. A group provides the social context for interaction between people—two or more individuals who are aware of one another's presence and who adjust their behavior toward one another. They may talk, laugh, cry, work, play, scream, fight, debate, struggle, or cooperate but, always, together. This interaction is the essence of the group experience. It is also the essence of what sociologists study.

In our mass society, there are people who have little more than superficial contacts with other human beings. Some have no informal contacts at all. However, while the old, traditional forms of social interaction represented by family and neighborhood may have weakened, they have been replaced by new patterns of interaction. As suggested in "College Fraternities: A Counteracting Force on Campus," students may depend a good deal on fraternities and sororities for finding others to date and for developing lasting friendships.

In addition to fraternities and sororities, there also seem to be growing numbers of unconventional groups called "cults." Sociologists have always defined cults as loosely structured and unconventional forms of religious groups, whose members are held together by a charismatic leader who mobilizes their loyalty around some new religious cause—typically a cause that is at odds with that of more conventional religious institutions. Using this definition, almost any new religious group that hasn't yet become institutionalized—whether benign or dangerous—could be regarded as a cult. From a sociological perspective, then, early Christianity during Roman times was a cult, but so were the Branch Davidians under David Koresh. Of course, the term *cult* has recently been used much more broadly to include any group—whether religious or not—that may be dangerous or destructive.

Some people need an excuse just to gather together with others. In the temporary alliances known as coalitions, individuals put aside their differences to collaborate for the sake of achieving common objectives. In "The Consequences of Coalitions," we see that many different groups of people have a stake in combating bigotry and hate. Their potential effectiveness in this regard becomes much greater when they form temporary alliances consisting of the range of such people who have been victimized.

In "Reunion, American Style," we discover Robert Merton's term *latent function.* He recognized that many of our social arrangements have not only a formal purpose but also an unintended and unrecognized consequence. Professional conferences, for example, frequently held on an annual basis, provide an opportunity for practitioners to exchange information in formal sessions. But the latent and therefore unintended, unrecognized effect may be even more important. In bars, restaurants, and hotel lobbies, participants from around the country reunite to chat.

Their informal conversations often provide the basis for exchanging ideas and collaborating on projects. In the same article, we see the manner in which patterns of behavior can become institutionalized. That is, aspects of the social order become widely accepted and organized. In our society, class reunions have become big business, a commercial success.

Speaking of big business and big organizations, "Children of the Organization Men" takes a look at two generations: first, those men (there were very few women who did this) who came of age in the 1950s and worked for most of their careers in large organizations. What happened to their children? Did they become organization men and women? Or did they choose to follow a different career path for themselves? A recent study of organizational offspring indicates that their fathers' loyalty to corporations and conformity to social order were hardly passed on to the next generation. Instead, the sons and daughters of organization men turned their attention to the self and cherished raw individualism.

"Thwarting the Bullies in Our Schools" offers a two-pronged strategy for reducing the prevalence of school murders committed by classmates against one another. First, we should take bullying seriously, viewing it as an abnormal practice that can and should be reduced rather than as part of the natural order of the school. Second, we should break the culture of silence so that students no longer feel it is socially unacceptable to inform on a peer who threatens to blow up the school or shoot students and teachers. Social influence can work either to damage the self-esteem of vulnerable children or to protect them from being harassed and humiliated.

# College Fraternities—
# A Counteracting
# Force on Campus

## Where Else Would Students
## Get to Know One Another?

Those who long for a return to a time of strong family ties, neighborliness, and a simpler life often invoke the term *mass society* to characterize a long-standing trend in American society that they deplore. The image of mass society is all too familiar to millions of Americans in the early 21st century—people who feel very much alone, city dwellers and suburbanites living in boxes, dissatisfied customers who talk on the phone to automated voices, rush-hour traffic that won't quit, and waiting in lines a mile long.

All of these forms of mass society are, indeed, a painful fact of life for millions of Americans. Yet at the same time that older types of social relations have diminished, they have been replaced by new, and sometimes deceptively effective, forms of intimacy and informality that compensate for the loss of traditional primary ties and counteract feelings of loneliness and isolation.

Technology has provided some degree of compensation. Even when friends and relatives are physically separated, they can still sustain primary contacts by telephone. Or as a postmodern form of social interaction, they can keep in touch by means of personal computer (Internet, e-mail, and electronic bulletin boards), even if they are thousands of miles apart.

Of course, such technological devices as long-distance telephones and computers hardly make up for the eclipse of community in America. Their essentially superficial forms of interaction cannot possibly compensate totally for the loss of profound friendship and family networks found in the neighborhoods or communities of another era.

This can be seen clearly in the case of millions of college students around the country who leave their families—perhaps for the first time ever—to take up residence on a campus, sometimes located thousands of miles from home. It should come as no surprise that these students, especially if they are on large and diverse campuses, often search for opportunities for intimacy and friendship. Some find the primary contacts they need in fraternities and sororities.

Membership in college fraternities and sororities seems to ebb and flow, depending on the social circumstances surrounding campus life at a particular point in time. In 1966, some 30% of all college students belonged to Greek-letter societies; by 1976, however, this figure had dropped to only 19% nationally. In fact, fully two thirds of these colleges had experienced declining fraternity enrollments. During the 1970s, on some campuses across the country, fraternities completely disappeared.

Apparently, the fraternity's ability to counteract mass society on campus was overruled, at least during this period of time, by a more powerful theme among the college-bound baby boomer generation. Many college students of the early 1970s regarded fraternity membership as thoroughly inconsistent with their interests in civil rights, student rights, antiwar activism, feminism, racial equality, and independence from institutional constraints.

James A. Fox and I conducted a study showing that the disappearance of college fraternities was short lived. By examining the fraternity and sorority membership figures around the country, we discovered a major resurgence of interest in campus fraternities. By 1981, almost one half of all colleges and universities had already reported seeing growth in fraternity enrollments. As more and more students sought structured opportunities to meet other students, date, and develop friendships, the fraternity began to make its big comeback. Especially on campuses where most of the students came from outside the immediate area, where there were few commuters, and where there was little else to attract students in the wider community, fraternity membership thrived and prospered. In some southern schools, fraternity membership reached 80%.

In a mass society, independence can be very lonely. For college students who miss the intimacy of family life, fraternities and sororities provide a new set of brothers and sisters and a home away from home.

# The Appeal of Cults

## If You Can't Get What You Need From Your Friends, You May Be Tempted to Join

W hat in the world is a cult, anyway? And how do you know it when you see one? Are we talking about Heaven's Gate and the dozens of people who in 1997 committed mass suicide so they could reunite on a spaceship? Or the more than 80 Branch Davidians who perished at Waco after their compound was stormed by federal agents? How about Jonestown, Guyana? In 1978, 912 people died there because their leader Jim Jones urged them to sip cyanide-laced Kool-Aid. Should we include transcendental meditators? Members of the Divine Light Mission? The Unification Church and Scientology, even though these groups have millions of members around the world? How about the Charles Manson "family"? In 1969, several Manson members killed seven innocent people.

Of course, many people nowadays use the term *cult* to refer to any new group they dislike—whether its members are organized around religion, race, flying saucers, psychotherapy, politics, or self-improvement. The despised cults are typically accused of engaging in devious practices. It is suggested, for example, that some of their members recruit in a deceptive way—they might, for example, lure unsuspecting students by promising them a free-of-charge get-together at some retreat, while they fail to inform the students of their true intent. Other cults are said to use methods of mind control or thought reform (i.e., brainwashing) for transforming their recruits into totally obedient zealots. According to this view, members of cults become dependent on an authoritarian group leader who claims to have some special knowledge, gift, or talent. In extreme cases, recruits are no longer allowed to make any important personal decisions without consulting their leader and must give up all relationships with old friends and family. Finally, it is rumored that the most dangerous of such cults have coerced their members into committing suicide, murder, or both.

Every once in a while, the behavior of a cult confirms the worst suspicions of its detractors. On March 26, 1997, for example, 39 members of the Heaven's Gate cult committed mass suicide in their rented mansion in Rancho Santa Fe near San Diego. Marshall Applewhite, the cult's leader, had convinced his followers—20 women and 19 men ranging in age from 26 to 72—that a spaceship traveling behind the Hale-Bopp comet was coming to pick them all up, just as soon as they could shed their vehicles or containers (also known as bodies). They were totally convinced that civilization on Earth was about to end but that they could enter a higher life form by killing themselves and then boarding a spaceship from what they called the next level. So, as instructed by their leader, they took poison and—just in case—placed plastic bags over their heads to asphyxiate themselves.

Not only did the Heaven's Gate suicide victims represent both genders and a wide range of ages, but they also consisted of blacks, Latinos, and whites who had come from all over the country. And these were not stupid, crazy, or uneducated people—they were computer skilled, musically talented, and scholarly—but they were also needy, lonely, and depressed. Many had abandoned their families and friends months or years earlier.

It is right, of course, to be concerned for the lives of people who are down on their luck when they are recruited by dangerous or deceptive cults. When someone has suffered a profound loss or has no place to turn for guidance and support, he or she is particularly vulnerable to the attempts of groups, dangerous or not, to influence their decisions through conformity and obedience to authority.

At the same time, it is pure myth to suggest that recruits typically lack any power to resist while under the spell of a madman. Even vulnerable individuals possess an *active self*—they are typically not brainwashed into misbehaving but comply willingly with the requirements imposed on their membership. From this viewpoint, there is a definite limit to the power of a charismatic leader to mold or shape the behavior and beliefs of his disciples. Most cult leaders are not in the category of a Jim Jones or Marshall Applewhite, even if they are extremely persuasive.

Over the past 20 years, there may have been as many as 20 million Americans involved for varying periods of time in some kind of cult. The reason such groups have widespread appeal is that they provide precisely what many Americans find lacking in their everyday lives—a sense of belonging and friendship; a feeling of power, control, and importance; and a more general sense of structure and certainty.

Of course, individuals who are taken by force—especially children and teenagers—may be especially malleable and easy to manipulate by those who exercise total control and claim to have special powers. In a sense, 14-year-old Elizabeth Smart was the perfect victim. On June 5, 2002, Smart was abducted at gunpoint, in the middle of the night, from her family home in Salt Lake City. Some 10 months later, she turned up alive just a few miles away, in the presence of a drifter and self-styled prophet, who once did handyman work in the Smart home, and his female companion.

Why in the world did the 14-year-old girl not attempt to flee her kidnappers when she had the opportunity to do so? What made her use biblical language and give a false name—Augustine Marshall—to the police who finally rescued her from her abductors? After months of living with her captors in a tent and being forcibly isolated from any other influences, Smart apparently began to identify with her abductors. The reality of their total control over her life was gradually transformed into an illusion of control that almost any healthy and decent 14-year-old girl would have come to accept. At first, she probably complied out of fear in order to survive. But it appears that she eventually succumbed psychologically.

Years earlier, 19-year-old Patty Hearst was vilified after being abducted by members of the Symbionese Liberation Front, who kept her in a closet for long periods of time and made her completely dependent on them. She was certainly tortured and perhaps sexually assaulted. Yet, after collaborating with her kidnappers to rob a bank, Hearst served almost 2 years behind bars. Not only was she found guilty in a court of law, but she also looked guilty in the court of public opinion. The point is that the average person saw Patty Hearst more as a villain than a victim. If only they could have understood her as a prisoner of war, she might have gotten more sympathy.

Actually, studies of prisoners of war who collaborated with the enemy suggest that mind control can be achieved by exerting absolute power and control over a prisoner's day-to-day experiences, establishing a bond between the prisoner and his captors, and showing the inmate that his only road to salvation is to comply with the enemy's demands. Cultists have employed the same psychological methods of torture in persuading their members to commit mass murder or suicide, kidnap children, or amass an arsenal of weapons.

Yet most cultists are not like Elizabeth Smart or Patty Hearst—that is, they are full-fledged adults who join a group voluntarily because they sincerely believe that their cult membership will give them everything that is missing in their miserable lives. At various times in our lives, all of us can fall into vulnerable states—we may be lonely, hurting, having a hard time socially, having academic problems, or feeling overwhelmed or confused. During such temporary periods of misery and loss—for whatever reason— another person can have more influence over us than during other periods of time. If the members of a cult come along and promise to show us the way out of our misery, we may very well be tempted to join them. If, however, we can instead count on a helping hand from our instructors, advisors, friends, clergy, resident assistants, family, and counselors, the most persuasive cult will seem totally irrelevant.

# Reunion, American Style

## The Ritual of Recommuning

In her novel of the same name, Rona Jaffe suggests that a class reunion is more than a sentimental journey. It is also a way of answering the question that lies at the back of nearly all our minds: Did they do better than I? Jaffe's observation may be misplaced but not completely lost. According to a study conducted by social psychologist Jack Sparacino, the overwhelming majority who attend reunions aren't there invidiously to compare their recent accomplishments with those of their former classmates. Instead, they hope, primarily, to relive their earlier successes.

Certainly, a few return to show their former classmates how well they have done (See Vinitzky-Seroussi, 1998); some enjoy observing the changes that have occurred in their classmates (but not always in themselves, of course). But the majority who attend their class reunions do so to relive the good times they remember having when they were younger. In his study, Sparacino found that, as high school students, attendees had been more popular, more often regarded as attractive, and more involved in extracurricular activities than those classmates who chose not to attend. For those who turned up at their reunions, then, the old times were also the good times! It would appear that Americans have a special fondness for reunions, judging by their prevalence. Major league baseball players, fraternity members, veterans groups, high school and college graduates, and former Boy Scouts all hold reunions on a regular basis. In addition, family reunions frequently attract blood relatives from faraway places who spend considerable money and time to reunite.

Actually, in their affection for reuniting with friends, family, or colleagues, Americans are probably no different from any other people, except that Americans have created a mind-boggling number and variety of institutionalized forms of gatherings to facilitate the satisfaction of this desire.

Indeed, reunions have increasingly become formal events that are organized on a regular basis, and in the process, they have also become big business.

Shell Norris of Class Reunion, Inc., says that Chicago alone has 1,500 high school reunions each year. A conservative estimate on the national level would be 10,000 annually. At one time, all high school reunions were organized by volunteers, usually female homemakers. In the last few years, however, as more and more women have entered the labor force, alumni reunions are increasingly being planned by specialized companies rather than by part-time volunteers.

The first college reunion was held by the alumni of Yale University in 1792. Graduates of Pennsylvania, Princeton, Stanford, and Brown followed suit. And by the end of the 19th century, most 4-year institutions were holding alumni reunions.

According to Paul Chewning, vice president for alumni administration at the Council for Advancement and Support of Education (CASE), the variety of college reunions is impressive. At Princeton, alumni parade through the town wearing their class uniforms and singing their alma mater. At Marietta College, they gather for a dinner-dance on a steamship cruising the Ohio River. At Dartmouth, alumni act as lecturers and panelists in continuing education courses for their former classmates.

Clearly, the thought of cruising on a steamship or marching through the streets is usually not, by itself, sufficient reason for large numbers of alumni to return to campus. Chewning contends that alumni who decide to attend their reunions share a common identity based on the years they spent together as undergraduates. For this reason, universities that somehow establish a common bond—for example, because they are relatively small or especially prestigious—tend to draw substantial numbers of their alumni to reunions. In an effort to enhance this common identity, larger colleges and universities frequently build their class reunions on participation in smaller units, such as departments or schools. Or they encourage affinity reunions for groups of former cheerleaders, editors, fraternity members, musicians, members of military organizations on campus, and the like.

Of course, not every alumnus is fond of his or her alma mater. Michelle Favreault, associate director of Alumni Affairs at Brandeis University, suggests that students who graduated during the late 1960s may be especially reluctant to get involved in alumni events. They were part of the generation that conducted sit-ins and teach-ins directed at university administrators, protested Reserve Officers' Training Corps (ROTC) and military recruitment on campus, and marched against establishment politics. If this generation has a common identity, it may fall outside of their university ties or even be hostile to them. Even as they enter their middle years, alumni who continue to harbor unpleasant memories of college during this period may not wish to attend class reunions.

Not all reunions are school affairs. People also reunite as an unintended consequence, a latent function of gatherings designed for other reasons. Hundreds of professional associations hold annual conferences or conventions to keep their members up-to-date with developments in their fields. Yet many of the professionals who attend pass up the formal sessions—the speeches and seminars—in favor of meeting informally in bars and hotel lobbies with colleagues from other cities and states.

Attendees are given an excuse to swap experiences with friends they haven't seen since the last meeting. Similarly, the manifest function—the intended and recognized purpose—of wedding ceremonies is to unite the bride and groom in matrimony. Yet weddings (as well as funerals, confirmations, and bar mitzvahs) also serve an important latent function: They provide occasions for scattered families and friends to reunite.

The poignancy of these meetings suggests a more general principle: If reunions make people cry, it is not, as Rona Jaffe proposes, because they have come out on the short end of things now. It is because they measured up so well 20 years ago, and they want to relive the good old days with tears of joy.

# The Consequences of Coalitions

## Responding to White Supremacist Leaflets

Several hundred residents of Sharon, Massachusetts, recently came together to participate in a candlelight vigil against hate, inspired by racist and anti-Semitic leaflets that were dumped, days earlier, on lawns across this Boston suburb. Local leaders held a daylong meeting to address the issue of bigotry and to find an appropriate long-term response. Many concerned Sharonites placed candles in their windows.

Why should so many people in a town like Sharon—a middle-class bedroom community—come together to protest such an apparently trivial event? After all, nobody was murdered, raped, or assaulted. There were no rocks thrown through the windows of synagogues; no crosses were burned. In fact, if any crime was committed at all, it was nothing more than littering. The answer is that hate thrives and prospers under conditions of silence and nonresponse.

The National Alliance, a West Virginia–based white supremacist organization, counted on its late-night distribution of fliers in Sharon to provoke widespread anxiety and division. But the hate group never counted on local residents to respond instead by coming together in a broad-based coalition—a temporary alliance of Muslims, Christians, and Jews—and by acquiring the strong backing of the Board of Selectmen, state representatives, School Committee, District Attorney's office, local police, recreation department, Sharon Clergy Council, Islamic Center of New England, Office of the Superintendent of Schools, Gay/Straight Student Alliance, Council on Aging, Sharon Community Youth Coalition, Anti-Defamation League, and many Christian clergy and congregations in town. The response of members of the

Sharon community could serve as a model for how to respond to hate incidents in general, even those that seem unimportant.

Where residents let the small incidents pass without response, hate can escalate into ever more serious offenses. Interpreting silence as support and encouragement, hatemongers are likely to take their tactics to a more dangerous level, stopping only when they have achieved their intended purpose.

Last month, for example, Donald Butler, a 29-year-old black resident of Pemberton Township, Pennsylvania, was targeted by two white supremacists who shouted racial slurs at him as he stood on the front lawn of his home. Perhaps seeing the verbal abuse against their neighbor as an isolated and trivial event, Butler's white neighbors did absolutely nothing to assure him of their support or indignation. Three weeks later, the same two hatemongers returned with baseball bats, this time invading Butler's home in the dead of night where they brutally beat him and his wife. The Butlers escaped with stitches and broken bones, but they also felt hurt and alone, as if no one really cared. They have since relocated to another community.

The National Alliance has been associated with more than just littering.

In the interest of establishing an all-white society, its members have distributed white-power rock music and recruited many racist skinheads to the cause. Moreover, its former leader, the late William Pierce, in his racist book *The Turner Diaries*, apparently provided the blueprint for Timothy McVeigh's 1995 murder of 168 innocent people in Oklahoma City.

Hate is more than just an individual offense. It can poison the relations between groups and escalate into large-scale ethnic conflict. When thinking of the consequences of hate, we are likely first to imagine the horrible violence in Bosnia, Israel, or Northern Ireland. Or we might recall the extraordinary murder of James Byrd, the black resident of Jasper, Texas, who was dragged to his death behind a pickup truck. But we should also never forget where hate begins—in the silence of ordinary people.

# Children of the Organization Men

## The New Individualists

For more than 30 years, William H. Whyte's *The Organization Man* (1956) was the most widely read book about organizational life. Focusing on middle-class Americans at midcentury, Whyte argued that bureaucratic organizations actually shaped almost every aspect of our lives. They dictated that employees be group minded. That is, they were expected to be flexible to the demands of others, to be completely loyal to the corporation, and to remain uncommitted to a set of values. In this view, organizations rewarded only those individuals who were good team players. Nothing else really counted, from the corporate point of view.

In collecting data for his book, Whyte followed his organization men (this is not a sexist slight; there simply weren't any organization women) into their offices, but he also visited their suburban homes, schools, and neighborhoods. He interviewed their wives and observed their children.

Whyte's description of the social role of the corporate wife is particularly telling. Any employee who aspired to be promoted to an executive position needed a wife who obeyed the corporate rules. She had to be willing to make frequent moves from city to city for the sake of her husband's job, to assume exclusive responsibility for household chores and child rearing, and to stay away from her husband's workplace. She must never gossip about the office with other corporate wives, never get drunk at a company party, never be too friendly with the wives of other employees whom her husband might pass on his way up the corporate ladder, and never show up her husband by being superior to him in any way.

Whyte observed the rise of a pervasive *social ethic*—a widely held belief that the group was the essential source of creativity and that belongingness was the basic human need: thus, the demand for yes-men, happy homemakers, family togetherness, and team players; hence, the worship of the organization.

For their book *The New Individualists: The Generation After the Organization Man* (1991), Paul Leinberger (whose father was an organization man interviewed 30 years earlier by William Whyte) and Bruce Tucker interviewed the sons and daughters of the original organization men as well as hundreds of other organizational offspring. They focused on baby boomer Americans—those men and women born between 1946 and 1964 whose fathers had worked for most of their careers in large organizations.

Included in their study were the middle manager chafing at the slow progress up the promotional ladder, the forest ranger dreaming of writing novels, the aging hippie getting by on marginal jobs, the gypsy scholar in today's brutal academic job market, the entrepreneur starting a software company, the corporate star rising rapidly, and the freelance consultant seeking autonomy.

Leinberger and Tucker found that the organizational offspring were very different from their fathers in terms of outlook, values, and motives. Children of organization men resembled one another with respect to attitude toward organizations, style of interpersonal relations, and patterns of consumption. But unlike their fathers, all of them were strong individualists. Whereas organization men admired the salesman, their offspring admire the artist. Whereas organization men were conspicuous consumers, their children cherish creativity. Whereas organization men were dominated by sociability, their offspring pursue self-fulfillment.

Leinberger and Tucker suggest that social change is partially responsible for the new norms embraced by organizational offspring. During the past 30 years, we have seen major changes in the conditions of work, leisure, economics, family life, and politics. The huge number of acquisitions and mergers in the late 1980s makes a lie of the concept of corporate loyalty; many longtime executives were summarily dismissed without any cause other than a need to reduce corporate expenses. The dual-career family introduces competing sources of allegiance between work and home. Foreign competition and reduced profits put new strains on American business.

The resulting generational differences are often profound. As soon as they finished school, organization men married, went to work, and began having children. By their mid-30s, the last of their 2 or 3 children was born. By contrast, children of the organization men often remain in school through their 20s, marry even later, and are in their 30s when they have their 1.8 children.

An obsession with the self can be observed as a major element in the individualism of the organizational offspring. At home, in schools, and through the mass media, the members of this generation were urged to enhance self-expression, self-fulfillment, self-actualization, self-assertion, self-understanding, and self-acceptance. Just as surely as their parents accepted a social ethic, the children of the organization men developed a *self ethic*.

The organization men were severely criticized for their almost robotlike obedience to corporate aspirations. But their children's individualistic ideal has also come under attack. According to Leinberger and Tucker, the offspring have created the most radical version of the individual in American history—a thoroughly isolated individual who can't make commitments, can't communicate, and can't achieve community. The exclusive emphasis on the self has left many people feeling alone and anxious.

To the extent that organizational offspring remain committed to the self ethic, they are unlikely to provide the human resources for a competitive American workforce—not unless the corporation adjusts to them. This is no small problem. There are approximately 19 million adult children of the organization men. What is more, as the offspring of the managerial class, they represent the middle and upper-middle classes—the very people who have historically dominated American business. The management philosophy of the organization man generation survives.

Into the 1990s, corporate managers continued to revere professionalism, control, teamwork, and order. At the same time, they had little patience with the ideas of leadership, substance, or vision. At midcentury, when American companies had no real competition, the organization man's view of corporate reality was viable enough. In the contemporary world of global competition and economic uncertainty, however, vision and leadership may be essential for survival. In the long haul, quality becomes more important than quantity.

Leinberger and Tucker present the grounds for believing that for children of the organization men, the future holds a better fit between their personal style and structural demands. If they are to succeed in the long run, organizations will be required to adapt themselves to a new generation of individualists—men and women who will soon be replacing their fathers in leadership positions. But just in case they don't adapt, perhaps it is time that we study the next generation, the grandchildren of the organization men.

# Thwarting the Bullies in Our Schools

## A Two-Pronged Strategy for Reducing School Violence

The fatal stabbing of a student at Lincoln-Sudbury Regional High School is obviously a tragic event; it is also an opportunity to examine the phenomenon of student-on-student violence.

The essential problem with the public reaction to this horrific act of violence is that we can't seem to get past the details of this particular crime in this particular school as perpetrated by this particular student, when we should instead be focusing on the larger picture. Until we are able to get beyond our obsession with easy answers, such as suspect John Odgren's Asperger's disorder or the psychotropic medications he takes, we will learn little about how to prevent violence at school.

The occurrence of a teen with Asperger's disorder who kills a schoolmate is so extraordinary that it may not happen again for generations. What will definitely occur time and again are episodes of school violence in which one youngster who has been teased, bullied, or humiliated kills another for revenge.

This revenge is not aimed at the student whose life he has taken but at students in general. It is almost never a single event that inspires an act of extreme violence. Instead, the young killer has typically spent months, if not years, being terrorized. He may reach the point where even an innocuous gesture from an innocent classmate is misunderstood as a threatening response.

Some students at Lincoln-Sudbury reported that Odgren had been teased for the way he dressed. But his parents suggested that he had been thoroughly miserable at his previous school, causing him to spend his evenings at home wrapped in a blanket and in tears.

There is an important lesson here—bullying in the schools should be totally unacceptable to students, teachers, parents, and school administrators. Let us see bullying for what it is: not a normal part of growing up but a potentially devastating series of events for any youngster who is different for a variety of reasons, including being overweight, being of a different race, having an accent, or having a physical or mental disability.

Intervention by an adult is the key. Rather than turning their backs on occurrences of bullying in the hallway, lunchroom, or playground, teachers, counselors, and school psychologists must intervene.

The easy response is to do nothing; the effective reaction is to become sensitive to what happens between students outside the classroom and to put a stop to anyone who is harassing another person with words or fists. Many schools have adopted antibullying programs in which students are taught to empathize with the victims of bullying rather than contribute to their victimization.

The second lesson to learn from the Lincoln-Sudbury tragedy is that we must break the culture of silence that so often exists among students in a middle or high school setting. In Boston, fear of physical retaliation has apparently caused many who witness violent criminal activities to ignore their responsibility to cooperate with police in identifying killers.

But in middle-class suburbs, students who overhear a threat in the hallway fear the social consequences. Snitching is not viewed as being cool, and students do not want to be rejected by their peers. Youngsters who prefer not to be labeled as a snitch will talk themselves into believing that someone else is bound to inform, so why should they get involved?

The establishment of a tip hotline in Lincoln-Sudbury makes sense but only if informing on schoolmates is positively sanctioned in the student culture.

Across the country, there have been fewer school shootings committed by disgruntled students thanks in part to the willingness of youngsters to put aside their social anxieties and inform a parent, a teacher, or a resource officer.

In such communities as Massachusetts's Marshfield and New Bedford, the culture of silence was reduced to the point where students cooperated with police to turn in threatening schoolmates before they carried out their murderous intentions.

By reducing bullying and breaking the culture of silence, we will dramatically improve the quality of life not only for those students who are victims of violence but also for all of our children. In the process, we may also prevent a slaying or two.

# FOCUS

## ✧ Suggestions for Further Reading ✧

Concerning "College Fraternities: A Counteracting Force on Campus," the original idea of counteracting forces in mass society can be found in Arnold Rose's article "Reactions Against the Mass Society" in the *Sociological Quarterly* (1962). For a recent treatment of the individual in modern, postmodern, or hypermodern society (depending on your personal view), read the fascinating account by George Ritzer in *The McDonaldization of Society* (2000). The eclipse of community is examined intelligently in Robert D. Putnam's *Bowling Alone: The Collapse and Revival of American Culture* (2000).

Opposing viewpoints concerning the efficacy of cults are represented in two recent treatments of the topic. On one side, there is the very interesting book *Why Waco? Cults and the Battle for Religious Freedom in America,* in which James Tabor and Eugene Gallagher (1995) present a compelling argument in favor of seeing cult recruits as possessing an active self that can be manipulated only so much. On the other side, Margaret Thaler Singer's (1995) *Cults in Our Midst: The Hidden Menace in Our Everyday Lives* takes the position that cultists are the victims of powerful mind control techniques. For a detailed examination of the details of the Heaven's Gate cult suicide in San Diego, read *Heaven's Gate* by Bill Hoffman and Cathy Burke (1997). In *Cults, Religion and Violence* (Bromley and Melton, 2002), a number of social scientists discuss the violence perpetrated by and against new religious cults. They also explore whether such dramatic conflicts can be foreseen, managed, and averted.

I collected information for "Reunion, American Style" by interviewing alumni personnel in a number of colleges and universities. I also relied on data gathered by the Alumni Administration Division of CASE. If you are interested in learning more about class reunions, I suggest getting in touch with CASE in Washington, DC. Concerning the functional argument used in this snapshot, Robert K. Merton's *Social Theory and Social Structure* (1957) is an important work in which he discusses, among many other things, the distinction between manifest and latent functions. He also discusses the role of serendipity in science, a topic that will be raised later in this book when we consider social change.

Coalitions are temporary alliances. As illustrated by the collaboration discussed in "The Consequences of Coalitions," the ordinary people in a coalition put aside their differences in order to pursue the goals and objectives that they have in common. At the turn of the 20th century, for example, labor unions developed out of a temporary alliance of newcomers from Ireland, Italy, and Poland who put aside their vast differences to join together for the sake of a common objective—higher pay and better working conditions. In the 1940s and 1950s, the civil rights movement began as a coalition of blacks and whites who regarded bigotry as a common enemy deserving of a united response. In the 1960s, a coalition of women and Americans of color successfully lobbied for affirmative action legislation at the federal level, a goal that neither group would in all likelihood have achieved by itself. And coalitions against bigotry, violence, and hatred can have a basis in initiating positive actions, rather than merely responding to negative actions, on their own behalf. See Todorov's *The Fragility of Goodness: Why Bulgaria's Jews Survived the Holocaust* (1999).

Concerning "Children of the Organization Men," the classic treatment of the midcentury lifestyle of the loyal and obedient corporate employee can be found in William H. Whyte's *The Organization Man* (1956). Conclusions in this snapshot regarding the children of organization men were drawn from *The New Individualists: The Generation After the Organization Man* (1991), by Paul Leinberger and Bruce Tucker. For an enlightening account of how bureaucratic organizations systematically hinder the careers of women, read Rosabeth M. Kanter's *Men and Women of the Corporation* (1993).

In the aftermath of a school shooting, there is a predictable tendency to do considerable "finger pointing." We want to place the blame on the killer's parents, medications, and illnesses rather than on situational factors that might reduce the likelihood of a similar occurrence of violence in the future. In "Thwarting the Bullies in Our Schools," there is no finger-pointing to be seen. Instead, a two-pronged strategy is offered, one that aims at changing important aspects of the student culture in which school shootings find encouragement and support.

## DEVELOPING IDEAS

### ✦ About the Group Experience ✦

1. Writing topic: Choose any book that focuses on a dangerous cult (e.g., Heaven's Gate, Jonestown, or Waco). Based on your reading, write an essay in which you discuss the aspects of the cult that were so influential in making members engage in dangerous behavior. In particular, focus on characteristics of both the leader and followers.

2. Research topic: Do college organizations really compensate for a lack of informal interaction? If so, students who spend much time with family, partners, or friends shouldn't join many clubs and organizations on campus; students who don't hang out with family, partners, or friends should make up the difference by joining. Interview a number of students on your campus to find out as much as you can about their social activities: how often they are with friends or family, how many campus organizations they belong to, and any leadership positions they hold in these organizations. What do your results indicate about college organizations as compensatory groups?

3. Writing topic: Examine an institutionalized practice—for example, a wedding or a funeral—for all of the latent functions it might perform.

4. Research topic: Just how restrictive is a formal organization? To what extent does holding a job in a large corporation necessitate a loss of personal freedom for the individual who works there? To provide a case study, visit a large company in your local community. For at least a few hours, observe the patterns of behavior, including dress, speech, arrangement of furniture in offices, any uniformity of color, hairstyles, cars in the parking lot, schedule for lunch and breaks, and so on. Don't forget to take notes concerning your observations in some systematic way. For example, before beginning, you might want to make a partial list of the patterns of behavior you expect to find, to be expanded during the study. You might even want to visit, only briefly, another large company, to get ideas about how employees conform. By the way, to avoid looking suspicious while collecting data, you might want to inform someone at the company of your purpose and ask permission to become a participant-observer.

5. Research topic: To what extent do coalitions of students exist on your college campus? Interview the leaders of various special-interest groups on campus to determine to what extent they have collaborated with the leaders of other special-interest groups on projects of common interest. During the academic year, for example, have various ethnic and racial organizations— Latino Center, African-American Institute, Muslim Students Association, or Hillel—cooperated to put on a multicultural food or music festival? Have the members of different groups come together in response to a hate incident or a sexual assault on campus? If student organizations have not formed coalitions, you might want to ask, "Why not?"

# PART IV

## Institutions

At a time when today's aging baby boomers were still hippies—during the late 1960s and early 1970s—I was just finishing up my graduate degree and making plans for the future. My primary objective was to teach at the college level. Yet not unlike many of my friends and fellow graduate students in sociology, I also thought long and hard about the possibility of dropping out of the mainstream of competitive American society and establishing instead an alternative lifestyle that would be less demanding and repressive. In retrospect, it sounds kind of silly, but at the time, it seemed to make sense.

During the late 1960s, many young people claimed to have given up on American institutions—the nuclear family, organized religion, capitalism, constitutional government, and traditional forms of public education—and it was relatively easy to find support and encouragement for going it alone. The more politically motivated students of the day referred to anyone in charge of almost anything—whether the police, the chair of the sociology department, or the president of the United States—as "pigs" and to conventional, middle-class political institutions, in the most negative sense possible, as "the establishment." Even among students who weren't inclined toward politics, the operating principle of everyday life seemed to be "do your own thing." Traditional institutions—the traditional ways of meeting basic needs—were often viewed as irrelevant, if not the enemy.

Of course, though many hip-oriented students paid lip service to the idea of an alternative lifestyle, most never went much beyond the hippie fashion (wearing love beads, jeans, and long hair) in seeking to throw off what they saw as the yoke of repression represented by American institutions.

Even the antiwar demonstrations and demonstrations for civil rights and women's rights were, for the most part, designed to reform, not overthrow, traditional institutional arrangements. After all, many of those young people who demonstrated loudly for equal rights or against the war were students enrolled in the very colleges and universities they were fiercely attacking. Moreover, only a relatively few young people actually left school to drop out of American society.

Over time, those who did leave to take up residence on a commune attempted to establish their own institutions—frequently, collective arrangements for feeding their families, building shelter, making clothing, teaching the basic skills of everyday life to children, and attending to their spiritual needs. Many communes failed to survive for more than a few months, however, because they also failed to develop collective ways for meeting their members' basic needs. To put it briefly, they never developed viable alternative institutions.

The collective ways developed by any society for meeting the economic, religious, familial, political, and educational needs of its members are known as institutions. The lesson to be learned from the failure of many hippie communes of the 1960s and 1970s is simply that a group of people cannot survive very long as a group without generating some set of effective institutional arrangements. The more recent demise of the Soviet Union was, in part, a result of a profound failure of its institutions in terms of meeting the basic needs of its members. It can happen to a small commune or to an entire society of millions of people.

How well do American institutions meet human needs? In "Who's Minding the Kids?" we find a very negative answer: Our families, schools, and religious institutions are so weak that the adolescent peer group has taken over. Young people now raise one another. As a result, violence among teenagers has taken on epidemic proportions.

Institutions often provide an efficient means of meeting human needs that would be impossible by sheer individual effort alone. But on the social psychological level, institutional responsiveness to difficult social problems also allows human beings to avoid dealing firsthand with what they desire to pretend doesn't exist—death, illness, disaster, disfigurement, and disability.

In "Let the System Do It!" this idea is introduced and illustrated. We have developed a set of institutions—schools, political systems, corporations, legal units, and religions—each of which now carries out specialized functions that used to be performed by family members. As a result, we, as individual members of society, escape the burden of having to face the entire range of human issues and frailties.

Another negative aspect of our institutions is contained in "Americans Are Moving to the Margins of Society." It isn't only government that has suffered recently with respect to loss of credibility; there is much evidence to suggest that faith and confidence in all mainstream institutions are on the decline.

One of the most important functions of the economic institution involves getting the unpleasant but necessary jobs done. In "Dirty Work," we are reminded that dirty work in America has traditionally been performed for low wages by poor people, newcomers, and minorities who have had few other choices. We also see that the dirtiness of a job has little, if anything, to do with its being physically unclean but can be changed profoundly depending on how much we pay people to do it.

# Who's Minding the Kids?

## Is Violence Filling the Void in Our Teenagers' Lives?

The headlines scream daily of hideous crimes—drive-by shootings, carjackings, and senseless murders—committed by our nation's teenagers. What makes violence so appealing to so many youngsters? Why is it that, in some quarters around the country, guns have replaced leather jackets and CD players as status symbols of choice? According to police reports to the FBI, the number of homicides committed by youngsters in their early teens skyrocketed between 1985 and 1991. During this period, arrest rates for homicide increased among 13- and 14-year-old males by 140% and among 15-year-old males by 217%. Then, thanks to a number of programs and policies that effectively addressed the needs of the teenaged population—after-school programs, community centers, tutors in the schools, and summer jobs—the teen murder rate declined for several years.

Since 2004, however, here has been somewhat of a reversal in the trend toward "good news" about youth crime, and the murder rate has once again climbed. Many of the recent budget cutbacks seen as necessary to balance the books at the state level have targeted the very programs and policies that were so effective through the 1990s in bringing down the rate of juvenile crime. In addition, larger numbers of inmates—men who were incarcerated during the late 1980s and 1990s as a result of the war on drugs—are now being released into the community. They have no job skills and little hope of making it in the legitimate system, so they are getting back into the gangs. As a result, murders committed by gang members are on the rise.

Actually, the problem is even worse than these dreadful trends in violent crime might suggest. Although relatively few of our youngsters are committing hideous murders, they are being tolerated—perhaps even honored—by their friends and classmates. Millions of teenagers may not be able to shoot or stab someone themselves, but they are fully capable of looking on as others do so.

Years ago, a case of bystander apathy raised enough concern to inspire the movie *River's Edge*. A teenager in Milpitas, California, murdered his 14-year-old girlfriend and then returned to the scene with a dozen classmates to show them the corpse. One student covered the body with leaves to keep it from being discovered; others threw rocks at it. None of them contacted the police or told their parents.

More recently, the nation was shocked to learn that an attractive New Hampshire school teacher, Pam Smart, had inspired her 15-year-old student and his friends to eliminate her husband, Greg, by shooting him in the head. Attorney Marsha Kazarosian subsequently filed a suit against the Winnecunnet, New Hampshire, school district on behalf of the families of the three youngsters convicted in the murder. Kazarosian claimed that Pam Smart's love affair with her student was made possible because she was negligently unsupervised by the Winnecunnet High School administration—that somebody in charge should have been keeping a watchful eye on Smart. Whether or not school officials should have known, it appears that they may have been the only ones at Winnecunnet High who didn't.

Statements made during the course of the police investigation indicate clearly that at least 1 month before the police finally broke the case, the corridors of Winnecunnet High were already abuzz with rumors implicating the three students and their teacher. Yet nobody bothered to inform an adult.

More incredibly, statements later made to law enforcement officials indicate that students at Winnecunnet High were talking about Greg Smart's murder for 2 months before it actually occurred. With a simple phone call, any one of them might have prevented a murder. But nobody wanted to snitch or tattle on a classmate. Everybody was concerned about being rejected by friends. So they all kept quiet and let the murder plot proceed according to plan.

Between 1997 and 2001, there was a string of school shootings in places like Littleton, Colorado, Springfield, Oregon, Jonesboro, Arkansas, West Paducah, Kentucky, Pearl, Mississippi, Williamsport, Pennsylvania, and Moses Lake, Washington, committed by students who felt belittled, harassed, or bullied by their classmates and teachers. In some of these murders, the apathy of students who overheard threatening words being spoken by classmates may have contributed to the problem. By contrast, a high school student in New Bedford, Massachusetts, turned in her friends before they could operationalize their plan to blow up their high school. In November 2001, Amy Bowman blew the whistle on the plans of her fellow students after realizing that the others were serious.

Too few of our teenagers are like Amy Bowman. Many more have become desensitized to the consequences of violence. They have been raised on a steady diet of slasher films filled with gory scenes of sex, murder, and mayhem. After school, they come home to an empty house where they spend hours daily listening to rap and heavy metal lyrics or watching MTV videos in which violence is glorified. For economic reasons, more and more of our teenagers are left to fend for themselves, unsupervised after school and during vacations.

Only a few of our youngsters are willing to shoot someone in the head. But many others participate from a distance. Even if breaking their silence might stop a murder, they do not want to get involved for fear of being rejected by their peers. Informing is viewed as snitching, and snitching is simply not regarded as cool.

In October 2007, just as Americans had become optimistic that school shootings were a thing of the past, a 14-year-old student in Cleveland, Ohio, who had been suspended from school, opened fire on his classmates and teachers, injuring four of them. Then, he took his own life. Within 24 hours, reporters were on the scene talking with a number of students who had heard the killer make threatening remarks but who never informed a teacher or a parent or never made an anonymous call to the police.

Marsha Kazarosian's lawsuit reflects an unpleasant truth about American society today. It isn't that TV, motion pictures, and popular music are so powerful. It is that our traditional institutions have become so weak. Our schools, religions, and families have lost their moral authority.

And in their place, we have allowed the peer group to fill the void in our youngsters' lives.

# Let the System Do It!

## Taking Care of Society's Problems Can Hurt

Less than a century ago, the middle-class family was still involved in almost every aspect of its members' lives. Mother, father, grandparents, and children all worked the farm (or in the family firm). Together, they educated the offspring, treated illnesses, and provided a role for elders. After death, family members were buried in the family plot in the backyard, not in some cemetery with thousands of strangers, located miles away.

In responding to social problems, we have similarly constructed hospitals, prisons, nursing homes, and "special" schools for the developmentally disabled and the emotionally disturbed. In the same way, we have built mental institutions, cancer wards, soup kitchens, and retirement communities, all in the name of efficiency and humanitarian motivation.

Clearly, there are compelling administrative, medical, and economic reasons that many of our thorniest human problems—illness, poverty, and old age—are better handled by specialized formal organizations than by families. But there may be other, less rational reasons as well.

One clue is to look at the sites where our nation's prisons and mental hospitals were first located. Many of them are now in middle-class suburban areas, an easy drive from the urban core. But at the time they were built, these same areas were quite different; they were almost invariably secluded rural settings, located many miles from large population centers and hidden from everyday view. Even cemeteries were typically built some distance from major cities, allowing friends and relatives to pay a visit but only on a limited basis.

Remember the cliché "out of sight, out of mind"? Let's face it: There are many problems that middle-class Americans would prefer to shuttle aside and put out of easy reach. Too often, the attitude is, "Let somebody else take care of it. We aren't trained and they are." Thus, our formal organizations help us isolate those things we simply don't want to see. By constructing a formal response, we are able to avoid the whole range of human misery that might otherwise disrupt our personal lives and make us feel very uncomfortable. By letting the formal system take care of terminal cancer patients, drug addicts, severely disfigured individuals, and Alzheimer's victims, for example, we increase the subjective probability that these hideous things won't happen to us or to our loved ones. By distancing ourselves from human frailty and misery, we are then free to pursue our individual goals and objectives—at work and at home—without fear that the same thing might (or will) happen to us.

Specialized institutions give us the false security of being able to go through life avoiding life's problems—until we are forced to deal with them. This may be one reason that community-based forms of treatment for mental illness, intellectual deficits, and juvenile delinquency have so often been opposed by Americans. In too many cases, even where their residents pose little if any risk to the neighbors, the thinking is that halfway houses belong on anybody else's block but mine.

Of course, not everyone opts to put his or her blinders on. Recognizing the myopic view of many Americans, educators are beginning to stress the importance of exposing young people to the entire range of social problems that they might otherwise not encounter. In one special program for high school students, for example, each teenager in the program spends one day working in a home for developmentally disabled children; each spends a number of hours in a jail cell; and each pays a visit to a morgue.

They may get sick to their stomachs, but they also learn about the possible consequences of their own behavior as well as the inevitable consequences of being human. They are forced to see the world the way it really is and not the way they'd like it to be. In the process, they may unexpectedly come face-to-face with themselves.

# Americans Are Moving to the Margins of Society

## They No Longer Trust Mainstream Solutions

What does the Oklahoma City massacre have in common with the mass suicide of 39 Heaven's Gate cultists near San Diego? Both of these tragedies provide examples of Americans who are turning, in ever-increasing numbers, to the margins of society—rather than to its mainstream—for solutions to their personal problems. Twenty or thirty years ago, citizens searching for spiritual guidance would, in all likelihood, have received comfort and reassurance from their church and family; those seeking a political answer would have found it in the Democratic or Republican party. Now they are more likely to join an obscure cult, go into the woods on Sunday afternoons to rehearse for the coming apocalypse, or simply barricade themselves in their homes rather than obey a federal court order.

This is exactly what Ed Brown and his wife Elaine, a prominent local dentist, did, when in January 2007, they were confronted by government agents who attempted to extricate them from their fortress-like Plainfield, New Hampshire, residence. The Browns had already been convicted of tax evasion; they owed the federal government back taxes on almost $2 million in unreported income. Arguing that the Constitution prohibited a federal income tax, the couple holed up in their rural residence and refused to permit federal authorities to enter. Finally, masquerading as a supporter of the antitax movement, an undercover federal agent was able to gain access to the Browns and put an end to the months-long standoff. The Browns are now serving a five-year prison sentence.

All of our traditional institutions are under attack. Postmodernists turn their backs on the scientific method, claiming that it has helped destroy civilization; skeptical patients experiment with herbal or homeopathic medicine, megavitamin therapy, acupuncture, or Tai Chi; and increasing numbers of parents have given up on the public schools, opting for a private-school alternative or for educating their youngsters at home.

For a brief period of time, the September 11 attack on the United States generated a renewed sense of confidence and trust in American institutions, including especially the police, firefighters, the military, and the presidency. Even the popularity of Congress temporarily soared. Indeed, public trust in government reached levels not achieved for three decades, rising from 42% in July 2000 to 60% in October 2001, just after the attack on the Twin Towers. By September 2002, however, public trust in government declined to 46%, nearly back to its pre–September 11 level.

In the latest Gallup poll, firefighters, the military, and the police continue to be popular with the American people. But the credibility of most of our other leaders has again plummeted, giving them the stature of stereotypical used-car salesmen. According to Gallup, only 9% of all adult Americans voiced a great deal of confidence in Congress, only 9% in the criminal justice system.

Outside of government, moreover, our institutions are faring only slightly better. When asked to evaluate the honesty and ethical standards of various occupational groups, less than 20% of the American people gave very high marks to labor union leaders, real estate agents, lawyers, stockbrokers, high school teachers, business executives, medical doctors, accountants, advertising practitioners, or even clergy. Part of the reason for the erosion of trust and confidence in traditional institutions involves the eclipse of community we have recently experienced.

Many Americans feel they have no place to turn when they get into trouble— they are unable to find a sense of belonging and importance at work, among friends, or in their own families. Children come home from school to an empty house. Anxious not to be fired or laid off, their parents are too busy at work to get to know their neighbors or participate in community activities. Those who have moved their residence for the sake of a job no longer have friends, family, or fraternal organizations to help them through tough times. Their support systems are now hundreds, perhaps thousands, of miles away. Even if they have remained in the same community, growing numbers of families are without the assistance of extended kin, especially grandparents, or of two parents who can share the tasks of child rearing and family breadwinning. As income inequality continues to rise, the eclipse of community becomes increasingly burdensome.

The decline in institutional credibility also involves a more than 30-year spiral of scandals involving leadership at the highest levels of government, business, and entertainment—Chappaquiddick, Abscam, Irangate, Watergate, S&L, Travelgate, Filegate, and Enron—not to mention the assumed and actual transgressions committed by Robert Packwood, Newt Gingrich, Bill Clinton, Michael Milken, Leona Helmsley, Martha Stewart, Larry Craig, Michael Vick, and Michael Jackson.

Having traversed the millennium, growing numbers of Americans are now thinking in apocalyptic terms. Some expect a spiritual transition to a higher plane, whereas others believe that the next few decades will bring the ultimate physical confrontation and destruction in a war of all against all.

We cannot do anything to alter the calendar—we hope, our nation will survive to new heights in coming years and decades. As individuals, we are almost as powerless to influence the course of our economy at the federal level. But all of us can assume a special sense of responsibility for what happens in our own backyard—at work, in our neighborhoods and schools, and at home. It is at the grassroots level that we might begin to repair the credibility of our traditional institutions. This is where we can make an effort on behalf of our fellow citizens in trouble so that they feel important, special, a sense of belonging, and that they really count. Bringing Americans back into the mainstream may be our only realistic chance to prevent more mass suicides and acts of domestic terrorism in the future.

# Dirty Work

## Who's Going to Do the Unpleasant Jobs?

E very society has its dirty work: jobs considered repugnant, undignified, or menial. They may also be regarded as absolutely essential for the well-being of society. Throughout the world, much of the dirtiest work of a society has been reserved for those individuals considered outside the mainstream: for example, Pakistanis in England, Iraqis in Kuwait, and Turks in Germany. At the same time, even the most prestigious occupations may include at least a few tasks that could be regarded as dirty.

As a historical trend, the increasing rationalization of American society has created a proliferation of specialized occupations from what was formerly thought of as merely another field's dirty work. Indeed, millions of Americans currently work in jobs that never even existed a few decades earlier: assistants to activity directors in nursing homes and daycare centers, emergency medical technicians, dental hygienists, data entry personnel, paralegals, associate producers, home care workers, audiovisual equipment aides, television and radio interns, computer technicians, and so on. To an increasing extent, therefore, one occupation's dirty work has become another's raison d'être! In the midst of the expansion of specialized occupational roles, some professionals have gained enough resources to subcontract much, if not all, of their dirty work to lower-paid specialists. For example, professors may assign the task of grading multiple-choice exams to their teaching assistants; many dentists have hygienists who perform routine dental care; and nurses often enlist nurses' aides to change bandages and bedpans. Accountants have their bookkeepers, physicians have physicians' assistants, and lawyers have paralegals.

What comes to be viewed as dirty work need not be the least bit dirty, at least in a physical sense. There is really nothing intrinsically repulsive about what we might choose to call dirty work. Instead, jobs are labeled as respectable or dirty based typically on a social construction: The members of a society share an understanding of the nature of their environment and apply that understanding to their definitions of occupational tasks.

In contemporary American society, for example, bankers are generally seen as holding a reputable occupational position. During the Middle Ages, however, the same job was regarded as too dirty for Christians to perform and was instead assigned to outsiders—specifically, to European Jews who were systematically excluded from respectable activities such as farming, owning land, and joining the guilds of craftsmen. Generally, Jews were restricted to the despised occupation of lending money at interest—an activity regarded as essential by the church and the nobility as a source of outside financing for building, farming, waging war, or engaging in political affairs.

Its economic importance notwithstanding, usury was absolutely forbidden to the Christian majority on religious grounds. As viewed by the church, the lending of money for interest was sinful regardless of the amount of interest charged or the purpose for which money was borrowed. Thus, any Christian who lent money during the Middle Ages would have committed a mortal sin. In the view of the medieval church, however, Jews were headed for hell anyway, so their participation in money lending could add little to the eternal punishment that already awaited them in the hereafter.

Traditionally, dirty work in America has been performed for low wages by poor people, newcomers, and minorities who have had few other choices. In the Southern colonies, slaves were forced to play the role of field hands or domestic servants, and indentured servants performed heavy labor to buy their freedom. During the 19th century, Chinese newcomers toiled to build the railroads and work the crops. At the turn of the 20th century, European immigrants performed unskilled, backbreaking labor for poor wages and under miserable working conditions.

Even today, many economic activities involving dirty work in areas such as restaurants, hospitals, and industrial agriculture continue to rely heavily on people from outside the mainstream—Americans of color and newcomers from Latin America, Asia, and Eastern Europe. According to sociologist Herbert Gans, these activities could not survive in their present form without depending on the substandard wages that they pay to their employees. More generally, Gans suggests that poverty may actually persist in part because it serves the important function of providing a low-wage labor pool that is willing to perform dirty work at low cost.

Of course, many respectable jobs also involve at least some tasks that most people would consider boring and unpleasant, even if they don't require getting their hands dirty. Take, for example, the role of police officer, which, according to the television image, consists exclusively of battling the forces of evil. Actually, the police spend much of their time and energy on more mundane matters, such as removing dead mice, controlling traffic, doing paperwork, helping citizens who have fallen out of bed, and answering false alarms. Many police officers actually go through an entire career without ever having to fire their weapons in the line of duty.

To complicate matters, the very meaning of what comes to be regarded as dirty work is partially determined by the prestige level of an occupation. Indeed, the same tasks may be considered dirty when performed for low wages but respectable and clean when performed for a lot of money.

Homemakers who are unpaid for providing services to the members of their family may occasionally feel bored with routine child rearing and the daily drudgery of preparing the evening meal, yet such tasks are not intrinsically boring. In fact, they are quite pleasant and satisfying when carried out by a well-paid teacher or by a chef in a gourmet restaurant. One can only wonder what might happen to the desirability ratings of cooking and child rearing if homemakers were paid a decent daily wage.

Many people are physically sickened by the image of doctors as they perform surgery on their patients or, worse yet, conduct an autopsy. More than a few neophyte medical students have been known to go rubbery at the sight of a cadaver being anatomized. Yet Americans would hardly identify the role of doctor with dirty work. Instead, physicians continue to enjoy extremely high status with the American public, invariably being ranked ahead of most other occupations with respect to prestige.

Apparently, even the most repulsive job is not necessarily thought of as dirty work. Is it a doctor's life-and-death struggle that makes the difference? In part, perhaps. But high income, prestige, and power can usually be counted on to turn the dirtiest work into good, clean fun!

# FOCUS

## ✧ Suggestions for Further Reading ✧

In "Who's Minding the Kids?" I suggest that the peer group has filled a void left by the absence of other strong institutions. To see the long-term trend in the rise of the peer group in relation to changes in the family, I recommend *The Lonely Crowd* (2001), by David Riesman, Nathan Glazer, Reuel Denney, and Todd Gitlin. Even after the passage of decades, this classic work continues to teach us about American social character.

Riesman sees the major source of socialization having changed with larger shifts in social character from tradition-directed to inner-directed to other-directed types. Until the mid–20th century, parents continued to be the primary agents of socialization for youngsters. Children internalized a set of normative criteria during their early years that remained with them for life to guide their behavior. More recently, however, parents were replaced by the peer group as the major source of values and norms.

Many youngsters became motivated not to please their parents but to gain the approval of their friends, associates, or contemporaries. They acted not so much out of an internal sense of what was right and wrong 25 out of a desire to do what the peer group believed to be right and wrong.

The effect of other-directedness can be extreme. From 1997 to 2000, there was a string of mass murders in high schools and middle schools across the country perpetrated by teenagers against their schoolmates and teachers. The most infamous of such incidents occurred in April 1999 at Columbine High School in Littleton, Colorado, where two students opened fire with their semiautomatic rifles, killing 12 of their schoolmates and a teacher. In several of these incidents, the killers had informed their friends and classmates of their intentions. One anonymous phone call to a teacher or the police might have prevented a massacre.

"Let the System Do It!" focuses attention on the rise of specialized institutions, which, for the sake of efficiency, may have reduced the psychological burden of death and illness in our daily lives. German sociologist Max Weber long ago discussed this trend in modern society when he wrote about "rationalization"—the process whereby our lives have become increasingly dominated by institutions dedicated to efficiency and to the domination of human beings by technology. Weber recognized that we pay a price for this efficiency: the dehumanization of everyday life. For a discussion of Weber's treatment of rationalization, see Stephen Kalberg's

"Max Weber's Types of Rationality: Cornerstones for the Analysis of Rationalization Processes in History," in the *American Journal of Sociology* (1980). Two excellent books by George Ritzer analyze modern life using Weber's concept of rationalization: *The McDonaldization of Society* (2007), about the fast-food industry, and *Expressing America* (1995), about our use of credit cards.

In "Americans Are Moving to the Margins of Society," I contend that the credibility of all conventional institutions has recently slipped. To see for yourself, in comparative terms, just how far institutional confidence has fallen over the decades, page through the latest version (it comes out annually) of the Bureau of Justice Statistics' *Sourcebook of Criminal Justice Statistics*. Look in the index for the section on "attitudes." Concerning "Dirty Work," I drew much of my discussion from an earlier project with Bill Levin, *The Functions of Discrimination and Prejudice* (1982), and a more recent project, *The Violence of Hate: Confronting Racism, Anti-Semitism, and Other Forms of Bigotry* (2007). Teresa Gowen (1998) examined the important role of homeless trash recyclers in San Francisco's trash collection and sorting system. Sociologist Everett Hughes investigated a particularly hideous form of dirty work in an article in *Social Problems* titled "Good People and Dirty Work" (1962). In this article, Hughes attempted to come to grips with the factors that led otherwise ordinary Germans to work in concentration camps during the Nazi regime. Dirty work as part of the division of labor in a society, what Émile Durkheim calls "organic solidarity," can be seen in Durkheim's classic book *The Division of Labor in Society*, which he wrote in 1933.

## DEVELOPING IDEAS

### ✧ About Institutions ✧

1.  Writing topic: Imagine that all institutions suddenly ceased to exist and that you personally had no choice but to take care of satisfying your own needs (and the needs of family members) on a daily basis. Write a short essay in which you describe a typical day in your life.

2.  Writing topic: As indicated earlier, *The Sourcebook of Criminal Justice Statistics*, published yearly by the Department of Justice, is a goldmine of data concerning Americans' attitudes toward conventional institutions. Using the information in the *Sourcebook* as a basis, construct a number of

tables showing how Americans have changed their opinion of the criminal justice system—police, courts, prisons, judges, and so on—since the 1970s.

3. Research topic: What is a family, and what is not? To study the range of family conceptions held by college students, construct a short questionnaire and give it to a small sample of students on your campus. One approach would be for you to give your respondents a list of possible family arrangements that you develop beforehand and then ask them to evaluate as a legitimate family form. For example, you might include (a) mother, father, and children; (b) mother and children; (c) father and children; (d) mother, boyfriend, and children; (e) father, girlfriend, and children; (f) gay couple and children; (g) mother, stepfather, and children; (h) woman living alone; (i) college roommates; (j) grandparents and grandchildren; and so on.

4. Writing topic: In a short essay, discuss changes in the structure and functions of the family over the past 30 years. If you have completed the research topic above, how do you think your respondents would have answered the same question about family 30 years ago?

5. Research topic: Traditionally, garbage collecting has been viewed as dirty work, not only because it was physically unclean but also because it was a low-paying job. Collecting garbage is still physically dirty, but is it still low paying? To see how the dirtiness of garbage collecting may have changed over the years, compare the average income of garbage collectors in your town or state, or nationally, now versus 10, 20, and 30 years ago.

Also determine whether the collectors are unionized and how often they have threatened to strike. If it is possible and makes sense, compare the racial or ethnic composition of garbage collectors over time. Why might you expect change in race or ethnic group? As a final possibility, examine in detail the circumstances of any strike that might have occurred among garbage collectors in your town. How long did it last? Just how much were garbage pickups missed during the strike? Did the strike disrupt business or school? How was the strike resolved?

# PART V

## Deviance

The last time I visited a state prison, it was to interview a notorious serial killer. As you might expect, our conversation began in a rather tentative manner. I tried to figure out what he was thinking; he tried to figure out what I was up to. I sized him up; he sized me up. Our first 30 minutes together consisted of an exchange of polite trivialities. We talked about most everything—everything, that is, except what I had come to discuss in the first place: the heinous crimes for which he had been convicted.

If you've ever visited a prison, you probably know how uncomfortable it can be to talk with inmates, at least initially. There is usually a great deal of anxiety, and it gets in the way of honest communication.

Part of the problem involves what sociologist Erving Goffman referred to as the management of spoiled identity. An imprisoned serial murderer has been stigmatized; he is totally discredited among those who live beyond the prison walls. He knows that I know, and I know that he knows that I know. There is no way for him to conceal the fact that he has been found guilty of murdering 12 young women, even if he continues to proclaim his innocence (which serial killers almost always do). The prison walls tell it all. So the best we can expect to do is to minimize the discomfort generated by his deviance—and that takes both time and effort.

Deviance refers to any behavior of an individual that violates the norms and values of a group or society generally. Many acts of deviance are rather harmless: for example, parking in a loading zone or breaking a curfew. Other acts of deviance are incredibly dangerous and violent.

When someone commits a severely deviant act, he or she may be stigmatized. In other words, the violation of society's rules is regarded as so extreme that an entire human being, and not just a particular behavior, gets discredited. Clearly, serial killers fit this category. But as suggested in "Fat Chance in a Slim World," so do individuals who are overweight by conventional standards—and they haven't broken any laws at all! Fat is too often regarded as a symptom of not just illness but a lack of moral fiber or willpower. To some extent, people who are too short, tall, or thin also bear the burden.

Mentally ill patients represent another group of stigmatized people. Some very depressed individuals would rather conceal their pain and suffering than risk being rejected by the important people in their lives. As suggested in "You Must Get Ill First; Then You Recover," those mental patients who are hospitalized also risk labeling. According to Erving Goffman, they may be thoroughly resocialized so that they can be easily managed and controlled. Goffman contends that new patients learn quickly what is required of them to get along while institutionalized and later to be released. Rosenhan's experiment in the same essay clearly indicates what happens when mental patients refuse to cooperate—they continue to be regarded as sick.

French sociologist Émile Durkheim once observed that deviant behavior actually helps unite the members of a society by focusing attention on the validity of its moral order. In the face of a deviant act—for example, a heinous crime—the members of a group feel challenged, even threatened. They no longer take for granted the important values that they share. Instead, they rally their forces to encourage and support the legitimacy of behaving correctly. Durkheim also suggested that punishing the individual who commits a deviant act similarly reconfirms behavior that conforms to a group's cultural standards. Punishment sends a message to every member of society: "Listen, buddy. Break the rules and the same thing will happen to you!" Numerous Americans, concerned about our soaring crime rate, would gladly base their support of capital punishment on Durkheim's view of deviance: Sending a killer to the electric chair also sends a message to potential killers everywhere. Thus, capital punishment is often justified by the fact that it might serve as a deterrent to violent crime. As indicated in "Is the Death Penalty Only a Vehicle for Revenge?" however, there is very little evidence to suggest that capital punishment actually deters future murders (although it definitely deters the condemned killer from killing again). Even if most Americans favor capital punishment, most criminologists seem to agree that the swift and certain imposition of a life sentence without parole is an effective alternative to the death penalty.

First-degree murderers should never be eligible for parole or furlough, and their sentences should never be commuted by a future governor who believes in their rehabilitation. As criminologist James A. Fox and I have argued, "We need a 'life sentence without hope.'" Let me pause, at this point, to once again raise the question of "value-free" sociology. In "Is the Death Penalty Only a Vehicle for Revenge?" I take a definite stand—based on evidence collected by criminologists but nevertheless a definite stand—on a controversial issue. You should be aware that some sociologists would cringe at the very thought of this. In their view, the advocacy role is antithetical to the goals of the "science of sociology." Not everyone would agree, however. Sociologist Howard Becker once argued just the opposite: that sociologists must take sides in favor of important values and pressing concerns. For him, the advocacy role is not only consistent with but essential to the work of sociology.

I am especially sure that the death penalty would have little impact on mass murderers. Those who kill several victims at a time would hardly be deterred by either a life sentence or an execution. Indeed, their killing spree is often an act of suicide anyway; but before taking their own life, they have decided to get even with all of those individuals they blame for having caused their problems—all women, all foreigners, all postal workers, and so on. Even if suicide is their intention, it is less often the outcome. About one third of all mass killers end up taking their own lives. Many more commit "suicide by cop," whereby they refuse to drop their weapon so as to force law enforcement to do what they could not—to gun them down. Still others decide to let the state do what they could not—they live long enough to be tried and convicted of first-degree murder and receive the death penalty.

Historically, the death penalty has been discriminatory in its application. For crimes of equivalent severity, black defendants were more likely than their white counterparts to be executed by the state. In 1972, the Supreme Court declared the death penalty unconstitutional because it was being applied in an uneven, capricious manner. In 1976, it was reinstated but only if applied under strict guidelines. Even today, there is evidence that the administration of the death penalty is uneven. Offenders who kill white victims are executed more often than offenders who kill black victims. Since 1976, on a national level, 223 black defendants have been executed for murdering white victims, but only 15 white defendants have been executed for the death of a black victim.

One of the more challenging yet important tasks of sociology is to be able to predict deviant behavior: for example, who will turn out to be a hardened criminal and who won't. Although we are still far from being able to make such predictions, a recent study, which I coauthored with Arnold Arluke, suggests that animal abuse may be a warning sign for violence committed against humans. In fact, our study indicates that cruelty toward animals may be linked with all forms of antisocial behavior, both violent and nonviolent. Of course, this clearly does not mean that every child who intentionally harms a dog or a cat will grow up to be a hardened criminal. Indeed, most will not. This leaves us in the uncomfortable position of understanding an important factor *symptomatic of* many forms of deviant behavior but of being unable to predict future behavior. The problem is one of false positives—many abusers grow up and out of their deviant behavior.

Of course, some youngsters don't wait to grow up before they exhibit criminal behavior. This was made painfully clear as investigators around the country—and especially in Southern states—attempted to solve the hundreds of cases of arson being targeted at America's churches during the 1990s. It very quickly became obvious that black churches were being disproportionately victimized, though many white churches had been burned as well.

As indicated in "America's Youngsters Are Responsible for Church Burnings," the overrepresentation of black churches gave some legitimacy to the opinion that many of the burnings were racially inspired. As it turned out, however, most of the burnings of black churches could not be pinned on any conspiracy on the part of organized hate groups. Sadly, most of the assailants represented America's future—its children.

Children are, however, more likely to be the victims than the perpetrators of criminal behavior. Across the country, states have imposed a series of measures to protect their youngsters from dangerous sexual predators who have served their sentences and have been released back into the community. As a result, sex offenders are required to register with the local police, may find their photos and addresses on Internet Web sites, may be restricted from coming within a specified distance of schools and playgrounds, and may be forced by irate neighbors to leave their jobs and homes. Many registered (and unregistered) sex offenders have, as a result, been ejected from shelters and now live on the streets, where supervision is totally lacking.

# Fat Chance in a Slim World

## We Believe It's the Size
## of a Book's Cover That Counts

A black woman in Philadelphia recently wrote me, complaining about the way she was treated by other people. Among other things, she rarely dated, had few friends, and was forced to settle for a job for which she was overqualified. Moreover, passengers on buses and trains often stared at her with pity or scorn, while workers at the office rarely included her in their water-cooler conversations.

The letter writer attributed these difficulties not to her gender or race but to the fact that she was vastly overweight by conventional standards. Her letter brought to mind the unfortunate victims of such illnesses as cancer, heart disease, and Alzheimer's disease who have the unavoidable symptoms of an illness over which they have little, if any, control. But they are typically treated with compassion and sympathy.

Curiously enough, fat people frequently receive contempt rather than compassion, unless their obesity can be attributed to some physical ailment (e.g., a glandular condition). Otherwise, they are seen as having caused their own problem by some combination of excessive impulsivity and lack of moral fiber. Not unlike prostitutes, ex-cons, and homeless people, they may be regarded as lacking in the self-control and willpower necessary to lead a healthy, normal life. In addition, this discrimination has been directed more often at women than at men over the years.

The term *fat person* is therefore more than a description of somebody's weight, body type, or illness; more often than not, it is also used to stigmatize or discredit an entire group of human beings by making their belt size an excuse for bigotry. The lady from Philadelphia may have been correct: Research suggests that people who are overweight by our standards are often viewed as undesirable dates and mates. They frequently have trouble getting married, going to college, obtaining credit from a bank, or being promoted. In short, they are excluded, exploited, and oppressed.

Stigmatizing fat people is, of course, only one expression of a much more general tendency in our culture: the tendency to judge others by their looks rather than their intelligence, talent, or character. Study after study suggests that what is beautiful is good. That is, attractive individuals are more likely to be preferred as dates, to be popular with their friends, to be cuddled and kissed as newborns, to achieve high grades in school, to be disciplined less severely by their parents, to be recommended for a job after a personal interview, and to have their written work judged favorably.

By conventional American wisdom, fat is as ugly and deviant as thin is beautiful. We are so infatuated with being slim and trim that it is indeed hard to imagine anything else. Yet the desirability of particular body types and body weight varies from culture to culture. Beginning with the ancient world, fat has not always been universally despised. Instead, fat people were often respected, if not admired, throughout history. Even Cleopatra was fat by our standards, although by the standards of her own time and culture she was a raving beauty. Renoir's French Impressionist masterpieces similarly portrayed a version of the female body that today would be considered massive, huge, and fat rather than beautiful. And in cultures where food was in short supply, obesity was often used to validate personal success. Under such circumstances, rich people could afford to eat enough to be fat and therefore to survive. Skinny was therefore a sign of neither good health nor beauty but a symptom of poverty and illness.

Until the Roaring Twenties, the large and voluptuous version of feminine beauty continued to dominate in our culture. But the flappers changed all this by bobbing their hair, binding their breasts, and, by some accounts, trying to resemble adolescent boys. While many women of the 1920s moved toward feminine power, others retreated from it by shrinking their bodies in fad diets. The result was that during this era, the suffragette movement succeeded and women got the vote, but many men felt threatened. All of a sudden, they preferred women who were small, petite, and thin, who looked powerless.

Given the importance of physical attractiveness in defining the value and achievement of females, it should come as no surprise that American women have come under extreme pressure to be unrealistically slim and trim. This may have made many women dissatisfied with their bodies and mistakenly convinced them that mastery was possible only by controlling their weight.

Women constitute 90% of those afflicted with the eating disorder anorexia nervosa and are the majority of those who join organizations such as Weight Watchers and Diet Workshop. Women are also more likely than men to suffer from compulsive overeating and obesity.

Since the women's movement of the 1960s, we seem to have become even more preoccupied with being slim and trim. *Playboy* centerfolds and contestants in the Miss America pageant have become increasingly thin.

Leading women's magazines publish more and more articles about diets and dieting. Physicians offer drastic medical cures, such as stomach stapling for obesity and liposuction surgery for problem areas like saddlebag thighs, protuberant abdomens, buttocks, love handles, fatty knees, and redundant chins. And the best-seller list inevitably contains a disproportionate number of books promising miraculous methods of weight reduction.

In the face of all this, signs of an incipient cultural rebellion against crash dieting and irrational thinness have emerged. A couple of decades earlier, popular books such as Millman's (1980) *Such a Pretty Face,* Orbach's (1978) *Fat Is a Feminist Issue,* and Chernin's (1981) *The Obsession: Reflections on the Tyranny of Slenderness* began taking their place in bookstores alongside the diet manuals. But rather than urge obedience to the conventional standards of beauty, these newer books exposed the dangers to physical and mental health due to rapid and repeated weight loss. Rather than focus on individual change, they placed the blame for our excessive concern with being skinny on sexism and the socialization of women to absurd cultural standards. In 2004, the newly established tradition was continued with the publication of Kathleen Lebesco's *Revolting Bodies?: The Struggle to Redefine Fat Identity.*

The merchants of fashion have also sensed a cultural change in the offing. Growing numbers of dress shops now specialize in designer fashions for size 14 and over and flattering designs in better plus-size fashions. Moreover, based on a good deal of evidence from around the world, physicians have revised their weight standards so that what was formerly considered 10 or 15 pounds overweight is now regarded as optimal. For the first time in decades, some popular female entertainers—Jennifer Lopez—are being revered for their derrieres.

As a final element in this dynamic, organizations such as the National Association to Advance Fat Acceptance (NAAFA) have helped fat people—even those considered obese—to gain a more favorable self-image. Rather than automatically advising its members to diet, NAAFA calls attention to the fact that fat people are often the victims of prejudice and discrimination. It recognizes the dangers in rapid and repeated weight loss and focuses instead on improving the way that fat people are treated on the job, as customers, and in social situations.

Taking its cue from black organizations, which reject words originating in the white community, such as *Negro* and *colored,* NAAFA prefers to use the term *fat* rather than *overweight* or *obese.* In this way, it refuses to conceal the issue in euphemisms, refuses to accept the stigma, and emphasizes that fat can be beautiful.

Unfortunately, however, our culture continues to give fat people a double message. On the one hand, we advise them to be themselves and to accept their body image regardless of social pressures to conform to some arbitrary standard of beauty. On the other hand, we urge them to go on a diet so that they will no longer be deviant. While the rhetoric may be confusing, it is also revealing. All things considered, our aversion is deeply embedded in our culture and is likely to remain with us for some time to come.

# You Must Get Ill First; Then You Recover

## Checking Out of a Mental Hospital May Be Harder Than Checking In

S ociologist Erving Goffman's study of the way patients were treated in a mental hospital yielded some frightening conclusions. He found that the hospital staff assumed absolute power to define how patients should think and behave. The institution gained total control over the terms by which its patients defined themselves. Inmates were thoroughly resocialized so that they could be easily managed and controlled.

According to Goffman, new patients learned quickly what was required of them to get along while institutionalized and later to be released. They were asked to discard their old self-concepts—those they had used on the outside—and to adopt a new set of self-definitions taught by the staff. First and foremost, inmates were to abandon the normal concept that they were sane or healthy and instead see themselves as sick and therefore in need of help. Admitting that they were psychologically ill was regarded as a patient's first step along the road to recovery. Conversely, any claim that an inmate was well was regarded as a symptom of severe mental disease.

As patients spent more and more time in the hospital, larger areas of their self-concept were turned upside down. Boredom was regarded as a sign of depression, anger as acting out, independence as rebelliousness and irrationality, and a desire for privacy as withdrawal. It took no time at all for inmates to recognize that being resocialized by the institution to accept the role of a mentally ill person was the only way to be rewarded while confined and then later regarded as cured. This meant not being a management problem for the staff—submitting to the hospital routines, which included cooperation in taking medications and going to therapy sessions. Otherwise, a patient might remain in the institution indefinitely.

Ideally, of course, whether a patient is defined by the hospital staff as healthy or sick and viewed as ready for release should be based strictly on his or her symptoms. In reality, however, the social setting of a mental hospital also comes into play in defining the situation. This brings up an interesting question that sounds very much like the plot from an old movie: If perfectly normal and healthy people were secretly admitted to a mental hospital, would they be able to convince the staff that they were well, that they didn't belong, and that they should be released? Or would they be defined by the rules of hospital life as rebellious, irrational, depressed, and therefore in need of continuing hospitalization? A classic study by D. L. Rosenhan looked at exactly this question. He had eight sane individuals—five men and three women representing a range of ages and occupations—secretly admitted to one of a number of mental hospitals across the country. Each of Rosenhan's pseudopatients was totally free of any symptoms of mental illness; all of them gained admission by complaining that they had been hearing voices. No hospital staff members were informed about the study.

Based only on this one symptom, hearing voices, all but one of the pseudopatients were diagnosed as suffering from schizophrenia. Moreover, once inside the hospital, the pseudopatients stopped expressing any symptoms of illness. They spoke and behaved normally for the entire duration of their stay.

When the pseudopatients expressed their desire to be discharged, they were told that release depended on the ability of a patient to convince the staff that he or she was sane. Yet despite their normal behavior, the average length of hospitalization for the group was 19 days. One of them failed to be released for 52 days. Finally, all of the pseudopatients were discharged— but with a diagnosis of schizophrenia in remission. In other words, not one was able to convince a hospital staff of his or her sanity, only that the symptoms of his or her illness had subsided.

In case you were wondering whether anyone, staff or not, would have been fooled by Rosenhan's band of pseudopatients, we have an answer for you. Believe it or not, some 25% of the other patients on the admissions wards accused the pseudopatients of faking insanity—the real patients guessed that the imposters were actually professors or reporters who were in the hospital to conduct a study!

# Is the Death Penalty Only a Vehicle for Revenge?

## An Ardent Abolitionist States His Case

Whenever I articulate my opposition to the death penalty, I feel like a voice in the wilderness. More than 65% of all Americans favor the death penalty, and the remaining 35% would probably be willing to make an exception if it meant eliminating the Jeffrey Dahmers and the John Wayne Gacys of the world. In fact, the United States has the dubious distinction of being the only remaining Western nation not to have abolished the death penalty for civil homicide.

Some proponents of capital punishment assert that legislators should enact death penalty laws because it is the will of the people. Well, it is true that the majority of Americans support capital punishment—*but only* if they are not given an alternative that they like better. When they are offered an option to capital punishment such as life without parole, their support for the death penalty drops to 50%—even lower when you throw in compensating the victim's family.

Unfortunately, many of our citizens really aren't informed enough about criminal justice policy to make a rational decision about crime and punishment. In one survey, pollsters found that only a fraction of the residents of Massachusetts—about 3%—even knew that the Commonwealth's penalty for first-degree murder was life without parole. One third of all Massachusetts citizens said they believed such offenders would be out of prison in fewer than 10 years; another 11% said they had no idea at all what happened to first-degree murderers in the state.

But the reason underlying much of the support of executions, according to a survey conducted for *ABC News* and the *Washington Post,* is usually revenge or retribution. Americans believe that the most serious crimes deserve the most severe punishment. As the Old Testament points out, "Thou shalt give life for life, eye for eye, tooth for tooth."

And, I admit, it's not hard to understand why revenge seems sweet. People are fed up with violent crime, believing that it is out of control and of epidemic proportions. They want to do something about it. Whether or not I agree with the extremity of the public reaction, I can understand why Gacy's execution by the state of Illinois was seen by many as a cause for celebration. The world lost one of its most despicable killers. Whether or not I believe it to be a proper sentence, I can see why Danny Rolling's execution by the state of Florida in 2006 brought a smile to the faces of concerned residents of the Sunshine State. After all, for nothing short of sadistic purposes, Rolling had butchered five beautiful young college students in the community of Gainesville.

The arguments for the death penalty, however, typically fall outside the realm of empirical inquiry. Instead, they are often emotionally charged, arguing that convicted killers deserve to die or that demonstrated by empirical inquiry. These three important issues involve cost, deterrence, and protection. Getting even is valuable as a measure of psychological compensation for victims and society. As an abolitionist, however, I rest my entire case on the weight of economic and social issues that can be tested for their accuracy.

Many people ask why we should spend hard-earned taxpayer money to imprison a murderer when we could just as easily execute him at much lower cost. But the fixed costs of running a maximum-security prison are little affected by the presence of a few additional inmates serving life sentences for first-degree murder. The warden still has to be paid, and the heat still has to be run. Moreover, because of the complex and lengthy trials, the large number of expert witnesses and forensic tests, and the appeals process required by the Supreme Court in capital cases, it actually costs less to imprison a killer than to execute one. In Florida, for example, the average cost of a case that results in execution is $3.2 million, whereas the estimated cost of imprisonment for 40 years is slightly more than $500,000. And to those who argue, "If it costs so much to carry out the appeals process, then take him out back and string him up," consider the number of errors that have been made under less stringent requirements: Since 1900, some 139 people have been sent to death who were later proven innocent. At least 23 of them were exonerated only after the executions had been carried out.

Proponents of the death penalty also claim that it deters violent criminals. They believe we need to execute murderers to send messages to potential killers that, if they can't control their murderous behavior, the same thing will happen to them.

Yet most of the evidence suggests that the death penalty has little if any effect on killings. In a study of 14 nations in which the death penalty was eliminated, criminologists Dane Archer and Rosemary Gartner report, for example, that abolition was followed more often than not by a reduction in national homicide rates. For example, homicide dropped 59% in Finland, 30% in Italy, 63% in Sweden, and 46% in Switzerland. In only 5 of these 14 countries did homicide increase at all. Even more ironically, research conducted by criminologist William Bowers suggests that the murder rate actually rises for a short period of time after the killer has been executed, producing what he calls a "brutalization effect." That is, would-be murderers apparently identify more with the state executioner than they do with the inmate.

The third argument, of course, is that capital punishment protects society by guaranteeing that killers like Charles Manson will never be paroled. And certainly, capital punishment would make sure that particular murderers never kill again. But before I support the death penalty, I would want to know whether an alternative exists for protecting society—for making sure that a killer isn't granted another opportunity—without taking human life. If the alternative in response to a brutal, hideous murder is life imprisonment with parole eligibility, I am indeed in favor of the death penalty. If, however, the alternative is a life sentence without the possibility of ever being paroled, capital punishment becomes unnecessary for the protection of society, and I am therefore against it.

In fact, I cringe whenever I hear that Charles Manson is being considered for parole, because I know what people will say: The criminal justice system is soft on murderers. We should be executing those who commit heinous crimes. Actually, Charles Manson did receive the death penalty.

But back in 1972, the Supreme Court struck down capital punishment because it was being applied in an uneven, capricious manner. At that point, any murderer on death row was instead given the next most severe sentence under state law. In California, that sentence was a life sentence with parole eligibility. As a result, Charles Manson was then eligible for parole after serving only 7 years.

A series of rulings by the Supreme Court in 1976 paved the way for states to restore the death penalty but only when applied under strict guidelines. In some states (e.g., California), those convicted of murder continue to become eligible for parole after serving only several years in prison, but if the court adds the "special circumstances" provision, the only possible sentences are either death or life imprisonment without parole eligibility.

Most states now have special-circumstances statutes for heinous crimes, such as multiple murder or murder with rape. Yet the "strict guidelines" under which the Supreme Court gave its blessings to capital punishment apparently have not worked. Racial discrimination continues to exist. The killers of white victims are much more likely than the killers of black victims to receive the death penalty. Moreover, innocent people continue to be condemned to die, often on the basis of faulty eyewitness evidence. This recognition recently led the former governor of Illinois—a staunch advocate of capital punishment—to declare a moratorium on the death penalty until such time that the state is comfortable that it is not executing innocent people. In some states (e.g., Massachusetts), all first-degree murderers are ineligible for parole, so no special statute is required. Under such conditions, the death penalty is unnecessary as a means for protecting society from vicious killers, because we can instead lock them up and throw away the key.

Actually, many proponents of the death penalty raise the issues of cost, deterrence, and protection of society only to rationalize what essentially is a thirst for revenge. This can be seen most clearly in the public response to heinous crimes.

In December 1987, Ronald Gene Simmons brutally murdered 16 people in Russellville, Arkansas, in the largest family massacre in American history. When the residents of Russellville learned that Simmons had suffocated the young children in his family and that he had had an incestuous relationship with his married daughter, cries for the death penalty were heard loud and clear throughout Arkansas. In 1989, Simmons was convicted of multiple murders and sentenced to die by means of lethal injection. Similarly, on December 26, 2000, Michael McDermott, a 43-year-old employee of Edgewater Technology in Wakefield, Massachusetts, shot to death seven of his coworkers. Public outrage quickly took the form of demands for Massachusetts legislators to enact a death penalty statute.

Florida certainly did get a measure of self-satisfaction in October 2006 by executing serial killer Danny Rolling; the same can be said for the state of Illinois when it executed John Wayne Gacy, the notorious serial killer, in 1994. For many Americans, the opportunity to get even with a serial killer is reason enough to apply the death penalty. But for those few who instead believe that capital punishment can be justified only to the extent that it protects society's members or serves as an effective deterrent, execution by the state is cruel and unnecessary punishment. In a civilized society, our best defense against wild animals is to lock them in cages so they can't get to the rest of us.

# Animal Cruelty and Human Violence

## Is There a Connection?

*Arnold Arluke and Jack Levin*

In the suburbs of Jackson, Mississippi, 16-year-old Luke Woodham allegedly killed two girls and injured seven other students before being subdued by a Pearl High School administrator. Earlier that day, Mr. Woodham's mother was found stabbed to death, and he was charged with the murder.

These killings have sparked nationwide attention in part because of bizarre plans by Mr. Woodham, "a self-proclaimed Satanist," and his fellow "cult" members to lay siege on the school, ignite explosives, cut telephone lines, and kill various people. A far more common event could have warned authorities that Mr. Woodham was ready to explode, but nobody paid attention to it.

More than 6 months earlier, the defendant and one of his friends repeatedly beat Woodham's dog, wrapped it in bags, set it on fire, and threw it into a pond. Mr. Woodham ostensibly wrote, "I made my first kill. . . . The victim was a loved one, my dear dog Sparkle. . . . I will never forget the howl she made. It sounded almost human." Research strongly suggests that understanding the causes and consequences of violence toward animals may be important in the effort to fight crime against humans. A link has long been suspected between cruelty to animals and human violence. In the 1960s, for example, psychiatrist John Macdonald first suggested that those individuals who later become homicidal begin in childhood by torturing small animals. Subsequent research on prisoners and abusive domestic partners supported Macdonald's position.

Indeed, a 3-year study we recently conducted with the Massachusetts Society for the Prevention of Cruelty to Animals examined the relationship between violence against animals and crime in the general population. We discovered that people who abused animals were five times more likely than those who did not to commit violent crimes against people—to assault, rape, or rob them.

Surprisingly, animal abuse was found to be linked with many types of nonviolent crimes as well. Abusers were four times more likely than nonabusers to commit property crimes and three times more likely to be arrested for drug-related offenses and disorderly conduct.

What can be done to reduce animal abuse and to recognize its value as a warning sign of future violence? We urge professionals—district attorneys, judges, police officers, doctors, social workers, teachers, and ministers—to take appropriate measures. Every year thousands of animals around the country are reported as victims of malicious cruelty. A resident of Manatee County, Florida, recently admitted beating to death a neighbor's 11-year-old Rottweiler with a 2-foot club. And, in Iowa, three teenagers were brought to trial and convicted for bludgeoning to death 16 cats in an animal shelter.

If these crimes were committed against children, the abusers would likely face stiff penalties in court, but this would not be so in one of the animal offenses. Even in the most extreme cases, a majority of the animal abusers are not found guilty in court. Most don't even get to trial. When they do, they typically get a slap on the wrist. In some states, only one in ten of those convicted receive jail sentences. And fines are minimal when imposed, averaging $132.

Most important, incidents of animal cruelty are typically viewed as isolated crimes, having no relationship to other human behavior, such as violence against people. The attitude among criminal justice personnel too frequently seems to be: "Suppose we make a concerted effort to wipe out animal cruelty—so what? When the money is spent, we will still be left fighting rape, murder, assault, burglary, and drug abuse."

There is strong public support to take effective measures. Eighty-one percent of all American adults approve strengthening the enforcement of cruelty laws. About 83% favor teachers, social workers, animal welfare officers, and law enforcement officials sharing information on juveniles who abuse animals as an early warning sign of criminal behavior. And 75% support the establishment of a system for tracking adult animal cruelty offenders as a tool for identifying other kinds of likely violent offenses.

Of course, not every child who tortures animals grows up to become a killer. In fact, many of them later grow up to be decent law-abiding citizens. Yet animal abuse is clearly a warning sign that deserves to be taken seriously in order to intervene before it is too late. A 6-year-old boy who enjoys causing the family pet to suffer deserves our attention. His abusive behavior is a clear-cut plea for help. Later on, he might progress from harming dogs and cats to harming people. The lesson is clear enough: By taking animal cruelty more seriously, we might help ourselves.

# America's Youngsters Are Responsible for Church Burnings

## It's Neither the Klan Nor the White Aryan Resistance

It is tempting to regard the wave of church burnings across the country during the 1990s as some kind of conspiracy involving white supremacist extremists. Yet the evidence suggests something much worse. Most of these racially inspired arsons seem to be the work of America's young people.

Collectively, scapegoating frequently takes the form of "protest by proxy," in which innocent victims substitute for the real source of economic hardship. As growing income inequality continues to take its toll, those Americans for whom the American Dream seems out of reach derive little satisfaction from blaming vague abstractions like global competition, corporate downsizing, or automation. Scapegoating minorities puts a human face on what otherwise would be a nebulous and unintelligible enemy.

Black Americans have always made especially effective scapegoats. Not only were they powerless to strike back effectively, but they had adequate visibility as well. Until 1930, the frequency with which blacks in the South were lynched increased as the value of Southern cotton declined. Black Americans were routinely blamed for downward economic fluctuations that might rationally have been attributed more to changes in the weather than to human intervention.

Criminologist Jack McDevitt and I have studied hundreds of serious crimes directed against individuals because they are different with respect to race, religion, national origin, or sexual orientation. If the recent strings of church burnings is at all typical of hate attacks generally, very few of them are being committed by members of organized hate groups. Instead, almost two thirds of the arsons will probably turn out to be thrill crimes committed by young people who go out looking to stir up a little excitement at someone else's expense. These youngsters aren't getting along at home, are doing poorly in school, or have dead-end jobs.

Typically they hate themselves as much as they hate their victims and are looking for someone to blame for their personal problems.

Though few arrests have been made, it thus far appears that young people have been disproportionately involved in the church burnings. In one case, a 13-year-old girl was arrested and charged for an act of arson that destroyed the Matthews Murkland Presbyterian Church in Charlotte, North Carolina. Three men in their early 20s were prime suspects in the burning of the Lighthouse Prayer Church in Greenville, Texas. Later on, two boys, ages 9 and 10, were charged with destroying Life Christian Assembly Church in North Charleston, South Carolina. A 17-year-old was charged in the burning of Pleasant Hill Baptist Church in Robeson County, North Carolina.

The good news about thrill hate attacks is that their perpetrators are generally not hardened hatemongers but only naive young adults and teenagers who hardly understand Nazi ideology or Klan slogans. Most of them don't know the Ku Klux Klan from the White Aryan Resistance. With a creative response including education and community service, we might reach many of these youthful offenders in time to turn their lives around and make them into productive citizens.

The bad news is that the string of church burnings reflects a more general trend toward escalating levels of bigotry and intolerance among America's youths. Too many of them feel important only to the extent that they are able to inflict pain and suffering on people who are different in terms of race, religion, or sexual orientation. So they burn, bash, and desecrate in order to feel superior.

In response to hurtful acts of intolerance, our mainstream leaders should send an unequivocal message that they will simply not tolerate intolerance. Strong hate crime laws for repeat offenders is, in this regard, an indispensable tool. Creative alternative sentencing for youthful first offenders—education, community service, and victim restitution—is also essential.

But the most effective approach by far would be to offer our bigoted youngsters some hope for the future. We must reach them with healthy alternatives to prejudice and violence, giving them some reason to feel good about themselves without terrorizing their neighbors.

# Keeping Children Safe
# From Sex Crimes

## The Community Approach
## Sounds Effective but May
## Do More Harm Than Good

Joseph Edward Duncan III, who allegedly bludgeoned to death three people in northern Idaho and kidnapped two children, killing one of them, represents a tremendous challenge to our criminal justice system. What are we to do with a dangerous Level 3 sex offender who has served his sentence but is likely to repeat his offense?

Duncan had served a 15-year sentence in a Washington state prison for raping a 14-year-old boy and was out on bail for molesting a 6-year-old boy. For every repeat offender who turns his life around, there are several others who commit even more hideous crimes. The typical child sex offender attacks more than 100 children. That is why legislators around the country have recently devoted so much time writing tougher laws to track, restrict, or sentence dangerous rapists and child molesters. While well motivated, almost all such legislation is bound to fail.

Sex offender registries have been ineffective. They make citizens feel safer but do little else. Many dangerous offenders never register. Others register but reoffend. Joseph Duncan was a registered sex offender.

Not even a strong national offender registry would discourage recidivism. Notifying the neighbors that an ex-con is in their community only ensures that he will be pulled out of mainstream society and pushed back into crime.

As soon as the word gets around, he undoubtedly will lose his job, be evicted from his apartment, and be shunned by his friends and neighbors. Then he will move to somebody else's city or town.

Some states have sought to put distance between sex offenders and children. At least 14 states have passed laws that provide buffer zones between convicted sex offenders and places where children congregate. The problem with such laws is that children are almost everywhere, not only in schools and at bus stops but also at daycare centers, zoos, swimming pools, churches, shopping malls, and playgrounds. It is almost impossible for offenders to live in a community and not be in proximity to children.

Last month, Florida and Oklahoma passed laws requiring electronic monitors using global positioning system technology for tracking sexual predators in the community. Legislatures in Pennsylvania, New Jersey, and New York are considering the same. Bills now being considered by Congress would require all repeat sex offenders to wear an electronic ankle bracelet for life.

In theory, electronic bracelets would help law enforcement to keep an eye on high-risk offenders who come close to places where children congregate. This approach would, in all likelihood, help prosecute sex offenders who violate the terms of their parole but would hardly prevent them from committing new offenses. Even Martha Stewart claims to have been able to dismantle her electronic monitoring bracelet. To this point, electronic monitoring has worked successfully for dissuading such low-level offenders as burglars, embezzlers, and drug offenders, not obsessed sex offenders from repeating their crimes. It would be an unmanageable task for authorities to monitor the hundreds of thousands of offenders who would wear electronic bracelets.

Recognizing that electronic monitoring, buffer zones, and registries don't work, states are seeking methods for keeping dangerous sex offenders incarcerated after they are scheduled for release. In January 2002, the Supreme Court ruled that dangerous inmates could be held indefinitely but only if they are proven to lack the capacity for controlling sexually harmful behavior; that is, they must suffer from a mental disorder.

The problem with this approach is twofold: First, many sexual predators have character disorders, not serious mental illnesses. They choose to do the wrong thing because they enjoy it and so are ineligible for indefinite incarceration. Second, psychiatrists and psychologists working for the state must decide who deserves continued incarceration, but they are generally less than effective at predicting dangerous behavior.

There is really only one way for the criminal justice system to protect our children from sexual predators: Give dangerous repeat offenders the life sentences they deserve. A first-time perpetrator probably merits a second chance. He serves a finite sentence behind bars and then resumes his life in the community. Everybody hopes he has learned his lesson. But a repeat offender has proven that he cannot be trusted with our children.

The rule for habitual rapists and child molesters should be: Commit two strikes and you're never out again.

# FOCUS

## ✧ Suggestions for Further Reading ✧

In the introduction to this section, I discussed the work of French sociologist Émile Durkheim. The frequency with which he appears in this small book should suggest just how much the work of Durkheim has influenced the direction of sociology. Durkheim's views of crime are found in *The Rules of Sociological Method* (1966).

Concerning "Is the Death Penalty Only a Vehicle for Revenge?" my argument relies on numerous studies by criminologists, most of whom find little or no support for the death penalty. For a major study of capital punishment, read William J. Bowers's book *Executions in America* (1974). A much more recent argument against the death penalty can be found in Jeffrey Fagan's 2005 testimony to a New York State Assembly Committee.

Dane Archer and Rosemary Gartner, in their important book titled *Violence and Crime in Cross-National Perspective* (1984), provide cross-national evidence. They found a reduction in homicide for most of the countries in which the death penalty was abolished. For a summary of the religious arguments, read Gardner Hanks's *Against the Death Penalty* (1997). And just in case you are interested in examining the views of a criminologist who sees both sides of the issue, take a look at L. Kay Gillespie's (2003) *Inside the Death Chamber: Exploring Executions.*

My snapshot about the death penalty takes a controversial position. I first raised the issue of value-free sociology in the introduction to this book; it should come as no surprise to see it again—especially in discussing how to deal with crime. In 1918, Max Weber gave a lecture at Munich University concerning the importance of value-free sociology.

You can find his speech reprinted in *Max Weber: Essays in Sociology,* edited by H. H. Gerth and C. Wright Mills (1946). For a different point of view regarding the place of values in sociological analysis, read "Whose Side Are We On?" by Howard S. Becker in *Social Problems* (1967). Becker argues that sociological research is always biased, never value free; in fact, every sociologist has a responsibility to take sides in support of important values and concerns.

For a perspective on and an interesting examination of the sociology of animals, read Arnold Arluke and Clinton R. Sanders's award-winning book *Regarding Animals* (1996). The sadism in many crimes against animals may be the link to similar acts of violence committed against humans. See Arnold

Arluke, Jack Levin, Carter Luke, and Frank Ascione's "The Relationship of Animal Abuse to Violence and Other Forms of Antisocial Behavior" in the *Journal of Interpersonal Violence* (1999).

Two books also seem especially relevant to the topic. First, Jack Katz examines the subjective experiences of doing crime in his fascinating book *Seductions of Crime: Moral and Sensual Attractions of Doing Evil* (1988). He looks beyond the practical and senseless motivational veneer of criminal behavior and focuses instead on its moral and sensual rewards. For a controversial and important explanation for criminal behavior, read Michael Gottfredson and Travis Hirschi's *A General Theory of Crime* (1990). Gottfredson and Hirschi present evidence for the position that an essential element in criminality is an absence of self-control, usually learned early in life. This is a factor that may very well be present in crimes against both animals and humans. For a discussion of animal abuse as a symptom of violence-proneness in serial killers and mass murderers, read Jack Levin and James A. Fox, *Mass Murder: America's Growing Menace* (1991).

In "America's Youngsters Are Responsible for Church Burnings," the blame for a rash of church burnings that occurred during the 1990s—especially arsons against black churches—is placed squarely on our youths. From the beginning, it appeared that many, perhaps most, were committed by teenagers who got a thrill out of causing trouble for the members of another racial group. Only in a few cases were organized hate groups involved. This finding is true of hate crimes in general, most of which are committed by teenagers who go out in a group to vandalize, bash, or assault people who are different. For a typology of hate crimes from which my analysis of church burnings was derived, see Jack Levin and Jack McDevitt, *Hate Crimes Revisited: America's War on Those Who Are Different* (2002).

Throughout this section, we have emphasized criminal behavior as a form of deviance. In closing this section, let me point out, once again, that crime is only one form of deviance and that deviance is actually a much broader concept. Many sociologists who specialize in deviance aren't primarily interested in crime at all and instead study various forms of deviant behavior, such as mental illness or physical disability.

In "Fat Chance in a Slim World," we are also told that, throughout history, people who would be considered overweight by Americans in the 1990s were instead respected, admired, and regarded as attractive. Rather than the epitome of feminine beauty, even Cleopatra of ancient Egypt was fat by our standards! In contrast, Americans who are overweight by conventional standards are stigmatized. Specifically, they are treated as lacking in moral fiber and character. As more food for thought about this topic, pick up Kim Chernin's interesting book *The Obsession: Reflections on the Tyranny of Slenderness* (1981). She suggests that women's acceptance of society's increasing demand for females to be thin reflects cultural pressure for women to dislike their bodies. For Chernin, rigid dieting and boyish fashions are forms of rejection of feminine power and equality. My snapshot depends a good deal on Chernin and on Marcia Millman's excellent sociological treatise about being fat in America, *Such a Pretty Face* (1980). I benefited greatly from Kathleen Lebesco's 2004 *Revolting Bodies?: The Struggle to Redefine Fat Identity*.

For the classic sociological treatment of the presentation of spoiled self, see Erving Goffman's *Stigma: Notes on the Management of Spoiled Identity* (1963). While reading Goffman, think about the influence that being fat or skinny or very short or very tall can have on a child's self-image.

Goffman has also written extensively about mental hospitals. His book titled *Asylums* (1958) is a classic in the field. David Rosenhan's excellent study of normal people gaining entrance into a mental hospital and then asking to be discharged is reported in his 1973 article "On Being Sane in Insane Places," which appeared in *Science*. For an excellent discussion of the social conditions implicated in mental illnesses, such as depression and anxiety, read *Social Causes of Psychological Distress* (1989) written by John Mirowsky and Catherine Ross.

Megan's Law, which gave legal sanction to sex offender registries, was based not on research conducted by criminologists but on the emotional activism of well-meaning grieving parents who wanted to implement a policy for ensuring that other children would not be victimized by sexual predators. In "Keeping Children Safe From Sex Crimes," I argue that Megan's law and other tactics in the community approach to sexual predators simply do not work and may even reduce the safety of our children.

## DEVELOPING IDEAS

### ✧ About Deviance ✧

1. Writing topic: Max Weber urged sociologists to attempt to be objective, even when their personal views were being contradicted. Gun control is a controversial issue—there are many proponents on both sides. In writing, state your own personal opinion—either for or against the restriction of firearms as a national policy. Then, in a short essay, defend the point of view that opposes your own.

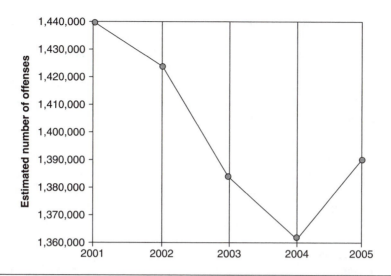

Violent Crime Offense Figure Five-Year Trend, 2001–2005

2. Research topic: Every year, the U.S. Department of Justice publishes the Uniform Crime Reports for the United States. In *Crime in the United States*, you will find a number of different statistics concerning the serious crimes reported to the FBI by local police departments. This book is easily available in libraries, from the U.S. Government Printing Office, or online at www.FBI.gov. As taken from the FBI data, the 5-year trend in violent crime is shown in the figure above.

Using *Crime in the United States* for a recent year, find monthly variations in murder and verify that murder rates peak during July, August, and December. Now do the same for property crimes such as larceny, theft, and burglary. Do these offenses also peak during the relatively cold month of December? Why or why not? Explain how the social climate may have more influence than the weather on monthly variations in homicide. Do you think that the social climate has the same effect on property crimes?

3. Research topic: Based on public opinion surveys, we know that most Americans favor the death penalty. But we also know that support for capital punishment decreases if people see an alternative that protects society just as well. For example, in a survey of Massachusetts citizens, William J. Bowers found that 54% prefer life without parole over the death penalty. Now, it's your turn. In a paper-and-pencil questionnaire, ask 20 students to indicate whether they support or oppose capital punishment. Now also ask the supporters of the death penalty to indicate whether they would support or oppose it under the following conditions: (a) if life imprisonment were the only

alternative sentence available; (b) if life imprisonment without parole eligibility were the only alternative sentence available; (c) if life without hope—that is, life imprisonment without parole eligibility, pardon, or commutation of sentence— were the only alternative available; or (d) if life imprisonment without parole eligibility plus victim restitution were the only alternative sentence available.

What do your results indicate about protection of society as a motivation for supporting the death penalty?

4.  Research topic: With your instructor's assistance, commit an act of deviance to see how others respond to you. Select an act that is neither illegal nor unethical. Also, make sure that your deviant behavior will not affect the way you are treated by others on a permanent basis! Because it isn't always so easy to think of a safe act of deviance, let me suggest one.

Simply mark your forehead with a meaningless symbol—for example, two blue and red circles. Then, walk on campus and observe the reactions (or lack of reactions). Do strangers and friends respond differently to you? Finally, try the same experiment, but this time walk on campus with two other students whose foreheads have been painted like yours. Do you notice a difference in the way you are treated? What do you think people assume when they encounter three students wearing the same unknown symbol?

5.  Research topic: Interview an individual who seems to be stigmatized because of his or her appearance (someone considered fat, short, tall, unattractive, and so on). In your interview, try to determine at what age your respondent first remembers being different. Have your respondent indicate the specific ways in which he or she has been discriminated against—at work, on dates, at school. Also try to discover how he or she manages the stigma (denial or avoidance?). Note: Please be careful not to approach a stigmatized person in a hurtful or an insensitive way. You might want to place an ad in your college newspaper asking for volunteers who have been labeled as too short, too tall, or too fat. Or you might invite volunteers from among your classmates. It may even be possible to locate an organization to which stigmatized people belong—for example, Little People of America or the NAAFA. In any case, it is obviously important to use extreme sensitivity in locating a potential respondent.

6.  Writing topic: Name a group in American society, other than fat people, whose members have been stigmatized. How do you think they would be treated in some other culture? Why?

7.  Research topic: Walk around for one day as a fat person to see how other people treat you. With the help of a friend, put on more than a few pounds— literally put on weight by wearing large clothing and padding yourself in a realistic way. Then, take written notes as to any differences you detect in the reactions of others.

# PART VI

## Social Inequality

"Can you spare some change for a cup of coffee, mister?" I never know what to do when I am confronted by a panhandler asking for a hand-out, especially if he looks like he's been drinking. If I give him what he wants, I might only be supplying him with his next drink of booze and his next hangover. But if I don't give him anything, I feel guilty. Who knows? Maybe he hasn't eaten in 3 days, and my small contribution will keep him going until the next handout comes along.

Homeless people in the streets of our major cities represent an extreme example of social inequality—the unequal distribution of wealth, power, and prestige among the members of society. At the other end of that distribution, there are entertainers and professional athletes who earn millions of dollars a year, enjoy tremendous popularity, and have a great deal of pull. But most of us fall between the panhandler and the famous ballplayer.

Clearly, we are not a classless society. In fact, social inequality in America is highly structured and passed from one generation to another. This characteristic of social inequality is known as social stratification. In fact, social inequality is definitely stratified. Sociologists have been able to identify a number of different social classes whose members share similar occupational positions, opportunities, attitudes, and lifestyles—an upper class containing the wealthiest and most powerful people in America, an upper-middle class consisting of the families of business executives and professionals who have high income, a lower-middle class consisting of average-income Americans, a working class containing primarily blue-collar workers, and a lower class consisting of the disreputable poor.

*Life chances* is Max Weber's term referring to an individual's probability of securing the good things of life. Sociologists are well aware that an individual's life chances definitely vary by social class. Regardless of their intelligence and steadfastness, people who are born into a low social class will likely benefit less from society's opportunities than people born into a higher social class. Members of lower classes are less likely to vote, obtain favors from politicians, go to college, receive adequate public services, be in good physical and mental health, have decent working conditions, or feel they have control over their everyday lives. They are more likely to give birth out of wedlock, grow up in single-parent families, be arrested and imprisoned after committing a crime, and die at an early age.

Many observers have suggested that the gap between rich and poor has widened over the period of the last decade or so. Clearly, there are now more homeless people on the streets of our major cities and more middle-class families whose members have skidded in terms of social class. In "The Economic Escalator," we find that intergenerational mobility seems to be moving in a downward direction. Consequently, millions of young people have begun to question the validity of the American Dream. Young adults have been particularly hard hit. As a result, they are staying in school longer, delaying their marriage plans, and moving back in with their parents.

Social inequality varies by gender, race, and age. African-Americans continue to be disproportionately represented in poverty. Affirmative action legislation may have helped create a large and viable black middle class, but it has hardly touched the lives of the members of the black underclass who continue to live in permanent poverty. In our postindustrial society, we lack the jobs that could propel young black males out of the underclass. And where such jobs do exist, they tend to be low-paying jobs that lead nowhere.

As suggested in "Gender Inequality Across Cultures," American women continue to earn less than their male counterparts. Moreover, when both husband and wife hold full-time jobs, it is usually the working woman who is expected to do the household chores and child rearing as well. She continues to be the main source of advice and guidance for her children and the one who is held responsible for cleaning and cooking.

Perhaps this fact of life helps explain the American female's disadvantage on the job: Because of the extra burden placed on her shoulders, the working woman is often unable to make the same commitment to her career that her husband can.

In the early 1980s, we were in the grip of a recession, and older Americans suffered more than their share of economic hardship. Some were eating dog food to survive. Perhaps fewer elders are now in critical economic condition, but their image continues to give them problems. In "The Stigma of Aging," I suggest that the old stereotype that all older people are poor, sickly, and incompetent has been joined by a new stereotype that they are also powerful and wealthy—perhaps too powerful and wealthy for their own good. The new view may turn out to be particularly dangerous, inspiring conflict between the generations for increasingly scarce economic resources. Indeed, there already exist political pressure organizations designed to minimize the influence of older people in the area of Social Security and health care. Americans for Generational Equity represents the interests of young people, and the Boomer Initiative represents the interests of middle-aged Americans.

In "An Apple Pie and an Open Mind," another segment of the population of the United States that suffered during the 1980s is highlighted. They were residents of rural areas—farmers, ranchers, miners, and people in the timber industry who were hard hit by recession and never quite came out of it. It is no coincidence that civilian militia groups have received a good deal of support from people in the rural areas of the country. Not only do many of them feel frustrated, but they also feel ignored by the rest of society.

The United States is in the midst of a possibly unprecedented period of immigration—and not everyone is delighted. In "Give Us Still Your Masses," Gordana Rabrenovic and I examine several of the misconceptions that have too often been used politically to frame the issue of limiting the flow of undocumented newcomers into the country. Our essay does not take a political position on illegal immigration, but it seeks to provide some accuracy in the collective perception of Americans regarding the immigration debate. In "Profiling Terrorists," law professor Deborah Ramirez and I suggest that immigrants who have a "Middle Eastern look" have been unnecessarily singled out by anxious Americans. Using the framework laid out by sociologist Lewis Coser (1956) in his modern classic *The Functions of Social Conflict*, it is also possible to suggest that immigrant bashing helps protect the leaders of a society from the unmitigated hostility of its citizens.

# The Economic Escalator

## Americans on Their Way Down

The term *downward mobility* is used to characterize the economic plight of an entire generation of middle-class Americans who are slipping and sliding their way down the socioeconomic ladder. Forget about the short-term effects of the recessions of 1991 or 2001; don't even think about all those people who lost their paper-profits in the stock market when the Internet bubble burst or who lost their homes when the real estate bubble exploded. According to political analyst Kevin Phillips, the culprit is an economic trend that began in the 1970s or 1980s and will likely continue indefinitely.

The rich really have been getting much richer—and apparently doing so at the expense of poor and middle-income Americans who have seen their status evaporate. Through at least the most recent three decades, the biggest losers have been blacks, Latinos, young men, female heads of households, farmers, and steelworkers, but almost everyone else has also suffered to some extent.

In a shift away from manufacturing toward services, we have been transformed into a postindustrial society. In 1959, production of goods represented some 60% of all American employment, but by 1985, this figure had dropped to only 26%. The trend toward service employment continued during the 1990s; some 90% of the job growth during this period was in private service industries.

As a result, the overwhelming majority of Americans are now employed in the service sector of the economy. During this transitional period, many new jobs were created, but in the main, these were poorly paid and provided few opportunities for upward mobility. Large numbers of Americans were forced to take a substantial drop in pay and, therefore, in their way of life.

Consistent with this view, Phillips suggests that the widening gap between rich and poor may have been encouraged by national economic policies of the 1980s, a period that represented a strong reversal of almost four decades of downward income redistribution. During the post–World War II era, a middle class began to emerge. Throughout the 1950s and 1960s, median income levels doubled, causing richer and poorer Americans to be drawn closer and closer together.

Then, beginning in the early 1970s, this trend came abruptly to an end and reversed direction. At the upper end of our class system, the after-tax proportion of income for the wealthiest 1% of Americans climbed from 7% in 1977 to 11% in 1990. Even when adjusted for inflation, the number of millionaires doubled between the late 1970s and the late 1980s, resulting in a record 1 million households reporting a net worth of at least $1 million. This trend continued through the 1990s, as a "new crowd" of Americans got richer for their investment in the communications media, biotechnology, and the securities markets. Between 1995 and 1997, for example, the average after-tax income of the 1% of tax filers with the highest incomes jumped by another 31%. The number of millionaires continued to climb until 2002, when the impact of a worsening economy finally put a dent in the resources of even the wealthiest Americans. Yet even as late as 2002, America's 400 top taxpayers represented 1.09% of U.S. income, a figure that is more than double the percentage in 1992, when they accounted for only 0.52% (Herman, 2003).

For families on lower rungs of the socioeconomic ladder, however, living standards have deteriorated. Since 1977, the average after-tax family income of the bottom 10% of Americans declined by 10.5% in current dollars. Recent government statistics reported by the U.S. Census Bureau indicate that this trend is likely to continue: During 1996, families in the bottom fifth of the income distribution nationally saw their incomes drop an additional 2%. But families in the top 20% gained another 2%. The imbalance in assets is even more striking than the imbalance in incomes. While the assets owned by the bottom 80% of the population of the United States has continued to decline, the top 1% has accumulated more than a third of the nation's wealth, and the highest 5% own almost 60% of it. These are the levels of inequality in wealth that existed prior to World War II (*News Batch*, 2007).

According to a study by Professor Timothy Smeeding of Syracuse University, the percentage of U.S. children living in poverty rose from less than 15% in 1978 to 20% today. Compared with seven other industrial countries (Sweden, West Germany, Australia, Canada, Britain, France, and the Netherlands), the United States has the dubious distinction of being the most unequal. That is, we have more poverty and fewer people who are middle class. By the year 2000, the United States was the world's richest nation, but—among Western industrial countries—we also had the largest gap between the rich and the poor.

Growing income inequality has already been linked with a worsening of our most stubborn and perplexing social ailments. Professor Henry Miller of the University of California notes that homelessness is a growing problem in our major cities—a problem that is not susceptible to easy solutions. He suggests that we were previously able as a society to assimilate many of the homeless into the military or industry. In today's economy, however, those who lack education or marketable skills remain permanently unemployed or take dead-end jobs. What is more, in the process of converting inexpensive rooming houses into high-priced condominiums for the affluent, the gentrification of urban areas beginning in the 1980s forced even more of the poverty-stricken onto the streets.

The continuing trends away from manufacturing and toward inequality between rich and poor are, of course, far from inevitable. But a reversal would necessitate a major commitment on the part of political leaders, business, and the public who recognize the urgency of finding a solution.

The urban underclass is now at least four times larger than it was during the turbulent 1960s, when our major cities were burning. It is conceivable that there will be riots of earthquake proportions within a few years in at least four major cities: New York, Chicago, Los Angeles, and Miami. At that point, there will undoubtedly be widespread support for making essential changes in our economy. The real question is one of timing: Will we be too late?

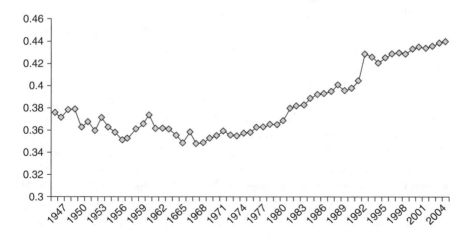

**Figure 6.1**    Income Inequality by Year, 1947–2004

# An Apple Pie and an Open Mind

## My Visit to a Patriot Potluck

J ust prior to the opening days of Timothy McVeigh's trial for his role in the deadly 1995 Oklahoma City bombing, militia groups were back in the news. McVeigh apparently had been associated with a civilian militia in Kingman, Arizona. His "bible" was the infamous *Turner Diaries,* a fictionalized account of a coming civil war, in which revolutionaries bring down the federal government by bombing federal buildings and disrupting public utilities.

I attended a "Patriot Potluck" attended by militia members, survivalists, and assorted right-wing political discontents. We met on a Saturday in an obscure dinner theater just north of Boston. I brought an apple pie and an open mind.

For the entire morning and much of the afternoon, I joined with members of the Patriot Movement as they swapped ideas, listened attentively to a parade of speakers, and lunched on pasta salad, sandwiches, and my apple pie. Along the sides of the room, vendors hawked their anti–New World Order T-shirts and conspiratorial literature. In unison, we sang patriotic songs and recited the Pledge of Allegiance.

I confess to feeling just a little nervous to be among people who are totally convinced that our federal government has been taken over by communists. I am not now, nor have I ever been, a member of any militia group, the John Birch Society, or the Pat Buchanan fan club. I decided to attend this gathering of political extremists in order to learn more about the militia movement, its members, and its causes. It never occurred to me, however, that I would learn even more about what is wrong with mainstream American institutions.

Civilian militias have long been linked, at least in the public mind, with violence and bigotry—with tragedies and near-tragedies at Ruby Ridge; Jordan, Montana; the Atlanta Olympics; and Oklahoma City. According to the stereotyped image, *all* militia members are nothing more than a collection of gun-loving, bomb-throwing hatemongers and terrorists.

That is why I was so surprised when the 75 men, women, and children who attended this meeting seemed so hospitable and friendly, even innocuous. From a distance, they could easily have been mistaken for a group of bridge players or a convention of social workers. Admittedly, I did hear a racist comment from a speaker and an anti-Jewish remark from one member of the audience. But, then, I also met a few dedicated members of the movement who were themselves black or Jewish.

I was also impressed by the utter boredom of their speeches. Through a 5-hour procession of speakers, I heard much less about guns and bombs than about economic survival. Speaker after speaker talked about money—about how to defeat the IRS through Common Law courts, how to withdraw from the Social Security system, the impact of free trade on the unemployment rate, and how to avoid going into debt. I got the strong impression that these were Americans—many from rural backgrounds—who had suffered through hard economic times and were looking for some way to explain their shared predicament. Their response was to blame the federal government, communists, the United Nations (UN), and international bankers.

Any group of Americans who believe that the enemy has surreptitiously taken over the White House, Congress, and the Supreme Court is potentially dangerous. These so-called patriots are no exception. But to treat the entire militia movement as consisting merely of a collection of crazies who deserve to be carted off to an asylum is just as dangerous.

Many of the issues addressed at the Patriot Potluck I attended were every bit as much the concerns of conventional, middle-of-the-road Americans who struggle daily to survive in the face of global competition and growing income inequality. They may not join a militia or stockpile weapons in anticipation of a revolution—they might not even attend a potluck meeting to voice their anxieties—but they are nevertheless convinced that the government is no longer working on behalf of ordinary citizens.

There is a natural tendency for government to respond to extremism with repressive measures, which give even more power to law enforcement agencies in their effort to investigate and infiltrate marginal groups. In the short run, such measures might prevent a violent episode or two.

In the longer run, however, they reduce the individual freedoms of all Americans and only push potentially dangerous groups underground. In the end, members of fringe organizations, already convinced that the government is out to get them, will be even more paranoid and delusional. As a result, they may actually become the menace they are perceived to be.

Of course, Americans of good will should be vigilant in response to a growing threat of terrorism perpetrated by our own citizens. But if we are careful to look past the stereotyped images of the Patriot Movement that frequently pass for reality, we might learn something about our country that needs to be repaired and is within our power to change: the need to work together as a nation in order to create a sense of trust and social responsibility that transcends the differences that divide us. If we are successful in this regard, the Patriot Movement will probably wither and die of its own irrelevancy. But if we are not, today's extremism could easily become tomorrow's version of moderation.

# Profiling Terrorists

## Lessons From the War on Drugs

### *Deborah Ramirez and Jack Levin*

Prior to the attack on the United States, racial profiling was considered a blatant civil rights violation. The practice of singling out racial or ethnic groups during traffic stops or at border checks was condemned by courts, civil rights groups, and the American public. In the aftermath of the September 11 attack, however, thousands of Arabs and Muslims complain that they are being unfairly scrutinized and harassed. A practice that was once considered intolerable is now accepted as a necessary tactic in the war on terrorism.

Profiling Arabs and Muslims represents a critical test for our multiracial, multicultural democracy. Must we sacrifice individual rights in order to avoid another terrorist hijacking? Will we adhere to the principle that people are to be judged by their acts, not by the group into which they were born? Or will we allow our fears to balkanize America? From our experiences with racial profiling in the war against drugs, we have learned a number of important lessons that can be applied now in fighting terrorism.

**First, using race or ethnicity as a proxy for involvement in crime is both too broad and too narrow to be effective.** Targeting people who appear to be Arabic is too broad because most of the millions of Arabs in the United States are loyal citizens, not dangerous terrorists. The profile is too narrow because there is no such thing as a "Middle Eastern" look.

Arabs come in all colors and sizes. Egyptians can be light-skinned and blue-eyed. Many Southern Sudanese people are of African descent. Indeed, numerous Americans who trace their heritage back to Mexico, Spain, Greece, India, and Italy share a "Middle Eastern" look.

**Second, criminals frequently modify their profile.** During the war on drugs, any drug courier profile the police created quickly became ineffective because drug distributors responded with an "anti-profile." If, for example, the police targeted blacks in out-of-state rental cars, the traffickers would begin to use female couriers in vans. Because federal agents have targeted "people of Arab appearance," it is highly unlikely that another terrorist attack will consist of Arabs who highjack planes and fly them into buildings.

**Third, by focusing on a particular group, we may overlook the criminal behavior of individuals whose appearance may not arouse our suspicion.** If we target blacks and Latinos in drug stops, we may miss the many white drug dealers. In the aftermath of the September 11 attack, we should fear that our narrow focus on "Arabs" will blind us to the presence of terrorists like Timothy McVeigh, the Unabomber, Eric Rudolph, or the white passenger in Tennessee who, weeks after September 11, slit the throat of a Greyhound bus driver.

**Fourth, profiling is widely employed by ordinary citizens in a destructive manner.** Perhaps taking their cue from law enforcement, white cab drivers don't always stop to pick up black men. Blacks and Latinos are frequently followed through stores by security guards who see them as potential shoplifters.

In a similar way, angry Americans have recently attacked dozens of individuals across the country, based only on the fact that their victim spoke with a foreign accent and had dark skin. In the weeks following September 11, 2001, the FBI investigated more than 40 anti-Arab and anti-Islamic hate crimes across the country. In addition, there were more than 300 reports of harassment and abuse filed with the Council on American-Islamic Relations. For several months following the attack on the United States, hate crimes directed against Muslim-Americans increased by some 1600%.

**Finally, when criminals share racial and ethnic traits with large urban populations, it is better to work with the community than against it.** When the police formed partnerships and collaborated with black and Latino residents in the war on drugs, they received information, intelligence, and support that enabled them to more effectively target and prosecute the criminals within those communities. Instead of casting the net wide and working as an occupying force against these residents, law enforcement could solve and prevent more criminal activity by working with them.

Perhaps instead of alienating the entire Arab-American population, we should cooperate with Arab-Americans to identify those members of their community who may be engaging in terrorist activities. Given their cultural and linguistic differences, Arab-Americans may be our best guides to what constitutes suspicious activity within the Arab population.

So, instead of trying to ferret out Arab-looking folks, perhaps we should focus on race-neutral responses that might improve our ability to detect terrorism from any source and by any person. Perhaps every passenger in an airport should be searched by wands. Or maybe we should select passengers to interrogate on a random basis. Perhaps all of us should consider carrying a national identification card.

Rather than settling for the false sense of security that racial profiling may provide, we should insist that the FBI and the CIA obtain better intelligence about potential terrorists and planned criminal activity in the United States and that all of us participate in the process of creating better security systems in our airports, bus terminals, public buildings, and urban skyscrapers. Only when we address these fundamental security problems will we truly be prepared to protect the homeland against terrorist attacks.

# Gender Inequality Across Cultures

## Both Men and Women Pay a Price

I recently had the occasion to speak with a sociology professor from Bucharest, Romania, who was visiting the United States for the first time. Her early impression of American life? She was shocked by what she called "feminism" or gender equality.

Knowing that women in the United States continue to suffer from discrimination, I was surprised to hear an outsider refer to the treatment of American women in such glowing terms. She was obviously unaware that according to the U.S. Department of Labor, the median weekly earnings of American women continue to be only 76% of the male median.

She was also unaware that only 14 of our U.S. senators are women; that the female inmates at state women's prisons around the nation continue to be subjected to psychological, physical, and sexual abuse; and that almost three out of every four of the victims of intimate partner homicide are women.

Everything is relative, of course, and it might put things in perspective to make some international comparisons. Since the September 11 attack on the United States, we have become vastly more aware of women's human rights issues around the world. Our military action against the Taliban regime in Afghanistan focused our attention on the plight of Afghan women. We learned they had been systematically prohibited from working in most occupations, forced to wear a garment covering them from head to toe, and banned from formal education beyond primary school. Less publicized was gender inequality in Saudi Arabia, where women are systematically denied access to jobs, forced to comply with restrictive dress codes enforced by the threat of public beatings, and segregated in public life; or the treatment of

Kuwaiti women, who are denied the right to vote, required to wear a veil in public, and segregated in public areas.

The list of discriminatory practices by country goes on and on. In Nigeria, Kenya, and Zambia, women are denied equal inheritance and property rights. In Thailand, women who marry non-nationals are not permitted the right to buy and own property in their own names. In Venezuela, women are prevented from marrying until 10 months after a divorce or an annulment. In Chile, husbands are legally granted control over household decisions and their wives' property.

Discriminatory practices often prevent women from escaping lives of abject poverty. In South Africa, female farm workers are far more likely than men to be seasonal or temporary workers who perform menial and low-paying jobs. In Ukraine, women work longer hours and are paid less than men. Kenyan women do most of the work when the land is first cleared for subsistence farming. Yet women in Kenya rarely own the property and are therefore denied access to the loans and extension services available to male landowners.

In Eastern European nations such as Bulgaria, Ukraine, Russia, Lithuania, and Armenia, pervasive hardships in the aftermath of the breakdown of national economic and political systems have resulted in a growing problem of trafficking in migrant women. Many of these women have turned to prostitution out of desperation, having lost their jobs at home and lacking the basic means of survival. A number had hoped to escape the poverty of their homelands, thinking that they would find legitimate work as maids, dancers, or waitresses in their host countries.

Instead, as soon as they arrive in the new land—in such countries as Poland, Bosnia, and Herzegovina—their immigration documents are stolen. Then, they are threatened and harassed and are kept as prisoners in a room where they are forced to have sex with clients.

Eastern Europe is not alone in failing to discourage trafficking. In Japan, women trafficked into the sex industry account for a large portion of the hundreds of thousands of undocumented migrants, many of whom have fled the deplorable economic conditions in Thailand for the sake of a better life. Israel has failed to provide human rights protections for trafficked women who serve as domestics, farm laborers, construction workers, and enslaved prostitutes. In Colombia, women being trafficked to European countries as forced laborers and prostitutes is an everyday occurrence, yet this is largely ignored by government authorities.

Violence against women is also pervasive. In Turkey and Jordan, under the assumption that the female victim had dishonored a male family member by committing immoral behavior, hundreds of girls and women have been murdered. In Zimbabwe, many women on farms and in rural areas are raped with impunity. In Uzbekistan, local officials have limited the number of divorces, coercing women into remaining with their abusive partners. In Ukraine, one in every three women suffers domestic violence.

In the former Yugoslavia, the Democratic Republic of the Congo, Indonesia, Guinea, and Tanzania, women—especially young women—have suffered large-scale episodes of rape and other forms of sexual and physical violence during periods of armed conflict and civil agitation.

Though recognized internationally as war crimes and offenses against humanity, such acts of abuse experienced by women have seldom been treated seriously by government officials. Perpetrators are rarely brought to justice.

There is a particularly brutal form of revenge against "an uppity woman" in which a husband, boyfriend, or suitor throws sulfuric acid into her face, scarring her for life. Many victims of acid attacks are forced to quit school and work, and the recovery is long and expensive. Such attacks, motivated by a woman's rejection of a man's advances, have been reported in Bangladesh, Egypt, England, India, Italy, Jamaica, Malaysia, Nigeria, and Vietnam.

Mexican authorities have recently revealed that a total of 258 women have been brutally killed since 1993 in the city of Juarez, across the border from El Paso, Texas. Almost 100 of the victims had been sexually assaulted.

In other cases, the motive is suspected to have been organ trafficking— that is, they were killed for their body parts. In addition, some federal agents have examined the possibility that violent religious groups or pornography dealers were involved in the killings (Tuckman, 2003).

It is no secret that gender inequality is a financial and social burden to women. It diverts resources from women's activities, rewards men for their gender-biased behavior, eliminates women's economic advantages, and reduces women's effectiveness in meeting their responsibilities. The amount that women contribute economically to society is frequently obscured or underestimated because they often work in the informal system where accounting is minimally applied. Ending gender inequality would sharply increase women's wages and well-being, but would it also enhance the quality of life more generally? Actually, it turns out that men also pay a price for women's second-class status. Eliminating gender discrimination would, according to a recent study, increase national income in Latin American countries by 5%. A study in Kenya suggests that giving female farmers the economic support now given to men would increase crop yields by more than 20%.

Limited access to medical care among the poor hits especially hard at the lives of female members of the family. Globally, the risk of death for impoverished men is twice that of their middle-income counterparts, but women trapped in poverty are 4.3 times more likely to die.

And the death of a woman can have a devastating effect on her impoverished family. A study in India determined that a mother's early demise can also mean the death of her family in both a literal and a figurative sense. The impact shows up in a greater likelihood for children—both boys and girls—to die, to drop out of school, or to be sent off to live with their grandparents.

Thus, inequality between men and women carries an economic and social cost. By neglecting gender inequality in the distribution of resources and responsibilities, we perpetuate the vicious cycle of poverty and despair, not only for women but also for their children. Men also pay a price. In combination with economic deprivation, gender inequality produces more intense forms of poverty for everyone.

# Give Us Still Your Masses . . .

## But Please Don't Send the Criminals and Terrorists!

### Jack Levin and Gordana Rabrenovic

T he voices of xenophobia once again reverberate throughout America. Anxious advocates of nativism envision huddled masses of impoverished, uneducated, disease-ridden criminals who sneak across our porous borders to steal jobs and murder our citizens.

Even in the early 20th century, when most newcomers were European, some part of anti-immigrant sentiment reflected widespread fear of job loss. Whenever the jobless rate soared, so did the forces of nativism.

But since September 11, 2001, stereotyped images of immigrants have turned decidedly more negative. Myths and misconceptions about newcomers have assumed the status of cultural truisms, as more and more Americans grow anxious about their personal safety and seek policies for effectively controlling our borders.

*Myth 1:* Criminals and terrorists are overrepresented among immigrants. Actually, they are vastly underrepresented. The National Center for Policy Analysis estimates that if native-born Americans had the same low probability of being incarcerated as all immigrants, our prisons would have one-third fewer inmates. El Paso, Texas, and San Diego, California, have extremely low homicide rates; not coincidentally, they also have large populations of immigrants. On the East Coast, 74% of Lawrence, Massachusetts's 95,000 residents are foreign born. In 2005, the Immigrant City had zero murders.

*Myth 2:* Unlike previous generations of immigrants from Europe, today's newcomers do not want to assimilate. In reality, every immigrant group has maintained its ties with the old country. At the turn of the 20th century, for example, Italian immigrants formed organizations of mutual assistance. Similarly, many Jewish newcomers settled in urban centers, where they established ghettos based on their shared religious identity. For all immigrant groups, assimilation generally came in the second and third generations.

*Myth 3:* Illegal immigration is uniquely associated with our present population of newcomers. It is true that illegal immigration has increased not only in the United States but around the world as well. According to the Pew Hispanic Center, 12 million immigrants to the United States are considered illegal. However, 40% of them crossed the border legally and overstayed their visas.

But illegal immigration is nothing new to the United States, nor is it restricted to Latinos. When legal immigration from Europe became limited by quotas in 1924, illegal immigration soared. Many Europeans migrated first to Canada or Mexico and then illegally slipped over the border. By the 1930s, the U.S. Border Patrol was established to exclude and deport illegal newcomers from Europe, *not* Mexico.

*Myth 4:* Unlike previous generations from Europe, most immigrants from Latin America and Asia are poor and uneducated. Actually, most newcomers through the centuries were destitute. In the mid-1800s, many Irish fled famine. In the United States, Irish women took jobs as servants or domestics; Irish men toiled in mines or built railroads and waterways. At the turn of the 20th century, millions of newcomers from Italy found a new life in America. Almost 80% were unskilled workers.

During the 1920s, psychologists of the day argued that the United States should protect itself by severely limiting the flow of newcomers coming from Eastern and Southern European countries. These specialists asserted that the uneducated and unintelligent immigrants from such countries as Italy, Poland, and Spain, because their IQs were lower than their counterparts from Northern Europe, would soon pollute the stream of American intelligence. Instead, as the children and grandchildren of these newcomers took advantage of educational opportunities, their IQs only continued to increase. As a result, some of the groups whose IQs were lowest when their ancestors arrived in the United States now have among the highest IQ scores.

Not unlike their predecessors, many present-day immigrants are poor and uneducated. Through hard work and perseverance, they can take advantage of opportunities in their adopted country.

Immigrants also create jobs here. Without the influx of foreign investment and skilled labor during the 1990s, our nation would have experienced economic stagnation or decline rather than growth.

Almost everybody agrees that immigration reform is desirable. Policy changes granting amnesty, erecting a wall along our Southern border, establishing guest worker status, or deporting illegal immigrants are debated daily on talk radio, on cable TV, and in Congress. It is to be hoped that the outcome will reflect a rational analysis of our national needs rather than hysteria based on stereotyped thinking.

# The Stigma of Aging

## Almost, but Not Quite,
## Elderly Enough

Yesterday I had the surprise of my life. The teller at the commuter rail station window asked which ticket I wanted—senior citizen or adult. Just a few years away from qualifying for the senior discount, I quickly, and with some relief, countered, "I'm really not eligible yet. One adult round trip please." Before that moment, it had never occurred to me that you were either an adult or a senior citizen and that you couldn't be both. I never realized that you were forced to give up your adult status when you were eligible for the senior discount. Thanks, but no thanks.

Everybody makes a fuss over senior citizenship. The press seems to love using the word *elderly* even when it is entirely redundant. In news articles presumably written by very young reporters, people still in their 50s are frequently referred to as such. For example, in one recent report, a 56-year-old man was killed in his home. He was also described gratuitously as "elderly." I doubt that he would have agreed.

Aside from children and teenagers, older people are the only age group to receive this "special" recognition in newspapers and on television. If a 38-year-old woman has a deadly accident, she is never referred to on the evening news as middle-aged. When a 20-year-old man robs a liquor store, he is never labeled as a young adult. But when someone 66 or 78 is described, not only is his or her specific age given but so is his or her stage of life.

Growing old must be a pretty big deal.

I know what some are thinking: "What's so wrong with getting older anyhow?" Well, nothing. Aging is part of the natural order, a gradual process that begins with birth and ends with death. But being *elderly* is a construction entirely invented by human beings. We decide when this stage of life begins by lobbing off a section of the life cycle and indicating—zap!—"now you're old." In our society, old age starts when you retire, take your Social Security check and your pension, and ask for your 10% discount at the local drug store.

Older people have long been stereotyped as chronically ill, unable to work, behind the times, slow thinking, and a burden on society. They are often regarded as existing in a period of second childhood, in which their ability to reason and make sound judgments has regressed to the level of a 6-year-old.

The mass media lend credence to this unflattering image by continuing to misrepresent or underrepresent elders. When they do appear in dramatic series or in commercials, older people are disparagingly connected with "Clap on! Clap off!" and "Help! I've fallen and I can't get up." And research shows that those who accept the elderly label are more likely to act the part; they tend to disengage, give up their important roles in society, and wait to die (sometimes for 30 or 40 years). On the other hand, those who continue to lead active lives tend to ignore the elderly status and maintain their self-image as functioning adults for as long as possible.

Moreover, the millions of older people who dye their hair, use antiwrinkle cosmetics, and undergo plastic surgery for the sake of a more youthful appearance may be operating less out of vanity and more out of a desire to escape age discrimination.

I have recently noticed a change in students' beliefs about elders but not necessarily for the better. In line with the traditional stereotype, most of my students routinely overestimate the percentage of the elderly who live below the poverty line or in nursing homes. For example, the average estimate was that 37% of all Americans 65 years or older are now residing in a nursing home, whereas the actual figure is only 4%.

Surprisingly, these same students also overestimated the percentage of senators, judges, and former presidents who were at least 65 years of age and the proportion of billionaires, chief executive officers (CEOs) of major corporations, and corporate stockholders who are elderly. The same students who were unrealistic about poverty and dependence exaggerated the wealth and power of the elderly: Less than 5% of major American corporations are actually headed by a CEO who is 65 or older, but the average estimated by the students was 43%. In this latter stereotype, older people are often seen as powerful and rich—perhaps too powerful and rich for their own good.

Traditionally, older people were blamed for their own plight; their poverty and dependence were regarded as an inevitable part of the life cycle. In the new view, however, the aged are seen as having disproportionate influence in the government, as having garnered too large a share of the country's economic resources, and as responsible for a national debt of unprecedented proportions and for health care costs that seem to be out of control.

The former view long justified encouraging the elderly to disengage from work, despite evidence that older workers are as productive as their younger counterparts. The new stereotype is potentially even more dangerous. It justifies organizing against the interests of the elderly, cutting the government expenditures that benefit them, perhaps even eliminating Social Security, and reducing efforts to keep the aged alive. In this view, because the elderly have so much wealth and political clout, they do not need the help of younger Americans.

Some have already begun to exploit the new stereotype. In politics, the interests of the elderly and the young have been pitted against one another as though they were in essential conflict—a substitute for the real battle that is so carefully avoided—that of the poor and middle class against the rich. Americans for Generational Equity (AGE), for example, argues that the status of the elderly has greatly improved at the expense of the well-being of the young. The leaders of AGE cite statistics showing high rates of poverty among children, a decline in real income among baby boomers, and a massive federal debt. AGE blames the elderly for consuming too much of the national budget and enjoying increases in Social Security benefits, while inflation-adjusted wages for the rest of the population have declined.

Even more disturbing is the extent to which this perception may be influencing medical personnel who make life and death decisions. Studies have shown that emergency room personnel tend to expend greater effort resuscitating younger patients. During his tenure in office, Colorado's former governor Richard Lamm said that the elderly have a duty to die because of the financial cost of health care needed to prolong the lives of the elderly. According to Lamm, it might cost too much to keep them alive.

It might be argued that now that the 76 million baby boomers are approaching their mid-50s, the term *elderly* will soon get a needed boost in the public relations department. This may be so but only if they continue to spend their money. More likely, older people will do what previous generations of older people have done: They will become more cautious consumers, more concerned about spiraling health care costs and maintaining their pensions than about gaining status in the eyes of others.

Recognizing this fact of life will be a rude awakening for the baby boomers, but it will probably make me feel better. When it comes to getting older, I am far from miserable. At the same time, I would certainly love the company.

## FOCUS

### ✦ Suggestions for Further Reading ✦

"The Economic Escalator" depended a great deal on Kevin Phillips's research in his books *The Politics of the Rich and the Poor* (1990) and *Wealth and Democracy: A Political History of the American Rich* (2002), as well as Jeffrey Madrick's argument in his book *The End of Affluence* (1995). I also based much of my argument on Katherine Newman's perceptive observations in *Falling From Grace: The Experience of Downward Mobility in the American Middle Class* (1988). As an anthropologist, Newman sees the downwardly mobile as a very special tribe. She conceives of the experience of generational downward mobility in American society as something foreign, as a phenomenon as strange to the members of American society as are the exotic rituals in New Guinea.

Yet there is more and more evidence to indicate that downward mobility for the American middle class will continue into the foreseeable future. Prognosticators argue that a number of factors will come together to maintain the middle-class slide: continued outsourcing of jobs, higher state taxes and declining state services, more costly public colleges and universities, higher health care costs, and shrinking stock portfolios (Stern, 2003).

The functional approach to social inequality no longer has the credibility among sociologists that it had in the 1960s and 1970s, yet some contemporary sociologists continue to argue that social inequality is functional and even necessary to the operation of a society. In an early article, "Some Principles of Stratification," in the *American Sociological Review* (1945), Kingsley Davis and Wilbert Moore suggested that at least some degree of social stratification is necessary as a means for rewarding the really important positions in a society. In his highly critical response to Davis and Moore, Melvin Tumin later wrote in his *American Sociological Review* article "Some Principles of Stratification: A Critical Analysis" (1953) that institutionalized social inequality was also dysfunctional for society. In other words, stratification has some negative consequences that were completely ignored by Davis and Moore. Herbert J. Gans took a modified version of the functional position when he argued in "The Positive Functions of Poverty," in the *American Journal of Sociology* (1972), that the presence of poverty aids in the survival of a society (e.g., poor people get the dirty work done, as we saw earlier in the book).

"An Apple Pie and an Open Mind" suggests that the inspiration for at least some part of the militia movement is economic—many members of the Patriot

Movement have suffered financial hardship and are looking for an explanation that makes sense to them. Representing rural poverty, they blame the federal government as well as a host of groups they believe to be in a conspiracy with the federal government to deprive them of their means of livelihood.

For an objective account of the rise of the militia movement in the United States, I recommend Jonathan Karl's *The Right to Bear Arms* (1995). Thomas Halpern and Brian Levin's *The Limits of Dissent* (1996) presents an interesting analysis of the constitutional status of armed civilian militia groups. And, for an examination of the militia presence that emphasizes its most dangerous aspects, read Captain Robert L. Snow's *The Militia Threat: Terrorists Among Us* (1999). It should be noted that the militia movement suffered serious decline after Timothy McVeigh's 1995 massacre of 168 people at a federal building in Oklahoma City. When McVeigh's connection with a civilian militia group in Arizona came to public light, many members of the movement were humiliated that so many children died in the explosion.

"Gender Inequality Across Cultures" examines various forms of discrimination being practiced against women around the world. Over the past 50 years, women's political and legal rights have grown in nations around the world. By 2000, 139 of the 185 UN Member States signed the 1979 UN Convention on the Elimination of All Forms of Discrimination Against Women. Despite gains in some areas, however, many women in a wide range of countries continue to be deprived of the legal and political rights enjoyed by men. Women do not have universal suffrage, nor do they have rights to own property or inheritance in all countries. Also, women continue to be vastly underrepresented in national decision making and hold only a small fraction of parliamentary seats and leadership positions. In 1998, women comprised 7.4% of cabinet ministers worldwide. As of March 2000, there were only eight female heads of state.

My evidence for "The Stigma of Aging" goes back to a paper titled "Powerful Elders," which I wrote with Arnold Arluke and William C. Levin for the 1992 meetings of the American Sociological Association and with William C. Levin in *Ageism: Prejudice and Discrimination Against the Elderly* (1980). For a summary of the traditional stereotypes associated with older people, see Robert Butler's excellent book *Why Survive? Being Old in America* (1975). By the way, it was Butler who coined the term *ageism*. There are also more recent treatments. In 1990, gerontologist Erdman Palmore wrote the book titled *Ageism: Negative and Positive,* in which he examines both the nasty and the supportive stereotypes and attitudes regarding older people. Todd Nelson's (2002) edited volume *Ageism: Stereotyping and Prejudice Against Older Persons* explores a broad range of issues related to current ageist attitudes. In her book *Young vs. Old: Generational Combat in the 21st Century,* Susan A. MacManus (1996) examines the complexities of generational conflict. Finally, Palmore, Branch, and Harris (2005) have recently edited a comprehensive volume in which a broad range of issues related to ageism is covered.

In writing "Give Us Still Your Masses," Gordana Rabrenovic and I relied a good deal on the numerous journalistic accounts in newspapers and magazines as well as scholarly reports. For a particularly comprehensive analysis of the worldwide movement toward immigration and its implications prior to the September 11 attack on the United States, see the special edition World Report section of the *Los Angeles Times* (October 1, 1991). The modern immigrant experience in America is described and analyzed in *Immigrant America: A Portrait* (1997) by Alejandro Portes and Ruben G. Rumbaut. For an excellent discussion of the post–September 11 newcomers to American society, see Vincent N. Parillo's *Strangers to These Shores* (2006).

For an examination of aspects of the lives of the new immigrant second generation, including their patterns of acculturation, family and school life, language, identity, experiences of discrimination, self-esteem, ambition, and achievement, read Alejandro Portes and Ruben Rumbaut's (2001) *Legacies: The Story of the Immigrant Second Generation.*

Anti-immigrant sentiment is certainly not confined to the United States. Across Europe, newcomers have been targeted for violence. Since the demise of the Soviet Union, East Germany has struggled to make the transition from Communism to a free-market economy, but its high unemployment inspired violent attacks on refugees and workers from Eastern European and developing countries. During the 1990s, there were thousands of attacks against foreigners, especially Turks, Africans, and Vietnamese. More than a decade later, a group of young Germans firebombed a block of high-rise apartments and a nearby Asian grocery store in the city of Rostock. The more than 100 residents of the building—all immigrants from Vietnam and other Asian countries—fled in panic across the rooftop to safety ("Four German Youths," 2003). In France, resentment against its 6 million Muslim immigrants has provoked the government to tighten controls against illegal immigration. In England, there were 2,000 racial attacks on immigrants over a recent 2-year period. Such xenophobic crimes ranged from swastikas spray-painted on the cars of Indian immigrants to the brutal murder of an Iranian refugee (Cracknell & Gadher, 2003). Even Scandinavian nations have been affected by the recent arrival of unprecedented numbers of immigrants. The growing presence of dark-skinned foreigners in Norway's big cities has inspired the Scandinavian version of the neo-Nazi skinhead movement to respond with violence (Cowell, 2002).

Lewis Coser's safety valve idea suggests that hostility toward immigrants may derive from citizens' dissatisfaction with their economic situation. Rather than direct their anger toward the true source of their deprivations (e.g., a president, a ruler, or a monarch), they focus their hostility on vulner-able people at the bottom (e.g., welfare recipients, underclass members, or immigrants). Coser's idea can be found in his classic work, *The Functions of Social Conflict* (1956).

In his enlightening book *The Rich Get Richer and the Poor Get Prison* (2006), Jeffrey Reiman, based on a conflict approach, presents a criminal justice version of the safety valve function. Reiman attempts to explain why the criminal justice system seems to be preoccupied with dangers usually threatened by violent offenders who are poor. He argues that our attention is diverted from the real source of crime, from the injustices of our economic system, and from those rich and powerful members of society who benefit most from the maintenance of the status quo. The dangerous activities of the rich are rarely defined by the legal system as crimes, he says, although such activities result in hundreds of thousands of deaths and the loss of billions of dollars. But the wealthy are weeded out at every stage of the criminal justice system. And in the failure of the criminal justice system, there is a victory for the rich: Hostility is redirected away from the top of the economic order and focused instead on the poor people in our society.

Of course, the terrorist attack on September 11, 2001, provided a new and more intense source of hostility toward immigrants in America, especially toward those newcomers *perceived* to come from Middle Eastern nations. I emphasize "perceived" to suggest that profiling Arabs and Muslims has resulted in some tragic mistakes and ineffective consequences. In "Profiling Terrorists," law pro-fessor Deborah Ramirez and I suggest that the ineffective profiling tactics recently employed to target black and Latino drivers in the war on drugs are now being used to locate terrorists—and with the same results.

## DEVELOPING IDEAS

### ✦ About Social Inequality ✦

1. Research topic: Make a list of 20 occupations representing the kinds of jobs that you and your classmates are likely to be doing after graduation. Give this list to several friends and ask them to rank all 20 occupations from 1 (most prestigious) to 20 (least prestigious). How much agreement is there regarding the prestige rankings of these jobs? What do your results indicate about the structured aspect of stratification?

2. Writing topic: Write a short essay in which you compare the everyday lives of two fictitious characters: a 25-year-old man who possesses extraordinary wealth versus a 25-year-old man who experiences extreme poverty. Specifically,

compare them on such things as (a) what they are likely to do at leisure, (b) where they are likely to live, (c) their family lives, (d) health care, and (e) their jobs. Explain how each man—the wealthy and the poor—got that way and what the poverty-stricken man might do to improve his social position.

3. Research topic: Popular culture often expresses our stereotyped images. Analyze any 10 birthday cards that you select from your local card shop or drug store. Choose only cards that make a direct reference to age. Are their messages—aside from Happy Birthday—positive or negative? How many refer, if only in a joking reference, to lack of sexual activity, lack of attractiveness, lack of intelligence, or lack of physical ability? How many joke about age concealment? How many make special mention of women's problems with aging? Does any card suggest that you might get better as you get older?

4. Writing topic: Make a list of all the tasks that poor people do for society—tasks that might otherwise not get done or might have to be done by middle-class types. For example, poor people buy day-old bread from thrift stores that might otherwise never be sold. Your turn. By the way, can you also suggest other ways to get these tasks accomplished without relying on poor people to do them?

5. Among the methods that sociologists use for assessing social status is the subjective approach, whereby the respondents are asked to place themselves in the stratification hierarchy. In 1949, Richard Centers asked a national sample of white adults, "If you were asked to use one of these four names for your social class, which would you say you belonged in: the middle class, the lower class, working class, or upper class?" Like many other sociologists, Centers found that the majority of his sample saw themselves as belonging to the middle class. Using the same question as Centers, take a sample of 20 people you know fairly well and determine how they see their social class membership as upper, middle, working, or lower. With which class does the majority identify? Explain your results.

6. Research topic: Every year, the U.S. Census Bureau produces a volume, easily accessible at most libraries or through the U.S. Government Printing Office, titled *Statistical Abstract of the United States*. To determine how inequality may have increased or decreased over time, compare at least 2 years (say, 1 year from the 2000s versus 1 year from the 1970s) on several indicators of economic well-being, such as unemployment rate, total personal income, families below the poverty level, and average annual pay. You can find these indicators in the table of contents of the book in sections on "Labor Force, Employment, and Earnings" and "Income, Expenditures, and Wealth." You may also decide to look in the section on "Business Enterprise" for business failure rate and employment growth by major industry. It might be interesting, in addition, to compare two groups—say, blacks and whites—on the same indicators of economic well-being over time.

# PART VII

## Social Change

I've been on a diet for the past 3 months. As of this date, I have lost 24 pounds and hope to lose another 10 or so. Twenty years ago, it would have been relatively easy for me to lose 34 pounds over a short period of time. I would simply have cut down a little on sweets and also reduced the quantity of what I ate at meals. Now that I have reached middle age, however, losing weight seems to require more than just a minor adjustment in my diet. It's not that I lack the will; it's that my metabolism has changed over the years. As a result, only a severe drop in calorie intake along with some kind of exercise regimen seems to make any difference. I really understand, on a gut level, why so many Americans suffer from middle-age spread. If you ask me, the more you age, the more you must reduce your intake of calories to maintain the same weight. Medical research supports my belief.

Just as the structure and functioning of the human body are modified with age, so too the structure of our social lives is capable of profound change. In a sense, the metabolism of our society changes over time. More and more women have entered the labor force, 25% of all college students are now over 30, and the homicide rate is once again on the rise. It was inconceivable, just a few years ago, that the Berlin Wall would come down or that the Soviet Union would crumble, and yet these changes are now taken-for-granted realities. By social change, then, we refer to modifications in either culture or social structure. Interestingly enough, much social change is orderly. Just as structure has discernible characteristics, so change often has patterns.

Theorists disagree as to precisely what that social change looks like. In the 19th century, theorists such as Herbert Spencer argued that societies inevitably evolve from the simple to the complex and always toward greater and greater progress. Karl Marx suggested instead that societies develop through a series of definite stages—from primitive communism, feudalism, and capitalism to socialism—depending on the organization of their economic institutions. Marx believed that all history is the history of class conflict. Finally, some sociologists saw a cyclical pattern in social change. They asserted that history repeats itself. Pitirim Sorokin, for example, identified three cultural themes—ideational, sensate, and idealistic—through which the pendulum of change swings back and forth.

This brief summary of social change theory is meant only to indicate its diversity. Most modern-day sociologists would agree that the earlier theories of social change were too simple. Spencer's views need to be modified: Not all change is for the better; some is for the worse. Progress is far from inevitable. Marx's views need to be modified: Not all conflict is class based. In modern life, we see conflicts between political alliances, age groups, countries, religions, racial groups, and so on. Many of these conflicts generate social change. Sorokin's views need to be modified: The pendulum of change doesn't necessarily swing on the course that he predicted.

Still, the idea of evolution continues to play an important role in our thinking about social change. There seems to be a strong tendency for culture and social structure to become more complex over time. Societies tend to move from small-scale and simple to large-scale and complex forms. Unlike living organisms, however, the evolution cannot be characterized as inevitable. Moreover, the direction and speed of change are not the same in all societies. Societies seem to evolve but on their own terms.

On an individual level, there are literally millions of people who go on diets and take up exercise programs to influence the course of biological change. Many avoid fatty foods, cut down on sugar, or give up red meat. Others buy treadmills and exercise bicycles or jog on a daily basis. Such efforts don't always work as well as we would like. In fact, some dieting plans have an incredibly high 90% failure rate over the long term.

Human beings have similarly sought to help social change along in one or another area of concern. Since 1960, for example, we have seen numerous programs and policies directed toward improving public education; reducing racial, age, and gender discrimination; combating violent crime; improving the economy; and aiding the mentally ill. As suggested in "The Boomerang Effect in Planning Social Change," not all of these efforts have succeeded as planned. In fact, some of them have only backfired by creating even more social problems for us to solve. The failure rate of programs and policies may not approach 90%, but our effectiveness could be better.

In the 1940s, sociologist Robert Merton recognized that unanticipated and anomalous results—perhaps even the boomerang effect—are rather commonplace in sociological research. Such unexpected, even surprising findings may not always generate the most effective proposals for change at the time, but they frequently have a positive consequence as well. In being forced to deal with inconsistencies and contradictions, sociologists must rethink their work, extend their inadequate theories, or create new theories that better explain the phenomena they seek to understand. In the long run, their serendipitous findings may become the basis for more powerful theories of social behavior and more effective social policies and planning.

One thing that I learned the hard way about dieting is that timing is everything. If you're not ready to make the commitment, don't bother trying. If you can't dedicate yourself to an exercise regimen, don't make the effort. You will only fail.

In "Fads," we observe that popular fads and fashions since the 1920s have depended on the timing of changes in the larger culture. Indeed, many fads are made possible by large-scale cultural change. For example, our shared ideas regarding sexuality had been modified so much during the 1960s sexual revolution that streaking became a widespread activity on college campuses and was usually considered a harmless prank or minor annoyance. Ten years earlier, however, the same act of public nudity would probably have been regarded as a major sexual perversion, and offenders would have been immediately shuffled off to serve long sentences in prison or in a mental hospital.

It is hard to believe that rioting could become a popular fad on college campuses across the country. Yet that is exactly what has happened. As indicated in "Keeping an Eye and a Camera on College Students," some excited college students have celebrated the victories of their favorite sports teams by overturning cars, setting fires, and throwing bottles. In reaction, the streets have swarmed with police personnel who attempt in vain to prevent major outbursts of violence. I propose instead the widespread use of well-publicized surveillance cameras in public places. Of course, many will rightly question whether the placement of such security devices represents an abridgement of civil liberties or privacy rights. I answer this question with another question: When hundreds, perhaps thousands, of police officers crowd the streets in anticipation of a riot, are our privacy rights also being reduced? I personally hate the idea of using surveillance cameras to fight crime and terrorism, but I also recognize their usefulness in reducing the need for a large police presence on the streets and on our campuses.

The aging of the human body is a mixed bag of developmental changes. For many people, advanced aging brings about an increase in verbal ability, a more mellow temperament, and more of a tendency to vote. But aging can also engender problems such as a worsening of both memory and hearing.

A major theme in "Riding the Rumor Mill" is that long-standing rumors about crime and disaster in suburban shopping malls actually mirror a trend in the aging of our society that many Americans view with alarm. Those social problems once associated with the inner city are now spreading to the suburbs, formerly regarded as bastions of middle-class respectability. Suburbanites often express anxiety about maintaining their lifestyle by contributing to unfounded rumors of the demise of the shopping mall. Though focusing on the safety of the mall, they actually express anxiety about more basic changes in their lives.

The human body is a system of interrelated parts. A change in one area has implications for other areas as well. Thus, a healthy diet and sensible exercise program will likely strengthen the functioning of the heart, kidneys, and lungs. The parts of our society similarly affect one another.

"Highway to Hell?" examines the effect of an item of American material culture called the sport utility vehicle on everyday forms of behavior: on the safety and security of members of society, both on and off the highways and byways. Anyone who routinely commutes in rush-hour traffic knows the meaning of the term *hot under the collar*. Unfortunately, the presence of thousands of pounds of steel in the control of angry and frustrated commuters helps create the conditions necessary for violent outbursts.

Even worse, some motorists who are already angry before they get on the highway decide to go for a drive to cool off. This creates an explosive mix.

Keep in mind that "Highway to Hell?" focuses our attention not on the personality characteristics of drivers but directly on a social situation—the act of driving on our roadways—as it influences differing conceptions of deviant behavior over the decades. But there is another important sociological issue to address: Exactly why did the automobile have such a profound influence on the shape of American cities? And why didn't Americans maximize the use of public transportation? Of course, it's not just the automobile that represents systematic changes over time. Change the structure of the American family (e.g., by increasing the number of dual-career families), and you change the economy as well. Change our political institutions, and you change the character of mass communication. Thus, "Enquiring Times" isn't only about newspapers and books. You don't have to read between the lines to see that celebrity gossip has become an important force in politics and mass entertainment. In the presidential campaign of 1988, for example, Gary Hart was a target; in a more recent election campaign, it was Bill Clinton.

Gossip was very much involved in the televised senate hearings to confirm Justice Clarence Thomas and in the televised rape trial of William Kennedy Smith. Millions of Americans eavesdropped on an entire cast of characters—Thomas, Hill, Smith—as they divulged the intricate details of their private lives. More recently, O. J. Simpson and the deaths of Nicole Brown Simpson and Ronald Goldman provided the focal point for small talk during prime-time. Then, just when we seemed to be experiencing a gossip lull, it turned out to be the lull before the gossip storm—the scandals involving President Clinton with Paula Jones and Monica Lewinsky. Even more recently, Idaho's conservative Senator Larry Craig became a target of the political grapevine when he pled guilty to engaging in a homosexual liaison in a public restroom. His subsequent denial and reversed decision to remain in the Senate fueled a lengthy round of gossip-mongering on radio talk shows and Internet blogs.

Some cultures will cut off your lips for gossiping. Here, we just put it on national TV! It is very possible to lose perspective while in the midst of significant social change. The September 11, 2001, attack on the United States colored our perception of the quantity and quality of the terrorist threat against us, making us vastly more vigilant and anxious but also distorting our view of terrorism. As suggested in "Terror American Style," we weren't safe before the attack, but we just didn't know it.

# The Boomerang Effect in Planning Social Change

## In the Social Arena, Good Intentions Sometimes Go Wrong

Usually, social policies and programs are a mixed bag; they have multiple effects. We should have learned this lesson from our experience with hard scientists who have long recognized the need to weigh costs against benefits in evaluating outcomes. Thalidomide probably eased the suffering of numerous pregnant women; unfortunately, it also produced serious birth deformities. Urea formaldehyde made an extremely effective form of home insulation; it also made some people sick. Antipsychotic drugs improve everyday psychological functioning, but when prescribed without caution, they can also produce an irreversible nervous disorder.

In the social arena, affirmative action legislation has opened doors for women and minorities who would otherwise have been summarily excluded from many decent jobs. It has also stigmatized its beneficiaries by giving the impression that blacks, Latinos, and women enjoy an unfair advantage and are not qualified for the jobs that they hold. Similarly, Social Security is, for many older people, the difference between survival and starvation; it also leads millions of young people to believe that they have no choice but to retire by the age of 65 or 70.

Aside from government intervention, multiple effects often confound those who give the rest of us advice. Marriage counselors who encourage troubled couples to air their differences may make their clients feel more comfortable with themselves; they may also inadvertently precipitate a divorce by escalating conflicts between husbands and wives. Nursing homes frequently provide humane care; they also foster dependence. And the voluntary rating system used by the motion picture industry provides guidance in the selection of movies appropriate for children; it also stimulates countless cinematic scenes of gratuitous sex and violence to justify a PG-13 or an R rating (the G rating is often the kiss of death for the commercial success of a film).

The same principle applies to the influence of the generations. To their credit, people who grew up in the 1960s were deeply involved in the civil rights and women's movements. But they must also take the blame for having weakened our resolve to teach basic skills to our youngsters. The demolition of the open classroom later marked our realization that we were producing a generation of well-adjusted functional illiterates. In some cases, intelligent people implementing intelligent policies are responsible for producing a boomerang effect; they actually create more of whatever it is they seek to reduce in the first place.

The boomerang effect has been achieved many times in recent years by men and women of goodwill. State legislatures around the nation have raised the drinking age back to 21 in an effort to reduce the prevalence of violent deaths among our young people. But such policies seem to have created the conditions for even more campus violence. Some underage college students who previously drank in bars and lounges under the watchful supervision of bouncers (not to mention owners eager to keep their liquor licenses) now retreat to the sanctuary of their fraternity houses and apartments, where they no longer control their behavior—or their drinking.

The boomerang effect has also played a role in attempts to reduce the availability of illicit drugs. During the 1980s, the federal government was quite successful in reducing the supply of, albeit not the demand for, such street drugs as marijuana. As fields burned and contraband was confiscated, the price of marijuana skyrocketed to a point where cheap alternatives (e.g., crack) began to compete in the marketplace. Unfortunately, the cheap alternatives were even more harmful than the illicit drugs they replaced. In addition, crack wars between competing dealers for territory and markets were responsible for escalating the violence on our city streets.

Our official response in the early 1980s was to wage a war against drugs, which meant filling our prisons to capacity with street-level dealers and addicts. Taking so many adult pushers off the streets left a vacuum in the illicit drug trade that was filled by alienated youngsters looking for an easy way to make lots of money. In order to protect their markets, teenagers began carrying guns. The result was a rate of teenage violence that soared out of sight.

The response of the courts to the rise in juvenile drug dealing was to try more teenagers as adults—not just those who had committed murder but also youthful burglars and drug addicts. But the assumption that severe sentences—spending decades behind bars—would reduce youth crime proved inaccurate. Recent studies—for example, by such criminologists as Donna Bishop—suggest instead that trying juveniles as adults only increases the likelihood of their recidivism. Adult prisons are schools for crime and a crash course in violence.

One final area should be mentioned in connection with the boomerang effect. Every state has now established a system of registering those ex-offenders who have committed sex crimes against minors. At the national level, moreover, Congress recently enacted legislation that creates a national registry to track released sex offenders when they move from state to state.

Establishing a database for the purpose of informing the local police or the FBI of a sex offender's presence may, of course, be useful for identifying potential suspects when a sex crime occurs. But notifying the neighbors that an ex-offender is in their community only ensures that he will be shoved out of mainstream society and pushed back into a life of crime. As soon as the word gets around, he undoubtedly will lose his job, be evicted from his apartment, and be shunned by his friends and neighbors. The crimes committed against sex offenders have ranged from harassment and arson to acts of violence. In Maine, an angry resident found the names and locations of two sex offenders in the state's sex offender registry and then shot both of them to death. In Washington state, two convicted child rapists were murdered. In September 2007, in the mountain town of Helenwood, Tennessee, two neighbors set fire to a tiny house on the block when they read in the newspaper that the owner had been arrested on child pornography charges. The intended victim lived, but his wife—who had not been charged with any criminal offense—lost her life in the fire.

Lest those who argue for a hands-off policy get too smug, I suggest that the failure to act also has its unanticipated side effects. Ronald Reagan's benign neglect in response to poverty in America during the 1980s may have helped cut double-digit inflation; it also reduced the size of the middle class and increased permanent poverty in our cities to an unprecedented level. The same tax-cutting policies throughout the 1990s and into the new millennium have helped ensure a healthy stock market, but they have also ensured the continued increase in income inequality.

Moreover, in what was euphemistically called "deinstitutionalization," we emptied our nation's mental hospitals in the 1970s without providing adequate services or supervision for the mentally ill individuals released into the community. Some of them joined the growing ranks of the homeless; others have found homes in prisons; many stopped taking the medications that had made possible their release from institutions.

Of course, not all policies are as well intentioned as they may appear to be. How do we ascertain another person's motives, let alone those of an organization? Was the ratings system initiated to help parents or to get government off the back of the movie industry? Did all those who supported emptying our mental hospitals really desire more humane treatment of the mentally ill, or were they merely trying to cut costs? Even motivation is often a mixed bag.

If a spokesperson for the cigarette industry claims that the link between smoking and lung cancer has not been established, we are suspicious. We may perceive a self-serving, biased assessment. Exactly the same skeptical mind-set is valuable in evaluating the effectiveness of social services and policies—skepticism without cynicism.

# Fads

## Is Goldfish Gobbling Next?

With the all-purpose response "I know, Mom, but everyone's doing it," millions of teenagers have sought to explain to their parents why they experiment with drugs or alcohol, color their hair purple, or wear multiple pierced earrings. Their desire to conform to fashions of their fellows is more than an excuse. Adolescents often do what everyone else is doing; they go along with a fad or fashion simply because they don't want to look different or to be seen as out of step with their peers.

Given their other-directedness, teenagers are especially sensitive to what is current versus passé, what is "in" versus "out." It should come as no surprise, therefore, that many fads and fashions originate in what is called adolescent subculture. By conforming to the latest crazes in haircuts, dress, music, and gadgetry, many teenagers hope to gain approval from their friends.

But peer approval is not the only appeal of such fads. While they hope to impress their friends with their compliance, teenagers also seek to distance themselves from their parents. As a result, behavior that appears to adults to be irrational and even dysfunctional may be valued by the young for exactly that reason: Such behavior is outrageous enough to the older generation. If, when young, their parents drank beer, the teenagers will try marijuana; if parents wore long hair and peace beads, their offspring will shave their initials into their hair or don spiked jewelry or join the Young Republicans; if parents wore their designer labels under their garments, their offspring will insist on wearing their labels outside.

Ironically, and of course unwittingly, even the most outrageous teenage fads touchingly reflect the tenor of their times. During the Roaring Twenties, for example, Charles Lindbergh and Amelia Earhart were busy setting records with their derring-do across the Atlantic. Rapid industrial growth and expanding capitalism generated intense competition for scarce economic resources. How did the flaming youth of the decade respond? With contests of skill and endurance: flagpole sitting, rocking-chair derbies, cross-country races, pie-eating contests, kissing and dancing marathons, and gum-chewing and peanut-pushing contests.

During the Sputnik era of the late 1950s, competition was once again intense. The United States and the Soviet Union vied for supremacy in science and technology, and American schools responded by attempting to raise their standards. Teenagers once more designed contests to set and break records. Throughout the decade, young people crammed themselves into hearses, Volkswagen Beetles, and telephone booths. They stacked dozens of students on a single bed and stuffed their rooms with papers.

Teenage fashion has also been affected by the culture of its period. During the 1920s, when American women were first allowed to vote, youthful flappers literally threw off the bras and corsets of their mothers' generation in favor of knee-length skirts, low-cut gowns, and bobbed hair. Some 40 years later, motivated by the women's movement of the 1960s, teenage girls wore miniskirts, cut their hair short, and burned their bras.

Conventional values influence adolescent fads in yet another way. They set the limits as to just how far those fads are permitted to go before adult society enforces sanctions against them. In 1974, undergraduates began to engage in streaking. To streak was to dash nude through a public place. Society's tolerance for streaking was a result of the sexual revolution of the 1960s. The same act would undoubtedly have received quite a different reception if it had occurred during the 1950s. Any student who had dared run naked through a college campus then would, in all likelihood, have been quickly locked away as a sexual pervert and a menace to society. In 1954, streaking could hardly have gained the popularity of a fad.

Even the most absurd practices can become the basis for an adolescent fad, given the right social climate. During the Great Depression of the 1930s, at a time when many Americans were having trouble putting food on the table, parents lost their appetites because of a fad that hit college campuses. From Massachusetts to Missouri, students had taken to swallowing goldfish. A Harvard freshman was the first to swallow a single live fish, while fellow students at the Freshman Union looked on in disgust. Three weeks of social change later, an undergraduate at Franklin & Marshall in Lancaster, Pennsylvania, ate three goldfish. New records for goldfish consumption were then set almost daily.

At the University of Pennsylvania, one intrepid soul swallowed 25; at the University of Michigan, 28; at Boston College, 29; at Northeastern

University, 38; at MIT, 42; and at Clark University, 89 were devoured at one sitting. One college student gained fame by coming up with the first recipe for a goldfish sugar cookie; the chef at the Hotel Statler put the dish on the menu as a special. But a pathologist with the U.S. Public Health Service cautioned that goldfish may contain tapeworms that lodge in the intestines and cause anemia, and by the spring of 1939, the goldfish-gobbling craze had gone the way of the dance marathon.

Teenagers in 1990 tripped over their own feet by wearing their sneakers unlaced; to this day, they continue to increase their susceptibility to illness by refusing to wear winter hats or raincoats and ruin their feet with pointed-toe shoes, all because these are in fashion. In general, they are seen as doing things that aren't very good for them—tattooing their bodies; piercing their tongues, noses, and navels; engaging in risky sports like skateboarding; and listening to Marilyn Manson. Most teenagers aren't swallowing goldfish yet, but for those who are too young to remember, that could very well be next.

# Keeping an Eye and a Camera on College Students

## A High-Tech Response to Celebratory Rioting

Violent social protests during the 1990s in response to police brutality or racism seem as much a distant memory as Rodney King. Nowadays, riots are likely to be celebratory, committed by middle-class college students who rejoice violently when their sports team wins an important game. During the last five years, happy college students on dozens of campuses across the country have participated in postgame looting, overturning vehicles, lighting fires, hurling bottles and rocks, and fighting.

Certainty of punishment is a powerful deterrent to illegal behavior. In order for authorities to eliminate postgame rioting, would-be violators must understand they cannot possibly escape being identified and punished. To this end, Boston Police Commissioner Kathleen O'Toole has promised to have officers from across the Commonwealth out in force for Super Bowl Sunday, and Mayor Thomas Menino has urged that colleges make clear they will discipline any student who participates in violent postgame celebrations. Referring to students who might decide to riot in the aftermath of a Patriots victory, Menino said, "Bad behavior will not be tolerated."

While worthwhile, such threats of formal punishment cannot by themselves possibly ensure tranquility following every championship game. Students must first be convinced that their participation in a riot will inevitably have negative consequences.

Yet being immersed in a crowd, participants often come to feel totally anonymous. No matter how severe the possible consequences, they simply do not believe they can be singled out and punished. Social psychologists refer to this phenomenon as "deindividuation" because people in a crowd—especially in a spontaneous gathering of excited participants—lose their individual identities.

To a limited extent, a far-reaching law enforcement presence reduces this feeling of anonymity. But, as we observed after the Red Sox's American League pennant victory in October, the presence of armed police on the streets can also exacerbate the danger, resulting in confrontations with students and even the death of innocent bystanders. In addition, it is all but impossible for the police to be in every area where rioting is likely to occur or to round up each and every violent student. Rioters know this, and it reduces their fear of being caught.

An alternative crime-fighting approach would be to supplement the police presence by installing tiny closed-circuit television cameras on street lamps and buildings in order to monitor those areas of the city densely populated by college students, where rioting is likely to occur.

To maximize the effectiveness of surveillance, potential riot areas must be blanketed with cameras. Their presence must be publicized throughout the academic community so that students become completely aware of their presence.

Many European countries now employ public video surveillance to discourage crime, drugs, and terrorism. More than 1.5 million closed-circuit television systems monitor the streets and roads of English cities and towns. In the United States, such major cities as Chicago and Baltimore have similarly made plans to electronically monitor and dispatch aid in response to crime, terrorist acts, and traffic problems.

Holyoke, Massachusetts, is in the process of installing closed-circuit television cameras in the crime-prone downtown area of the city. In Boston, surveillance cameras were installed in 2004 to identify terrorist threats during the Democratic National Convention but have not been used extensively as a crime-fighting apparatus.

Concerned about an erosion of personal privacy, civil libertarians have opposed the widespread presence of surveillance cameras to fight crime but fail to recognize that a pervasive police presence on the streets has a similar impact.

Moreover, rioting occurs not behind closed doors but in public places where everyday behavior can be easily observed. In England, where the ubiquitous closed-circuit television cameras have significantly reduced criminal activities and have made possible the identification of terrorists, there is surprising support among citizens for video surveillance.

It is too late for surveillance cameras to be effectively installed and publicized prior to this year's Super Bowl. But there is time to make preparations now for the possibility of violence after future sports events, including Boston's Beanpot tournament, the NCAA Final Four, and October's World Series.

Rioting has become a fad among college students, taking the place of the goldfish swallowing, flagpole sitting, panty raids, and streaking practiced by previous generations.

At some point, today's college students will tire of rioting and move on. In the meantime, we should keep an eye and a camera on them.

# Riding the Rumor Mill

## Our Basic Anxieties Are
## Projected in Various Tall Tales

Rumors frequently touch on our important fears and anxieties. Where food shortages exist, individuals circulate stories about the supply and distribution of provisions; where access to economic resources depends on tracing descent through uncertain genealogies, they gossip about one another's ancestors; where witchcraft is a cultural belief, they spread tales about who is and is not a witch; and when economic times are bad, workers depend on the office grapevine to forecast management changes.

Temple University's Ralph Rosnow suggests that rumors on a national level prey on our basic anxieties about death, disaster, and illness. Thus, a number of celebrities have reportedly died in the face of overwhelming evidence to the contrary (including their personal denials): Paul McCartney, Jerry Mathers of *Leave It to Beaver* fame, Scott Baio, Life Cereal's Mikey, James Earl Jones, and Whitney Houston. More recently, rumors spread that pop idol Britney Spears had been killed in a car accident that also left her former boyfriend Justin Timberlake in a coma. On the other side of the ledger, some who have, by all credible accounts, actually died—Elvis, Jim Morrison, John F. Kennedy, Selena, and Hitler—have been seen alive! In addition, many rumors have incorrectly reported the contamination of popular food: for example, spider eggs in bubble gum, candy that explodes when eaten with a carbonated beverage, worms in hamburgers, mice in Coke bottles, rats in fried chicken, and cats in Chinese food.

Most of the time, it is impossible to track a rumor to its original source. Once in a while, however, a rumor can be traced. In 1998, for example, a medical researcher tried to extort millions of dollars from a fast-food hamburger company by claiming that he had found a french-fried rat tail in his son's meal. The researcher was convicted of fraud by a federal jury after it was learned that he had placed the rat tail in his son's french fries. In 2005, a San Jose woman claimed to have found a fingertip in her Wendy's restaurant chili bowl. Her charges against the fast-food chain later turned out to be a scam—the customer had purposely inserted the finger, taken from a dead friend, in order to sue the restaurant. Then in September 2005 she and her husband pleaded guilty to conspiring to file a false claim and attempted grand theft.

According to Tulane sociologist Fredrick Koenig, author of *Rumor in the Marketplace: The Social Psychology of Commercial Hearsay* (1985), rumors do not necessarily reduce anxiety; instead, they often confirm our worst suspicions. But in one sense, such doomsday stories can also be comforting; for at the very least, they confirm the validity of our perception of the world, especially if we see that world as dangerous.

The anxiety multiplies when the danger is seen as encroaching on our personal safety. Take living in the suburbs, for example. For decades, young families scrimped and sacrificed, denying themselves all but the barest necessities to accumulate the down payment on their dream house in East Norwich, New York; Longmeadow, Massachusetts; or Glencoe, Illinois. By moving to the suburbs, they had hoped to escape the poverty, crime, and congestion associated with city living.

But during recent times, the suburban version of the American Dream has seemed to slip away, as real estate values and property taxes skyrocketed, the quality of local services declined, energy costs remained high, and crime invaded the outer reaches of suburbia. On a daily basis, newspapers increasingly reported incidents of the very crimes that anxious suburbanites had left the city to escape—forcible rape, aggravated assault, school violence, missing children, and automobile theft. Facing severe tax restrictions at the local level, suburban school systems began laying off teachers, firefighters, and police. Public roads and buildings were left in a state of disrepair. And in the process, the suburbs increasingly began to resemble the pathologies associated with urban decay.

In 1979, tension surrounding an invader of the suburbs, Reverend Sun Myung Moon's Unification Church, the so-called Moonies, which purchased real estate in Gloucester, Massachusetts, manifested in a classic rumor. Hearing stories of teenagers coerced into the Moonie cause, people began believing that the regionally powerful Entenmann's bakery was owned by the Unification Church and that its products were tainted. Although Entenmann's was then actually owned by the Warner-Lambert Corporation, that detail didn't stop hundreds of customers from complaining to store managers who carried Entenmann's products.

Moreover, church bulletins, letters to the editor, and callers to radio talk shows all warned about Moonie ownership of the bakery and urged everyone to boycott Entenmann's products. As they attempted to deliver their goods, Entenmann's drivers were physically assaulted by angry customers. The bakery's sales declined. So long as public anxiety remained at a high level, Entenmann's continued to serve as a convenient, albeit innocent, target of hostility.

Eventually, the anxieties fueling the Entenmann's rumors faded into the distance. In its place, rumor-mongering about the deterioration of suburbia coalesced around images of the shopping mall as dangerous and threatening, as a place where the most pernicious influences of the inner city had altered suburban life. After all, the mall had previously represented the heart and soul of the suburban lifestyle, being inaccessible except by automobile, protected from crime by security guards, sheltered by its physical isolation, and attractive to a largely homogeneous segment of the middle-class customers who spent their days leisurely strolling through the corridors spending money. If crime and poverty invaded the tranquil, secure confines of the suburban shopping mall, absolutely nobody was safe.

In western Massachusetts, there surfaced a story about a "woman" shopping at a local mall who asked various customers for a ride home. It was said that when authorities finally apprehended her, she turned out to be an axe-wielding man wearing makeup and a wig to protect his true identity. Similarly, in the early 1980s, Connecticut residents picked up various stories about a young girl who suddenly disappeared while walking with her mother in a mall. According to this tale, worried security guards later found her in a restroom, where she had been given a short haircut and dressed in boys' clothing. Within a period of two or three years, some version of these mall stories had spread all over the country from New York to Texas to California. Only the name of the shopping center and some of the details of the crime varied from location to location.

The rumors of abduction and crime in suburban shopping malls, although not completely gone, have receded somewhat. But in their place, there are new reports around the country that newly constructed shopping malls are in imminent danger of being transformed into underground shopping centers; they are, it is said, structurally unsound and literally sinking.

In the most recent episode, the mammoth three-story Emerald Square Mall in North Attleboro, Massachusetts, has been the target of unfounded rumors since it opened more than 10 years ago. Among the most widely told tales are those that contend that the mall has already sunk 6 inches, that its third floor has been closed, that the top floor of the adjoining parking garage has been closed, that the garage has separated from the main building, that many of the windows have shattered, that the mall will soon close, and that the mall will be torn down and rebuilt. Although there is no truth in any of this, that hasn't prevented customers from phoning the mall's building inspector with wild stories, excitedly discussing the rumors in shops and restaurants, and, in some cases, taking their business elsewhere.

Those who attempt to explain such rumors of sinking shopping malls might point to some offhand, ill-informed remark made by an engineer or the presence of a neighboring shopping center that really did have structural problems. People sometimes do get confused by the facts. But for those who take a long-term view, the sinking-mall rumors are merely a new variation of an old theme, beginning with the stories of children allegedly being abducted from mall restrooms and continuing with the axe-wielding woman. You don't have to be Freud to figure it out: It really isn't the shopping mall sinking we worry about—it is our whole way of life.

# Highway to Hell?

## Fear and Loathing on the Road

Travel any highway into a major city during rush hour. While waiting to move, you are bound to observe at least a half dozen drivers talking to themselves, singing along with a tune on the radio, or scratching themselves.

Automobiles give an illusion of privacy. So long as drivers remain behind the wheel, they travel in isolation. Enclosed by steel and glass, they are physically independent of the thousands of other motorists with whom they share the road. No matter how jammed the highway is with vehicles, drivers feel alone, and in a social-psychological sense, they are. As a result, they may engage in bizarre, even deviant, behavior.

Having been associated with deviance ever since the advent of mass motoring, automobiles have long contributed to the direction of social and cultural change. In the 1920s, many Americans for the first time owned a family car. And it was the automobile that critics blamed for what they saw as a precipitous decline in national morality. Newly freed from the rigid restrictions of previous generations, the flaming youth of the decade regarded the family's tin Lizzie as their apartment on wheels—a place where they could kiss, neck, and pet.

Sex researcher Alfred Kinsey reported that young women of the 1920s were far more likely to have premarital intercourse than were those who had reached sexual maturity before World War I. Not surprisingly, the automobile was blamed—and with cause. In Robert and Helen Lynd's 1929 classic community study, *Middletown*, the overwhelming majority of teenagers in Muncie, Indiana, reported that the automobile was the most common place to pet.

In a more extreme version of immorality, the automobile of the 1920s also became a brothel on wheels, providing ladies of the night from red-light districts around the country a secure and secluded place where they might escape police oversight and ply their trade. The use of the automobile for purposes of prostitution posed a serious setback to the vigorous antivice campaigns of the World War I period. The police were not yet equipped to patrol city streets and country highways.

By the 1950s, teenagers around the country were holding their submarine races in lovers' lanes and drive-in theaters. The game of chicken became a deadly contest between males who sought to impress their dates. During subsequent decades, young people relied on their automobiles as a safe haven in which to drink beer, have sex, and smoke dope.

Teenagers aren't the only drivers who play chicken. Every year, some 46,000 Americans from all age groups are killed in motor vehicle accidents. Another 1.8 million are disabled. Among the leading causes of such fatal crashes are drinking and speeding—two human factors that could be totally controlled. In some single-victim automobile accidents, the lack of control is deliberate: The driver purposely veers into a tree or off a bridge to commit suicide. These victims choose an automobile as an instrument for taking their own lives to save their families the embarrassment that accompanies more obvious forms of suicide.

But most deaths and injuries are avoidable. Such accidents happen because the automobile offers power, especially to the powerless. The automobile is a vehicle that satisfies the desire to be in charge. Even the most timid and passive individuals (or perhaps especially the most timid and passive individuals) may become fearless bullies and criminals as soon as they get behind the 3,000 pounds of steel that separate them from the rest of humanity. Not only do they feel anonymous; they also feel invulnerable caught up in an illusion of their own omnipotence. At the extreme, unbridled power turns nasty, and arguments between drivers erupt into violence.

The advent of sport utility vehicles (SUVs) has given new meaning to the term *unbridled power*. Most SUV owners do not need the capacity to carry seven passengers; some 80% never do off-road driving. Yet SUV drivers apparently feel that they benefit profoundly—the wide appeal of these vehicles can be found in their military appearance, massive proportions, and high center of gravity. Occupants literally sit above the traffic, giving them an even more exaggerated sense of power and control. Unfortunately, these are the same features that make SUVs so destructive.

SUVs waste billions of gallons of gas and emit vastly more carbon monoxide, hydrocarbons, and nitrogen oxide than do passenger cars. SUVs seem to be especially dangerous to the drivers of other passenger cars, blocking their vision at intersections and on highways, blinding them at night by headlights placed high on the vehicle, making parking garages into obstacle courses, and causing a disproportionate number of fatalities in accidents with them. Moreover, according to the Insurance Institute for Highway Safety, SUVs are predisposed to overturning in an accident and are disproportionately involved in single-vehicle crashes.

For commuters, of course, the frustrations of driving in rush-hour traffic go well beyond the presence of SUVs. In most major cities, parking places have become as rare as pollution-free air, and traffic jams at 5 p.m. are common. Our roads are beginning to resemble never-ending parking lots. For visitors, the problems associated with negotiating traffic are exacerbated by a lack of street signs and the presence of one-way streets without pattern or logic. Then, there is the growing *density* of traffic—the number of miles driven increased by 35% between 1988 and 1997, but, over the same period of time, only 1% more roads were constructed. In addition—commuting time—a measure of how congestion affects the daily routines of drivers—increased by about 12% from 1990 through 2000 (Siggerud, 2003).

The problem of traffic volume is in part a result of growing population density in urban areas across the nation. According to Federal Highway Administration data for the year 2000, an urban area with a population density of 5,000 (such as Los Angeles) will have traffic volumes per square mile almost three times that of an urban area with a population density of 1,000 (such as Nashville).

No wonder that 80% of all drivers are now angry most or all of the time, at least according to a 1997 survey conducted by a Michigan firm, EPIC-MRA. Moreover, some drivers are already frustrated and angry before they get behind the wheel of their vehicles. They decide to go for a drive to cool off after arguing with their boss, their spouse, or their friends. According to University of California psychologist Joseph Tupin, people with aggressive impulses frequently take their cars out for a spin as a release from the tensions of the day. They get into a minor confrontation on the highway and explode. The result is pervasive road rage. Between 1990 and 1996, episodes of road rage contributed to 218 deaths and 12,610 injuries. Moreover, such violent incidents increased by almost 7% each year within that 6-year period (Dittmann, 2005).

Of course, the most pervasive effects of the automobile are at the level of social change. As we have seen, the presence of the family car, beginning in the 1920s, significantly altered the ability of young people to achieve independence from their families. At the same time, the opportunities for deviant behavior became much more difficult to challenge.

Moreover, the pattern of commuting traffic in most major cities has determined, for the most part, the clustering of skyscrapers, the placement of sports arenas and convention centers, work schedules, the direction of suburban sprawl, and the aesthetics of urban life generally. In a few cities (e.g., Los Angeles), the urban landscape is virtually dominated by the presence of interconnected networks of freeways.

Americans continue their love affair with their cars. No matter how efficient, public transportation will probably never quite take the place of the beloved automobile. After all, the gargantuan automobile industry (not to mention all of the peripheral industries that it has spawned) literally cannot afford for that to happen and so continues to spend incredibly large amounts of money for advertisements and commercials in which the virtues of driving are extolled. It is perhaps no exaggeration to suggest that the automobile is now as American as apple pie. Of course, so is violence.

# Enquiring Times

## The Tabloidization of Hard News

I confess to having thumbed through a copy or two of the *National Enquirer* and the *Star,* usually while waiting in line at the supermarket checkout counter. It takes little more than a cursory reading to discover that the two-headed-baby stories—the gory items for which they are notorious—have all but disappeared. According to an article in *Journalism and Mass Communication Quarterly,* the tabloids now print profiles; 61% of their articles focus on celebrities (singer Michael Jackson's obsession with children, Dolly Parton's diet, President Clinton's affair with Monica Lewinsky) and 37% on the accomplishments of ordinary people who do extraordinary things (the man who lost 350 pounds by stapling his stomach, the 87-year-old woman who gave up her Social Security check to feed the homeless, the man who swam for 4 days in shark-infested waters).

For those who prefer the gore, there are still a few, relatively obscure tabloids that specialize in it. The *Sun* and the *Weekly World News* can be counted on for a story featuring a human pregnant with an animal or an animal pregnant with a human. But the most popular supermarket tabloids—the *National Enquirer,* the *Star,* the *Globe,* and the *National Examiner*—have removed most of the grisly pieces, and they still attract some 10 million readers.

These tabloids continue to run into thorny ethical problems, however, mainly concerning their aggressive methods of reporting and their reliance on hearsay rather than hard news. Hollywood celebrities often claim that *Enquirer* reporters invade their privacy, rely on unreliable informants, and fabricate information about their personal lives. Some continue to believe that overly aggressive tabloid paparazzi following Princess Diana's automobile contributed to the crash that killed her. As a result, tabloids continue to have only marginal status among print journalists. Yet mainstream journalists must be aware, and are perhaps even envious, of the tremendous popularity of supermarket tabloids. At a time when newspapers around the country are shutting down, publishers are looking for new models that might keep them in business.

Because of their vast appeal, the supermarket tabloids have provided such a model. Many mainstream papers have become *tabloidized;* that is, they have imitated not only the tabloid's size and shape but its sensational headlines. Some have begun to rely more on hearsay and ethically questionable investigative techniques. The *National Enquirer* continues to be the butt of criticism from Hollywood celebrity types, television talk show hosts, and the public. It remains a whipping boy of mainstream journalists, even as they imitate its content and format.

Before we blame the messenger for sending a message we detest, let us recognize that the tabloidization of news reflects a large-scale social change: Gossip about powerful people has assumed an important place in the American psyche. During the 1960s, we treated our rich and famous like royalty. They could do no wrong, and if they did, we would look the other way. John F. Kennedy's acts of infidelity in the White House were well known yet summarily ignored by the press. Whatever their faults and frailties, the rich and powerful were still regarded as paragons of virtue and exemplars for the ethical and intellectual standards we hoped to impart to our children. Nobody wanted to make our heroes into monsters.

In the wake of Watergate, Chappaquiddick, Abscam, Irangate, Jim and Tammy Bakker, Leona Helmsley, Ivan Boesky, Whitewater, Bob Packwood, Paula Jones, the savings and loan scandal, Enron, and Martha Stewart, however, public naiveté gave way to widespread skepticism, if not outright cynicism. We could no longer trust the people who ran things—the national politicians, Hollywood celebrities, and New York business tycoons. They were caught too often literally with their pants down. A recent Harris national survey of more than 1,000 Americans indicated that almost 25% of all Americans have recently deleted some national figure from their list of heroes, mainly because of unethical conduct. Half of all respondents were unable to identify any living public figure whom they considered to be heroic (Clark, 2001).

In response to an apparently insatiable appetite for gossip, information about the private lives of public figures has become a mainstay of front-page news, just as it has long been the backbone of tabloid journalism. It was not the *Star* or the *National Examiner* but the legitimate *Las Vegas Sun* that first revealed that Liberace was dying of AIDS. It was not the *National Examiner* but the *Miami Herald* that snooped on Gary Hart to expose his affair with Donna Rice. Gossip about the lives of such celebrities as Bill Clinton, Kitty

Dukakis, Nancy Reagan, Barney Frank, Ted Kennedy, John Edwards, Martin Luther King Jr., Eliot Spitzer, and John F. Kennedy Jr. has been featured in front-page stories, not only in the *Star* but in local newspapers around the country. Gossip about Bill Clinton's womanizing was featured not only in mainstream newspapers and magazines such as *Newsweek* but also on network newscasts and Web sites. Indeed, during the first days of allegations concerning Clinton's affair with a 21-year-old White House intern, his press secretary's news conference was considered important enough by TV producers that it preempted regularly scheduled programs.

Some people still remember Carol Burnett's successful mid-1970s lawsuit against the *National Enquirer*. She was able to show that the tabloid had acted with reckless disregard for the truth when it published defamatory information about her. According to University of Arkansas law professor Rodney Smolla, the establishment press tried, in the wake of a verdict favorable to Burnett, to dissociate itself from such tabloids as the *Enquirer*.

Tabloid journalism uses hearsay—the anonymous source—as a method for collecting information about celebrities' private lives. Establishment newspapers are known for their reliance on eyewitness accounts and interviews with participants. But legitimate print and broadcast journalists have made mistakes of their own, some of which rival, perhaps surpass, the *Enquirer's* shoddy treatment of Burnett. Increasingly, libel cases have been successfully aimed at mainstream news ranging from *60 Minutes* to *Time* magazine.

Northeastern University sociologist Arnold Arluke and I tried to determine the prevalence of hearsay in legitimate front-page journalism. To this end, we examined the front page of the *New York Times* Sunday edition over a period of 12 months. We found that as many as 70% of these front-page stories were unattributable. Many were so vague that they could have referred to almost anyone: sources close to the investigation, officials, intelligence sources, a key official, critics, campaign strategists, and the like. Some reporters even admitted to using third-hand sources or obtaining information over the phone from an unknown person.

The reliable source has always been an important and legitimate technique of investigative journalism. (Without "Deep Throat," we might never have learned of the Watergate cover-up.) In the 1970s, unadulterated hearsay could be found in only 35% of the front-page articles published in the *New York Times*. But by the 1990s, the anonymous source had become common in gathering information for front-page stories. Taking their cue from more traditional sources of gossip, celebrity gossip blogs have often reported on the dark side of celebrity lifestyles, frequently without disclosing any source at all.

When *Enquirer* reporters use an anonymous source to get some dirt on Carol Burnett, they harm one individual. When a daily newspaper uncritically accepts the word of an anonymous source concerning an international event, it may damage the reputation of an entire country or the relationship between nations. When the *Star* bases a story about Michael Jackson on a source close to the celebrity, we are skeptical. When the *New York Times* or the *Washington Post* relies on an off-the-record comment to develop a front-page story, we think of it as hard news. In the era of the tabloidization of news, the distinction between supermarket tabloids and legitimate daily newspapers has blurred in fact, if not yet in the public mind.

# Terror American Style

## Have We Changed Since September 11?

More than 7 months before the September 11 attack on the United States, white supremacist Leo Felton walked out of prison, having served his 11-year sentence for assaulting a black cab driver. Now 30 years old, Felton moved into an apartment in the town of Ipswich, Massachusetts, and got a job doing construction.

Yet only 3 months later, Felton was back in prison, beginning a 21-year sentence for committing acts of racial terrorism. The prosecutor in the case argued that Felton had been plotting to use violent terrorist actions, such as blowing up the U.S. Holocaust Museum in Washington, DC, and the Leonard Zakim Bridge in Boston. He had hoped to ignite a racial war, a racial holy war that would bring about a new, all-white Christian nation.

And in a letter that Felton wrote to the judge, after he had been found guilty, he confirmed that his ultimate goal was to establish a politically independent white nation somewhere in North America. The interesting thing is that Leo Felton's father is black—but that didn't discourage him from joining up with the white supremacists.

The case of Leo Felton illustrates that Americans share an important misunderstanding about terrorism. They believe incorrectly that the September 11 attack initiated a new and more dangerous era of vulnerability in the United States. And admittedly, the incredibly large body count involved in the attack was unprecedented.

Just as clearly, however, we were never immune from terrorism; it's just that we didn't know it until September 11, 2001. Apparently, the loss of six lives at the World Trade Center in 1993 didn't attract our attention. The body count simply wasn't large enough to generate much interest or publicity.

And according to the FBI, there were almost 500 acts of terrorism in this country between 1980 and 2001—before the September 11 attack on the United States. The majority of these attacks were committed—as Leo Felton intended—with explosives or bombs. Terrorism is really nothing new to the United States—it's just that its form has changed.

A second misconception is that terrorist attacks on our citizens have been typically committed by organizations originating in Middle Eastern or Asian countries—organizations such as Hamas, al-Qaeda, or Hezbollah. In fact, the largest number of terrorist acts in the United States have come from our own citizens, whether right-wing extremists like Leo Felton, left-wing extremists, radical environmentalists, or the like. In fact, only 36% of all acts of terrorism since 1980 have been international in origin. All the rest have traditionally originated on American soil and have been perpetrated by American citizens who hate the federal government, despise certain kinds of people who live here, or want desperately to feel a sense of their own importance.

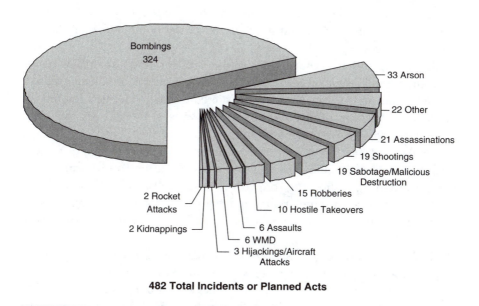

**482 Total Incidents or Planned Acts**

**Figure 7.1**     Terrorism by Event, 1980–2001

*Note:* Figure 7.1 includes the events of September 2001 which are counted as one incident.

Few acts of terrorism since September 11 have been perpetrated by Americans with Middle Eastern connections. The overwhelming majority of Americans of Middle Eastern origin simply do not want to blow up the United States; they have too much at stake in this country. Arab-Americans are better educated and wealthier than their non-Arab counterparts. More than half of all Arab-Americans own their own homes; 41% are college graduates; 42% are employed in managerial or professional occupations; and their median family income is more than $52,000.

Why would such prosperous and well-educated people want to destroy what they have worked so hard to build? Most of them are loyal Americans, just as most Japanese-, German-, and Italian-Americans were loyal citizens during World War II.

By contrast, Middle Easterners who have relocated to European countries have had a far less satisfactory experience. In general, they are poorly schooled and thoroughly impoverished. Many of them feel persecuted, exploited, or left out of things.

Most terrorist attacks have been committed by American citizens. In 1995, American citizen Timothy McVeigh bombed the Oklahoma City federal building, killing 168 people; in 1996, American citizen Eric Rudolph allegedly caused the deadly explosion that ripped through Centennial Olympic Park in Atlanta and is suspected in the bombing of an abortion clinic and a gay nightclub.

In 1999, Indiana University college student and American citizen Benjamin Smith went on a rampage, shooting to death a Korean graduate student and an African-American basketball coach. He also injured six Orthodox Jews. It turned out that Smith was a member of the white supremacist group World Church of the Creator.

In April 2000, an unemployed immigration lawyer and American citizen, Richard Baumhammers, drove from location to location in suburban Pittsburgh, shooting to death five people in five different places. He hated minorities, immigrants, and Jews, so he killed someone Jewish, someone Vietnamese, someone Chinese, someone Indian, and someone African-American.

In 2003, American citizen Clayton Lee Waagner was charged with mailing anthrax hoax letters to women's clinics around the nation.

In 2006, seven men—all but two American citizens—were arrested in Miami on charges of conspiring to bomb the Sears Tower in Chicago and the FBI building in North Miami Beach.

And in 2007, Russell Defreitas, an American citizen and a native of Guyana, was accused by authorities of plotting to attack New York's John F. Kennedy International Airport.

Unlike terrorist acts committed in Latin America, Europe, and the Middle East, terrorism American style often comes more from psychopathology than politics. The homegrown terrorist wants to send a message but not necessarily about our national policy. He has led a life of frustration, failure, and obscurity, and he now seeks to tell the world—through the barrel of a high-powered firearm or a bomb—that he is an important and powerful individual. In a sense, he is playing God. There are marginalized and alienated American citizens who feel like victims of injustice and who see our mainstream institutions as the enemy.

One such terrorist was Theodore Kaczynski, the so-called Unabomber, who was responsible for an 18-year killing spree in which he sent bombs through the mail to blow up and destroy the leaders of what he called our dehumanized, technological, postindustrial society. Kaczynski had no links to the Middle East, but he saw himself as some kind of high-tech Robin Hood whose mission was to save us from ourselves.

And terrorists don't always look like the monsters our culture warns us about. In April 1999, two young men at Columbine High School in Littleton, Colorado, who identified with the Nazi movement, selected Hitler's birthday to shoot to death 12 of their schoolmates and a teacher. But their plan was much larger than just a killing spree at school. Were Eric Harris and Dylan Klebold terrorists? According to the diary they kept, after blowing up their school, the Columbine shooters had planned also to hijack a plane and crash it into the New York City skyline! Who knows, maybe the September 11 terrorists were inspired by the Columbine shooters.

Even the anthrax contamination that, in 2001, killed five people—was possibly the work of American terrorists, not Middle Easterners. It is interesting that all of the senators to whom anthrax was mailed were liberal Democrats. Maybe it was a coincidence, but it seems very unlikely that terrorists from the Middle East would make the political distinction between Republicans and Democrats—but American citizens might. If anything, international terrorists might instead have gone after conservative Republicans who have supported the war in Iraq and the state of Israel.

And just after the attack on America, some of the racist big shots in white supremacist groups castigated their members for letting Middle Eastern terrorists do what they said proud Aryan-Americans should have been doing long ago. Maybe this is the reason why some law enforcement personnel suspected that the anthrax attack was the work of some white supremacist group in the United States.

In September 2001, Americans witnessed the most violent single incident of hate-motivated violence in our country's history. This horrendous event demonstrated the power and devastation that hate is capable of generating.

It taught us that to ignore hate is to risk the potential for unimaginable tragedy. Knowing that terrorism has a long history in the United States and that much of terrorist activity is homegrown, we should also learn to look for terror in the right places. If it is rational to keep an eye on suspicious foreigners in our midst, we should also keep an eye on one another.

# FOCUS

## ✧ Suggestions for Further Reading ✧

Which came first, the chicken or the egg? In sociology, the debate is frequently between religion and the economy. For a classic account of the influence of Protestantism on capitalism, read Max Weber's *The Protestant Ethic and the Spirit of Capitalism* (1958). To examine the opposite view, that the state of the economy determines the direction of the religious institution, read Karl Marx and Friedrich Engels's *On Religion* (1964).

As discussed in "The Boomerang Effect in Planning Social Change," even the best intentions sometimes go awry. Robert Merton's essay concerning unanticipated findings is found in *Social Theory and Social Structure* (1957). For a slightly more recent discussion of the boomerang effect, read Samuel Sieber's book *Fatal Remedies* (1981).

Concerning "Fads," I owe much to Ernie Anastos's *Twixt: Teens Yesterday and Today* (1983). He provides an engrossing photo history of changing adolescent fashion, hairstyles, dances, and heroes since the 1920s. For a discussion of fashion as it relates to gender roles and aging, I also recommend Alison Lurie's readable, intriguing, and often sociological book *The Language of Clothing* (1981). *American Fads* (1985) by Richard Johnson provides a description of 40 fads, from Silly Putty and swallowing goldfish to hot pants and Hula Hoops. So does Mark A. Long's more up-to-date *Bad Fads* (2002). For a broader look at fads, see Martin J. Smith and Patrick J. Kiger's *Poplorica: A Popular History of the Fads, Mavericks, Inventions, and Lore That Shaped Modern America* (2005).

My discussion of changing shopping mall rumors in "Riding the Rumor Mill" was based in large part on ideas developed by psychologists and sociologists over a span of 50 years. I gathered the details of particular rumors by talking with the reporters who covered the stories and by reading their newspaper accounts. Psychologists have long defined rumor as a message passed by word of mouth that becomes increasingly distorted as it travels from person to person. See Gordon Allport and Leo Postman's "The Basic Psychology of Rumor" in *Readings in Social Psychology*, edited by G. E. Swanson, T. M. Newcomb, and E. L. Hartley (1952). From a sociological point of view, however, rumor can be regarded as an informal source of news, a collective experience that the members of a group employ to define an extraordinary situation. After an earthquake hits an area, for example, you came to count on the spread of rumor to fill gaps in public anxiety until official information is finally available. This sociological conception can be found in Tamotsu Shibutani's pioneering work *Improvised News* (1966). The Link between anxiety and rumor mongering was made clear in Ralph Rosnow and Gary Fine's early book *Rumor and Gossip: The Social Psychology of Hearsay* (1976). For an insightful account of the spread of commercial rumors, read Fredrick Koenig's *Rumor in the Marketplace: The Social Psychology of Commercial Hearsay* (1985). Patricia A. Turner's (1993) work on rumors in African-American culture can be found in her book *I Heard It Through the Grapevine*. More recently, she coauthored with Gary Fine (2001) *Whispers on the Color Line: Rumor and Race in America,* which analyzes racial rumors to reveal the subtle and not-so-subtle components of race relations in America.

"Highway to Hell?" focuses attention on the impact of technology (in this case, the automobile) in determining the direction and quality of social change. For a pop culture treatment of how the automobile is implicated in what many observers now call "road rage," see "Road Rage," in the January 12, 1998, issue of *Time*.

During the last few years, enormous SUVs have taken the place of the big-finned, chrome-bumpered automobiles of the past in helping destroy our environment and maintain our dependence on foreign sources of oil (I'll probably lose many of my friends who drive SUVs, but I have to call it the way I see it). During the 1950s and 1960s, humongous gas-guzzling automobiles dominated the highways. It took pervasive pain and suffering in the form of an Organization of the Petroleum Exporting Countries–generated energy crisis for American consumers in 1973 to take seriously the benefits of fuel efficiency at home and on the roads. Made personally uncomfortable by double-digit inflation and long lines at gas station pumps, they began insulating their homes, turning down their thermostats, and driving smaller, fuel-efficient automobiles.

In the same way, the escalating price of gasoline since the September 11 attack on the United States has forced car manufacturers into the reality of focusing on fuel conservation and efficiency. Recognizing a 21% drop in demand, Ford discontinued production of its 8,000-pound Excursion SUV in 2004. Moreover, many of the largest SUVs are being downsized and made more fuel efficient.

Still, some of the most popular features of SUVs—their weight, spaciousness, and high center of gravity—are being incorporated into family cars. Moreover, about 25% of all cars purchased in this country continue to be SUVs.

Long before Americans began driving SUVs, many theorists emphasized the role of technological change, beginning with William F. Ogburn's

(1950) classic treatment titled *Social Change,* which he originally published in 1922. To illustrate the power of technology in the process of social change, Ogburn suggested that slavery in the United States was greatly encouraged by the invention of the cotton gin in 1795. By increasing productivity and therefore profits, this single technological innovation—the gin—depended on large numbers of laborers to work the cotton fields. The plantation economy quickly dominated the Southern landscape, where it remained in full force for more than 100 years.

Concerning "Enquiring Times," much of the research was taken from my work with Arnold Arluke as reported in *Gossip: The Inside Scoop* (1987). For this book, we interviewed gossip columnists and tabloid reporters and studied supermarket tabloids, popular celebrity biographies, and the front page of the *New York Times.* For an excellent treatment of the role of gossip as an agent of social control cross-culturally, try Sally E. Merry's chapter "Rethinking Gossip and Scandal" in *Toward a General Theory of Social Control,* edited by Donald Black (1984). More recently, Robin Dunbar (1997), in *Grooming, Gossip, and the Evolution of Language,* suggests that gossip is the human equivalent of primate grooming—an essential part of social order and cohesion.

In "Terror American Style," I contend that while in the midst of a national crisis, we may have lost perspective and accepted a number of myths about our new national reality—myths that have spread far and wide to color the perceptions of our citizens and to serve as a major turning point in our lives. For a treatment of the social construction of terrorism, see Philip Jenkins's (2003) *Images of Terror: What We Can and Can't Know About Terrorism.*

At the same time, the horrific attack on the United States had a tragic reality—some 3,000 innocent people lost their lives. And a majority of Americans continue to say that September 11 had a greater impact on this country than any other event of the last four decades, including the assassination of President Kennedy, the end of Soviet Communism, or even the Vietnam War. Nearly three out of four Americans still support tightening immigration restrictions against Arabs and Muslims. And a national poll taken in August discovered that a large number of Americans have become phobic about terrorism. They avoid large crowds and national landmarks; they are suspicious of people of Arab descent. Some 20 million Americans now refuse to fly, but millions more are terrified when they do. And because of September 11, many Americans have bought guns or have canceled their vacation plans. September 11 continues to be on our minds and in our hearts and decisions, even years later.

# DEVELOPING IDEAS

## ✧ About Social Change ✧

1. Research topic: This task requires some library work. Find a best-selling magazine that has been around for several decades and contains advertisement photos featuring men and women. Take at least a couple of different time periods—for example, war versus peacetime, prosperity versus recession. Examine each ad photo to determine how changes in the larger society may have influenced fashions of the day. Be sure to keep a written record of important information, such as the year, the magazine title, whether the model in an ad was a man or a woman, and so on.

2. Research topic: Do a kind of sociological family tree that might inform you about social changes over the generations. For example, go back in your own family at least two generations, comparing yourself with your parents and your grandparents. Compare the generations on variables such as (a) last year of school completed, (b) jobs held, (c) place of birth, (d) favorite music, (e) the racial composition of neighbors on the block while growing up, (f) attitudes toward family life, and (g) cost of a single-family home or monthly rent.

3. Writing topic: After conducting research in Exercise 2 above, write a short essay in which you discuss social changes over three generations, using your own family to illustrate.

4. Writing topic: The role of the automobile as an item of material culture in social change has been discussed. Unlike Canada and many European countries, America never developed its system of public transportation to its maximum potential. In a short essay, develop the argument that the automobile industry is largely responsible for maintaining our love affair (or should I say marriage) with the automobile, to the exclusion of alternatives such as public buses, trains, and subways.

5. Research topic: This is a project to determine changes in the importance of gossip in election campaigns. Go to the library and locate files of a daily newspaper that has been around for a few decades. Compare the front-page newspaper coverage of any presidential election campaign before 1970 versus the coverage of the 1992 or the 1996 campaign. You might want to limit yourself to reading the front page of Sunday papers beginning with the Iowa caucus or the New Hampshire primary and ending with Election Day. How many references do you find concerning the personal lives of the candidates? How many references do you find regarding their moral character? How have the issues changed?

6. Research topic: Have Americans' attitudes toward children and teenagers changed in any important way? To address this question, select several issues of a leading general-interest magazine that has been published for decades (e.g., *Reader's Digest*). Choose several issues from a very recent period (say, six months of issues from 2007) and from the same period a couple of decades ago (say, six months of issues from 1987).

   Compare the magazine for these two time periods in terms of the percentage of all articles devoted to exploring issues related to children and teenagers. Were more articles about children printed in the 2007 issues? Also, examine the qualitative differences between periods of time. In 1987, what issues or problems did most of the articles about youngsters discuss? How did those issues or problems differ from the ones addressed in the 2007 articles?

# Into the Future

O ne of the most important goals of sociology as a social science is to make accurate predictions. In *Forecasting Crime Data* (1978), my colleague James A. Fox long ago provided an important example of the way in which sociologists can successfully make projections into the future based on demographic data. He correctly predicted the soaring crime rate we experienced until 1980. Then, he correctly predicted the decline through the mid-1980s. Unfortunately, no criminologist, including Fox, was able to foresee a sudden upswing in serious crimes beginning in the mid-1980s and continuing into the early 1990s. Then, from the mid-1990s on, the rate of serious crime took a plunge. Again, many criminologists were surprised. See Alfred Blumstein and Joel Wallman, *The Crime Drop in America* (2000).

So sociologists aren't psychics; we don't pretend to have perfectly clear snapshots of the future (we are doing well to come up with clear pictures of the present). Like economists and political scientists, we may be willing occasionally to take an educated guess as to the direction of society, admitting that there are too many variables to make precise predictions about almost anything. Sure, X will grow, unless, of course, Y suddenly declines. Sure, A will improve, assuming, of course, B isn't modified first. We don't always know Y and B, so our projections about X and A are less than perfect. And we haven't even mentioned the assumptions we make about C, D, E, F, G, H, I, J, K, L, M, N, O, P, Q, R, S, T, U, V, W, and Z—the many other important variables that influence changes in social structure and culture.

It's not just sociologists, of course, who are imperfect prognosticators. Few economists were able to predict the energy shortage that began in 1973 or the plummeting stock prices beginning in 2000; even fewer political scientists forecast the crumbling of the Berlin Wall or the toppling of the Soviet Union. The September 11 attack on the United States seemed to come out of nowhere, as far as the literature of social science is concerned.

By the year 2007, the leading edge of the baby boom generation was into its early 60s, and their children were approaching young adulthood and middle age. Like every other generation, the baby boomers are making plans to retire from the labor force. However, they won't feel quite so pressured to do so. First of all, the stock market decline took its toll on pension plans.

In addition, during the second and third decades of the new century, they are likely to be offered incentives to remain in what is likely to become an ever-shrinking labor force. At this point, you can expect the typical retirement age to move from 65 to 70, or even older. Early retirement will, in all likelihood, all but disappear as an option.

The children of the baby boomers have become deeply entrenched in the crime-prone age group—late teens through early 20s. As a result, the rate of violent crime may once again soar, but that is not all. For the same reason, college admissions requirements are likely to remain quite competitive, at least for a few more years. Academically marginal and older students (those often called nontraditional by college administrators) will have to compete against growing numbers of traditionally defined college-aged students—children of the baby boomers between the ages of 18 and 22. Academic late-bloomers are likely to lose out, as they are no longer wooed by formerly eager admissions committees.

We have recently crossed into the new millennium. And at the end of every century (not to mention every millennium), organized groups emerge to prophesy the end of the world. This millennial myth can be traced back to ancient Biblical writings, which predict that a cosmic cataclysm orchestrated by God will destroy the ruling powers of evil and raise the righteous to a new existence in a messianic kingdom lasting 1,000 years. This is the prophesied millennium.

We certainly observed the impact of this kind of thinking during the closing years of the 20th century. As Phil Lamy (1996) suggested in his book *Millennium Rage,* not all contemporary millennialists sat back and waited for God to destroy the old system and usher in the new. Their vision of apocalypse went far beyond any vision of a spiritual New Age metamorphosis. For some of these new apocalyptic thinkers, a declining rate of economic growth since 1970 was the result not of abstract forces such as global competition and automation but of active behind-the-scenes covert manipulation by human beings with a purpose—international bankers, the United Nations, the federal reserve system, and one-world-order types who benefited at the expense of the average American. Their notion of apocalypse was just as active and just as physical—all-out war, nothing more, nothing less.

Other apocalyptic thinkers gave death a helping hand. In 1994 and 1995, 69 members of a doomsday cult known as the Solar Temple perished in fires set in Canada and in Switzerland. Maybe you remember reading about it. Then, in 1997, five more members of the Solar Temple committed mass suicide in a burning house in Quebec. On March 26, 1997, 39 members of the Heaven's Gate cult committed mass suicide in their rented mansion in Rancho Santa Fe near San Diego.

Marshall Applewhite, the cult's leader, had convinced his followers—20 women and 19 men ranging in age from 26 to 72—that a spaceship traveling behind the Hale-Bopp comet was coming to pick them all up soon after they had shed their vehicles or containers (i.e., bodies). They were totally convinced that civilization on Earth was about to end but that they could enter a higher life form by getting rid of their bodies and boarding a spaceship from what they called "the next level."

The good news is that we have gotten several years into the new millennium without experiencing cataclysmic worldwide upheaval. Yes, we experienced the attack on the United States and the war in Iraq, but tidal waves have not enveloped the seven continents, and earthquakes have not yet taken the lives of hundreds of millions of people. We have seen catastrophe—but "normal" catastrophe, not on a global scale. There should be a noticeable reduction in dangerous cult activity over the next few years, as the millennial thinkers fade into the woodwork.

Most aging baby boomers will be very little affected, in any personal sense, by the new calendar. Instead, they will continue to be like every generation to precede them by reducing their spending and their use of credit cards. As they actually begin to retire from the labor force, the boomers will, as a result, finally forfeit their cultural clout as well. Just as members of the 20-something generation presently feel they are playing second fiddle to the boomers, so more and more young Americans in the future will resent the presence of huge numbers of retired Gruppies (gray urban professionals) who live on their Social Security checks and require expensive health care insurance to survive.

By the second decade of the new millennium, multiculturalism will become a focal point of social change. Growing numbers of immigrants and minorities—African-, Asian-, and Latin-Americans—will ensure that the white Anglo-Saxon majority is no longer the majority. In our postindustrial society, there will be growing conflict among groups for scarce economic resources.

In their important effort, *The Good Society* (1991), Robert Bellah, Richard Madsen, William Sullivan, Ann Swidler, and Steven Tipton argue that we can solve our growing social problems by transforming our institutions—our schools, families, corporations, churches, and state. As they so eloquently did in *Habits of the Heart* (1985), Bellah et al. decry the rise of raw individualism in American society. Calling for public debate concerning our social ills, they propose a blueprint for the future of American society. In *The Good*

*Society,* they assert that we are fully capable of making changes in our values and of taking responsibility for our economic and political institutions.

The technological outlook may be even rosier, according to Gene Bylinski. In a 1988 article in *Fortune* titled "Technology in the Year 2000," he was sanguine regarding our ability to employ future technological discoveries to heal the human body and help us live fuller lives. Unfortunately, like so many before him, Bylinski was not totally accurate in predicting the timing of innovation.

Still, we have seen, in recent years, significant progress in understanding *genes* (the hereditary material in cells), making possible the successful identification of the genetic defects involved in some diseases. Physicians hope that understanding genes will lead to new methods for treating or preventing diseases. Moreover, medical researchers have recently developed a variety of devices to aid in the diagnosis, treatment, and prevention of diseases. In many cases, doctors can now perform microsurgery through tiny incisions using small precision instruments. This technique reduces the trauma of surgery and shortens or avoids long periods of hospitalization.

Finally, medical researchers have made significant progress in replacing worn or damaged body parts, including artificial limbs, joints, and heart valves. New and improved imaging techniques, such as MRI, CT, and positron emission tomography (PET), produce highly detailed views of internal body structures. The only problem with such medical innovations is that they are not always available to those members of our society who lack the economic resources to pay for them. Social stratification in America continues to determine that the best-quality health care goes to the wealthy.

We have witnessed tremendous growth in nonmedical technological innovations during the past quarter century. Since the early 1980s, the lives of millions of Americans have been dramatically impacted by such inventions as the Internet, cell phones, personal computers, fiber optics, e-mail, digital cameras, high-definition television, hybrid cars, memory storage discs, nanotechnology, voice mail, ATMs, DNA fingerprinting, and air bags in automobiles (CNN.com, 2005).

Sociology has often been regarded as subversive, and in a sense, it is. That is, sociologists often challenge our taken-for-granted assumptions, the status quo, and, more precisely, the people in charge of things. No wonder totalitarian societies rarely permit their college students to study the field of sociology; or when they do, they keep it under rigid controls. For the same reason, even in societies that permit greater freedom of choice, sociologists aren't always welcome or appreciated. They might rock the political boat. They might advocate expensive programs and policies. Their research might be useful to reformists who agitate for social change.

The importance of the field of sociology, or, more precisely, the collective respect for it, varies according to the urgency of our social problems and the extent of our prosperity as a society. In popular-culture terms, we have to believe that we need sociologists, but we also have to feel that we can afford them. The hip generation of the 1960s and early 1970s, for example, was a heyday for the field. By 1973, the number of college students earning their bachelor's degrees in sociology had reached a record high of 35,996. Inflation was relatively low, the economy was growing, and there were several important social issues to inspire interest.

Civil rights, feminism, and war were on almost everybody's mind. Our inner cities were burning while thousands marched through the streets to protest, demonstrate, or riot. As a result, millions looked to social scientists

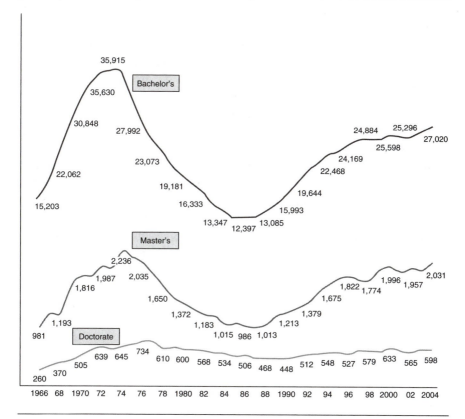

**Figure C.1**     Sociology Degrees Awarded by Degree Level, 1966–2004 (Number of Degrees)

*Source:* U. S. Department of Education, National Center for Education Statistics (NCES), *Integrated Postsecondary Education Data System (IPEDS) Completions, 1995–2004* (Washington, DC: NCES, 2006). Retrieved October 26, 2006, from http://caspar.nsf.gov

to give them advice about how to run society, how to solve the urgent problems of the day—not that anyone in charge often implemented the answers that sociologists provided, but at least we were asked.

In the February 3, 1992, issue of *Newsweek*, reporter Barbara Kantrowitz, in her article "Sociology's Lonely Crowd," summarized some of the problems and prospects of the discipline at that time. She reported that by 1989, the number of students receiving bachelor's degrees in sociology had dwindled to only 14,393. Long holding a reputation as being among the more liberal of the arts and sciences, sociology apparently did not fit very well into the cultural milieu of the 1980s. Students turned to majors such as business and engineering—majors they considered more practical. Moreover, many undergraduates enrolled in specialized professional programs—criminal justice, social work, urban studies, and market research—which began in and are actually offshoots of sociology.

In the last decade, however, we have seen a major reversal of this trend. There are now more students taking sociology courses, more students majoring in sociology, and more standalone sociology departments (Spalter-Roth, 2003). As shown in the figure above, there are increasing numbers of students who graduate with bachelor's and master's degrees in sociology (U.S. Department of Education, 2006). Apparently, there are also growing numbers of undergraduates who recognize that sociological training is connected to a range of attractive career paths, from doing significant work in a federal agency to running a successful consulting business (Levine, 1997). Moreover, we are just beginning to recognize the need to address growing social problems such as homelessness, crime, and poverty. If present trends continue unabated, it is safe to predict that sociologists will again gain greater prominence. The United States continues to struggle with long-standing problems that reduce our quality of life and frustrate our collective aspirations. Finding effective solutions will require that we put aside our differences and pull together as a society. We can only hope that Americans will rise to the challenge.

# References

Allport, Gordon, & Postman, Leo. (1952). The basic psychology of rumor. In G. E. Swanson, T. M. Newcomb, & E. L. Hartley (Eds.), *Readings in social psychology.* New York: Holt.

Anastos, Ernie. (1983). *Twixt: Teens yesterday and today.* New York: Franklin Watts.

Archer, Dane, & Gartner, Rosemary. (1984). *Violence and crime in cross-national perspective.* New Haven, CT: Yale University Press.

Arluke, Arnold, Levin, Jack, Luke, Carter, & Ascione, Frank. (1999, September). The relationship of animal abuse to violence and other forms of antisocial behavior. *Journal of Interpersonal Violence, 14,* 963–975.

Arluke, Arnold, & Sanders, Clinton R. (1996). *Regarding animals.* Philadelphia: Temple University Press.

Asch, Solomon. (1952). Effects of group pressure upon the modification and distortion of judgment. In G. E. Swanson (Ed.), *Readings in social psychology.* New York: Holt, Rinehart & Winston.

Ball-Rokeach, Sandra, & Cantor, Muriel. (1986). *Media, audience, and social structure.* Beverly Hills, CA: Sage.

Barcus, F. Earle. (1983). *Images of life on children's television: Sex roles, minorities, and families.* New York: Praeger.

Bateson, Mary Catherine. (1990). *Composing a life.* New York: Plume.

Becker, Howard S. (1967). Whose side are we on? *Social Problems, 14,* 239–247.

Becker, Howard S., Geer, Blanche, Hughes, Everett C., & Strauss, Amselm L. (1961). *Boys in white.* Chicago: University of Chicago Press.

Bellah, Robert, Madsen, Richard, Sullivan, William, Swidler, Ann, & Tipton, Steven. (1985). *Habits of the heart: Individualism and commitment in American life.* Berkeley: University of California Press.

Bellah, Robert, Madsen, Richard, Sullivan, William, Swidler, Ann, & Tipton, Steven. (1991). *The good society.* New York: Knopf.

Blass, Thomas. (2000). *Obedience to authority: Current perspectives on the Milgram paradigm.* Mahwah, NJ: LEA.

Blumstein, Alfred, & Wallman, Joel. (2000). *The crime drop in America.* New York: Cambridge University Press.

Bowers, William J. (1974). *Executions in America.* Lexington, MA: Lexington Books.

Breines, Winifred. (1994). *Young, white, and miserable: Growing up female in the fifties.* Boston: Beacon.

Bromley, David G., & Melton, J. Gordon. (2002). *Cults, religion and violence.* New York: Cambridge University Press.

Brookhaven Citizens for Peaceful Solutions. (2001, April 24). *Violence against immigrants.* Farmingville, NY.

Butler, Robert. (1975). *Why survive? Being old in America.* New York: Harper & Row.

Bylinski, Gene. (1988, July 18). Technology in the year 2000. *Fortune.*

Cantor, Muriel, & Pingree, Suzanne. (1983). *The soap opera.* Beverly Hills, CA: Sage.

Chernin, Kim. (1981). *The obsession: Reflections on the tyranny of slenderness.* New York: Harper & Row.

Chudacoff, Howard. (1989). *How old are you?* Princeton, NJ: Princeton University Press.

Clark, Kim. (2001, August 21). Heroes. *U.S. News & World Report* online.

Comstock, Gary D. (1991). *Violence against lesbians and gay men.* New York: Columbia University Press.

Conrad, Peter. (2007). *The medicalization of society.* Baltimore: Johns Hopkins University Press.

Cooley, Charles H. (1902). *Human nature and the social order.* New York: Scribner.

Coser, Lewis. (1956). *The functions of social conflict.* New York: Free Press.

Cowell, Alan. (2002, January 3). After black teenager is slain, Norway peers into a mirror. *The New York Times*, p. 1A.

Cracknell, David, and Gadher, Dipesh. (2003, January 26). Labour is warned of asylum backlash. *Sunday Times*, p. 8.

Currie, Eliott. (2005). *The road to whatever.* New York: Metropolitan Books.

Davis, Kingsley, & Moore, Wilbert. (1945). Some principles of stratification. *American Sociological Review, 10,* 242–249.

Dittmann, Melissa. (2005, June). Anger on the road. *Monitor on Psychology, 36,* 6, 26.

Dunbar, Robin. (1997). *Grooming, gossip, and the evolution of language.* Cambridge, MA: Harvard University Press.

Durkheim, Émile. (1933). *The division of labor in society.* New York: Free Press.

Durkheim, Émile. (1951). *Suicide: A study in sociology.* New York: Free Press.

Durkheim, Émile. (1966). *The rules of sociological method.* New York: Free Press.

Economic inequality. (2007, January). www.newsbatch.com/econ.htm

Ehrlich, Howard J. (1990). *Campus ethnoviolence and the policy options.* Baltimore, MD: National Institute Against Prejudice and Violence.

Erikson, Erik H. (1950). *Childhood and society.* New York: Norton.

Fagan, Jeffrey. (2005). *Deterrence and the death penalty.* Testimony to the New York State Assembly Committee on Codes (January 21).

Ferguson, Andrew. (1998, January 12). Road rage, *Time Magazine*, p. 23.

Fine, Gary Alan, & Turner, Patricia A. (2001). *Whispers on the color line: Rumor and race in America.* Berkeley: University of California Press.

Fisher, Marc. (2007, July 18). AARP tunes into radio's discarded audience. *The Washington Post*, p. 5.

Four German youths sentenced for anti-foreigner attacks. (2003, January 24). *Deutsche Presse-Agentur.*

Fowler, Rebekah I., & Fuehrer, Ann. (1997, August). Women's marital names: An interpretive study of name retainers' concepts of marriage. *Feminism & Psychology.*

Fox, James A. (1978). *Forecasting crime data.* Lexington, MA: Lexington Books.

Gans, Herbert J. (1972). The positive functions of poverty. *American Journal of Sociology, 78,* 275–289.

Gerbner, George. (1998). Fairness and diversity in television. Screen Actors Guild Report.

Gerbner, George, Gross, Larry, Morgan, Michael, & Signorielli, Nancy. (1982). Charting the mainstream: Television's contributions to political orientations. *Journal of Communication, 32,* 100–127.

Germany: Green cards, violence. (2000, September). *Migration News, 7*(9).

Gerth, H. H., & Mills, C. Wright (Eds.). (1946). *Max Weber: Essays in sociology.* New York: Oxford University Press.

Gillespie, L. Kay. (2003). *Inside the death chamber: Exploring executions.* Boston: Allyn & Bacon.

Glazer, Myron Peretz, & Glazer, Penina Migdal. (1989). *The whistleblowers: Exposing corruption in government and industry.* New York: Basic Books.

Goffman, Erving. (1958). *Asylums.* New York: Anchor.

Goffman, Erving. (1963). *Stigma: Notes on the management of spoiled identity.* Englewood Cliffs, NJ: Prentice Hall.

Gottfredson, Michael, & Hirschi, Travis. (1990). *A general theory of crime.* Stanford, CA: Stanford University Press.

Gowen, Teresa. (1998). American untouchables: Homeless scavengers in San Francisco underground economy. In Amy Wharton (Ed.), *Working in America: Continuity, conflict, and change.* Mountain View, CA: Mayfield.

Granfield, Robert. (1986). Legal education as corporate ideology. *Sociological Forum, 1,* 514–523.

Halpern, Thomas, & Levin, Brian. (1996). *The limits of dissent.* Amherst, MA: Aletheia Press.

Hanks, Gardner. (1997). *Against the death penalty.* Scottdale, PA: Herald Press.

Harris, Marvin. (1979). *Cultural materialism.* New York: Random House.

Herek, Gregory, & Berrill, Kevin. (Eds.). (1992). *Hate crimes: Confronting violence against lesbians and gay men.* Newbury Park, CA: Sage.

Herman, Tom. (2003, June 6). Richest Americans got even richer. *Wall Street Journal* online.

Hoffman, Allan M., Schuh, John H., & Fenske, Robert H. (1998). *Violence on campus: Defining the problems, strategies for action.* Gaithersburg, MD: Aspen.

Hoffman, Bill, & Burke, Cathy. (1997). *Heaven's gate.* New York: Harper.

Hughes, Everett. (1962). Good people and dirty work. *Social Problems, 10,* 3–11.

Jaffe, Rona. (1986). *Class reunion.* New York: Dell.

Jenkins, Philip. (2003). *Images of terror: What we can and can't know about terrorism.* New York: Aldine de Gruyter.

Johnson, Richard. (1985). *American fads.* New York: Beech Tree.

Jones, Landon Y. (1980). *Great expectations: America and the baby boom generation.* New York: Ballantine.

Kalberg, Stephen. (1980). Max Weber's types of rationality: Cornerstones for the analysis of rationalization processes in history. *American Journal of Sociology, 85,* 1145–1179.

Kanter, Rosabeth M. (1993). *Men and women of the corporation* (2nd ed.). New York: Basic Books.

Kantrowitz, Barbara. (1992, February 3). Sociology's lonely crowd. *Newsweek.*

Karl, Jonathan. (1995). *The right to bear arms.* New York: Harper.

Katz, Jack. (1988). *Seductions of crime: Moral and sensual attractions of doing evil.* New York: Basic Books.

Kaufman, Debra Renee. (1991). *Rachel's daughters.* New Brunswick, NJ: Rutgers University Press.

Keen, Sam. (1986). *Faces of the enemy: Reflections of the hostile imagination.* San Francisco: Harper & Row.

Kennedy, Daniel, & Kerber, August. (1973). *Resocialization: An American experiment.* New York: Behavioral Publications.

Koenig, Fredrick. (1985). *Rumor in the marketplace: The social psychology of commercial hearsay.* Dover, MA: Auburn House.

Kohn, Alfie. (1990). *The brighter side of human nature.* New York: Basic Books.

Kollock, Peter, & O'Brien, Jodi. (2001). *The production of reality* (2nd ed.). Thousand Oaks, CA: Pine Forge.

Kooistra, Paul. (1989). *Criminals as heroes: Structure, power, and identity.* Bowling Green, OH: Popular Press.

Kuhn, Manford. (1960). Self-attitudes by age, sex, and professional training. *Sociological Quarterly, 1,* 39–55.

Lamy, Philip. (1996). *Millennium rage.* New York: Plenum Press.

Largey, Gale, & Watson, David. (1972). The sociology of odors. *American Journal of Sociology, 77,* 1021–1034.

Larson, Mary Strom. (1996, July). Sex roles and soap operas: What adolescents learn about single motherhood. *Sex Roles: A Journal of Research, 35,* 97–110.

Lebesco, Kathleen. (2004). *Revolting bodies?: The struggle to redefine fat identity.* Amherst: University of Massachusetts Press.

Leinberger, Paul, & Tucker, Bruce. (1991). *The new individualists: The generation after the organization man.* New York: HarperCollins.

Levin, Jack. (1993). Misery as a turning point for academic success. *Journal of Research in Education, 3,* 3–6.

Levin, Jack. (2007). *The violence of hate: Confronting racism, anti-Semitism, and other forms of bigotry.* Boston: Allyn & Bacon.

Levin, Jack, & Arluke, Arnold. (1987). *Gossip: The inside scoop.* New York: Plenum.

Levin, Jack, Arluke, Arnold, & Levin, William C. (1992, August). *Powerful elders.* Paper presented at the annual meeting of the American Sociological Association.

Levin, Jack, & Fox, James A. (1991). *Mass murder: America's growing menace.* New York: Berkley.

Levin, Jack, & Levin, William C. (1980). *Ageism: Prejudice and discrimination against the elderly.* Belmont, CA: Wadsworth.

Levin, Jack, & Levin, William C. (1982). *The functions of discrimination and prejudice* (2nd ed.). New York: Harper & Row.

Levin, Jack, & Levin, William C. (1991). Sociology of educational late-blooming. *Sociological Forum, 6,* 661–680.

Levin, Jack, & McDevitt, Jack. (2002). *Hate crimes revisited: America's war on those who are different.* Colorado Springs, CO: Westview Press.

Levin, Jack, & Rabrenovic, Gordana. (2004). *Why we hate.* Amherst, NY: Prometheus Books.

Levine, Felice J. (1997). Sociological lines of work. *Footnotes, 25,* 2.

Long, Mark A. (2002). *Bad fads.* Toronto: ECW Press.

Löwenthal, Leo. (1961). *Literature, popular culture and society.* New York: Prentice Hall.

Lurie, Alison. (1981). *The language of clothing.* New York: Random House.

Lynd, Robert S., & Lynd, Helen M. (1929). *Middletown: A study in American culture.* New York: Harcourt Brace.

MacManus, Susan A. (1996). *Young vs. old: Generational combat in the 21st century.* With Patricia A. Turner. Boulder, CO: Westview Press.

Madrick, Jeffrey. (1995). *The end of affluence.* New York: Random House.

Marx, Karl, & Engels, Friedrich. (1964). *On religion.* New York: Schocken.

Mead, George Herbert. (1934). *Mind, self and society.* Chicago: University of Chicago Press.

Mecca, Andrew, Smelser, Neil, & Vasconcellos, John (Eds.). (1989). *The social importance of self-esteem.* Berkeley: University of California Press.

Merry, Sally E. (1984). Rethinking gossip and scandal. In Donald Black (Ed.), *Toward a general theory of social control.* Orlando, FL: Academic Press.

Merton, Robert K. (1957). *Social theory and social structure.* Glencoe, IL: Free Press.

Milgram, Stanley. (1974). *Obedience to authority: An experimental view.* New York: Harper & Row.

Millman, Marcia. (1980). *Such a pretty face.* New York: Simon & Schuster.

Mirowsky, John, & Ross, Catherine. (1989). *Social causes of psychological distress.* New York: Aldine de Gruyter.

Montalbano, William D. (1991, October 1). World on the move: An overview. *Los Angeles Times,* p. 1.

Nelson, Leif, & Simmons, Joseph. (2007, November 15). What's in a name? Initials linked to success, study shows. *Science*Daily. http://www.sciencedaily.com/releases/2007

Nelson, Todd. (2002). *Ageism: Stereotyping and prejudice against older persons.* Cambridge, MA: MIT Press.

New ranking names America's cough and cold capitals. (2004, November 7). *Nursing Home and Elder Business Week,* p. 78.

Newman, Katherine. (1988). *Falling from grace: The experience of downward mobility in the American middle class.* New York: Free Press.

Noguera, P. A. (2001). Finding safety where we least expect it: The role of social capital in preventing violence in schools. In W. Ayers and R. Ayers (Eds.), *Beyond zero tolerance.* New York: Teachers College Press.

Ogburn, William F. (1950). *Social change.* New York: Viking. (Original work published 1922)

Oliner, Samuel. (2003). *Do unto others: How altruism inspires true acts of courage.* Boulder, CO: Westview Press.

Orbach, Susie. (1978). *Fat is a feminist issue.* New York: Paddington.

Owen, T. Ross. (2003, June). Retention implications of a relationship between age and GPA. *College Student Journal,* 1–9.

Palmore, Erdman. (1990). *Ageism: Negative and positive.* New York: Springer.

Palmore, Erdman, Branch, Lawrence, & Harris, Diana K. (1995). *Encyclopedia of Ageism.* Binghampton, NY: Haworth Press.

Parillo, Vincent N. (2006). *Strangers to these shores* (8th ed.). Boston: Allyn & Bacon.

Phillips, Kevin. (1990). *The politics of the rich and the poor.* New York: Random House.

Phillips, Kevin. (2002). *Wealth and democracy: A political history of the American rich.* New York: Broadway Books.

Portes, Alejandro, & Rumbaut, Ruben G. (1997). *Immigrant America: A portrait.* Berkeley: University of California Press.

Portes, Alejandro, & Rumbaut, Ruben G. (2001). *Legacies: The story of the immigrant second generation.* Berkeley: University of California Press.

Putnam, Robert D. (2000). *Bowling alone: The collapse and revival of American community.* New York: Touchstone.

Reiman, Jeffrey. (2006). *The rich get richer and the poor get prison.* New York: John Wiley.

Riegel, Henriette. (1996, Spring). Soap operas and gossip. *Journal of Popular Culture.*

Riesman, David, Glazer, Nathan, Denney, Reuel, & Gitlin, Todd. (2001). *The lonely crowd* (Revised ed.). New Haven, CT: Yale University Press.

Ritzer, George. (1995). *Expressing America.* Thousand Oaks, CA: Pine Forge.

Ritzer, George. (2007). *The McDonaldization of society.* Thousand Oaks, CA: Pine Forge.

Rose, Arnold. (1962). Reactions against the mass society. *Sociological Quarterly, 3,* 310–319.

Rosenhan, David. (1973). On being sane in insane places. *Science, 179,* 250–258.

Rosenthal, Robert, & Jacobson, Lenore. (2003). *Pygmalion in the classroom.* New York: Crown House.

Rosnow, Ralph, & Fine, Gary. (1976). *Rumor and gossip: The social psychology of hearsay.* New York: Elsevier.

Russell, Maureen. (1995). *Days of our lives: A complete history of the long-running soap opera.* Jefferson, NC: McFarland & Company.

Sampson, Robert, & Laub, John. (1994). *Crime in the making: Pathways and turning points through life.* Cambridge, MA: Harvard University Press.

Shibutani, Tamotsu. (1966). *Improvised news.* Indianapolis, IN: Bobbs-Merrill.

Sidel, Ruth. (1994). *Battling bias.* New York: Penguin Books.

Sieber, Samuel. (1981). *Fatal remedies.* New York: Plenum.

Siggerud, Katherine. (2003, September 26). Highway infrastructure. Testimony before the Subcommittee on Highways and Transit, Committee on Transportation and Infrastructure, House of Representatives.

Singer, Margaret Thaler. (1995). *Cults in our midst: The hidden menace in our everyday lives*. San Francisco: Jossey-Bass.

Smith, Martin J., & Kiger, Patrick J. (2005). *Poplorica: A popular history of the fads, mavericks, inventions, and lore that shaped modern America*. New York: Collins.

Snow, Robert L. (1999). *The militia threat: Terrorists among us*. New York: Plenum Press.

Spalter-Roth, Roberta. (2003, February). Has sociology suffered the declines predicted ten years ago? *Footnotes*, 2.

Stern, Linda. (2003, July 6). For American middle class, it's all downhill for now. *Boston Sunday Globe*, p. D2.

Tabor, James, & Gallagher, Eugene. (1995). *Why Waco? Cults and the battle for religious freedom in America*. Berkeley: University of California Press.

Todorov, Tzvetan. (1999). *The fragility of goodness: Why Bulgaria's Jews survived the holocaust*. Princeton, NJ: Princeton University Press.

Top 25: Innovations. (2005, March 1). www.cnn.com/2005/Tech/01/03CNN25 .top25.innovations/index.html

Tuckman, Joe. (2003, May 11). After 10 years of fears, a new theory. *The Houston Chronicle*, p. 21A.

Tumin, Melvin. (1953). Some principles of stratification: A critical analysis. *American Sociological Review, 18*, 387–394.

Turner, Patricia A. (1993). *I heard it through the grapevine*. Berkeley: University of California Press.

Vinitzky-Seroussi, Vered. (1998). *After pomp and circumstance*. Chicago: University of Chicago Press.

Weber, Max. (1958). *The Protestant ethic and the spirit of capitalism*. New York: Scribner's.

Wharton, Amy. (Ed.). (1998). *Working in America: Continuity, conflict, and change*. Mountain View, CA: Mayfield.

Whyte, William H. (1956). *The organization man*. New York: Simon & Schuster.

Wright, Charles, R. (1986). *Mass communication: A sociological perspective*. New York: Random House.

Zimbardo, Philip C. (2007) *The Lucifer effect: Understanding how good people turn evil*. New York and London: Random House.

Zimbardo, Philip C., Haney, Craig, & Banks, William C. (1973, April 8). A Pirandellian prison. *New York Times Magazine*.

Zerubavel, Eviatar. (1981). *Hidden rhythms: Schedules and calendars in social life*. Chicago: University of Chicago Press.

# Index

# About the Author

Jack Levin is the Irving and Betty Brudnick Professor of Sociology and Criminology at Northeastern University. He has authored or coauthored a number of books, including *Elementary Statistics in Social Research, The Functions of Prejudice, Gossip: The Inside Scoop, Hate Crimes: The Rising Tide of Bigotry and Bloodshed,* and *Serial Killers and Sadistic Murderers: Up Close and Personal.* Levin's work has appeared in professional journals, including *Youth & Society, Criminology, The Gerontologist,* and *Sex Roles,* as well as in *The New York Times, The Boston Globe, The Dallas Morning News,* the *Chicago Tribune, The Washington Post,* and *USA Today.* He has lectured on campuses around the country about serial murder, hate crimes, and domestic terrorism. A dedicated educator and social advocate, Levin received Northeastern University's Excellence in Teaching Award and was honored by the Council for Advancement and Support of Education as its Professor of the Year in Massachusetts.